The Real Cheese Companion

A GUIDE TO THE BEST HANDMADE CHEESES OF BRITAIN AND IRELAND

Sarah Freeman

sphere

SPHERE

First published in Great Britain in 1998
by Little, Brown and Company (UK)
This edition published by Time Warner Paperbacks in 2003
Reprinted by Sphere in 2007

A CIP catalogue record for this book
is available from the British Library

ISBN 978-0-7515-3532-1

Papers used by Sphere are natural, recyclable products made from
wood grown in sustainable forests and certified in accordance with
the rules of the Forest Stewardship Council.

Typeset in Janson by M Rules
Printed and bound in Great Britain by Clays Ltd, St Ives plc
Paper supplied by Hellefoss AS, Norway

Sphere
An imprint of
Little, Brown Book Group
Brettenham House
Lancaster Place
London WC2E 7EN

A Member of the Hachette Livre Group of Companies

www.littlebrown.co.uk

CONTENTS

ACKNOWLEDGEMENTS	vi
INTRODUCTION	vii
CHAPTER 1: SOUTH-EAST ENGLAND	3
CHAPTER 2: SOUTH-WEST ENGLAND	43
CHAPTER 3: IRELAND	128
CHAPTER 4: WALES	163
CHAPTER 5: THE MIDLANDS	184
CHAPTER 6: THE NORTH OF ENGLAND	228
CHAPTER 7: SCOTLAND	270
INDEX	301

ACKNOWLEDGEMENTS

This book is a co-operative effort: I could not have written it without the help of the cheesemakers included, who not only offered me hospitality and gave me their time but also made the research more fun than anything I have ever attempted. I thank them all most warmly and sincerely. I also owe particular thanks to the late James Aldridge, Piers Feilden, Matthew Organ, Iain Meliss, and Polly Freeman for help of various kinds; to Eurwen Richards for technical advice; to David Natt for his contribution on wine; to Randolph Hodgson and Gerd Seeber for supplying photographs which show that cheese has a visual interest at least equal to its gastronomic appeal; to Vivien Bowler, Julia Charles, and Arianne Burnette at Little, Brown for their patience, humour, and – well, for being just wonderful; and finally to my husband, who came with me on some of my visits and ultimately made the whole project possible.

INTRODUCTION

The past two decades have seen a wonderful, if overdue revival of British handmade cheeses. I was brought up on post-war mouse-trap and loved it, never having tasted anything better. Then came the revelation of Brie, Camembert and other imported French cheeses, followed by Mary Holbrook's rich goats' and sheep's cheeses, Veronica Steele's Milleens, the Curtises' Bonchester, flowing and creamy, from Scotland, and a little later Anne Wigmore's hard and semi-soft sheep's cheeses. Meanwhile, Patrick Rance launched a campaign for Real Cheese with *The Great British Cheese Book*, which Randolph Hodgson of Neal's Yard Dairy, James Aldridge at Beckenham, and others took up, scouring the country for traditionally made, unpasteurized cheeses. During the period of wartime rationing, only seven varieties, all hard and all pasteurized, were permitted: recovery did not begin for another generation, but now hundreds are made, ranging from fresh or mould-ripened soft, washed-rind, and blue to hard and semi-hard.

I set out to write this book in the spirit of discovery – not so much to discover the cheeses themselves, most of which I already knew, but to find out where and how they were made and what makes each different, in the belief that knowing a little about them enhances enjoyment. The result has turned out to be longer than I anticipated because every cheesemaker's method is individual and all have something particular to contribute. For reasons of space, it has not been possible to include them all, and I apologize to those I have omitted; however, the majority, in all their diversity, are here. A few come from families who have made cheese for generations; some are dairy-farmers who became depressed by the milk lake or saw cheese as a way of adding value to their quota; and others, rejecting the nine-to-five routine, have adopted it as a creative form of downshifting – although, as all would confirm, the hours they work are far longer than the office day.

In the course of my visits, just about every conceivable subject connected with cheese was discussed, from the importance of hygiene to the problems of marketing. The standard of hygiene everywhere, in small and larger dairies alike, is truly impressive and indeed is one of the reasons for the long hours cheesemakers work: washing and disinfecting the floor, vat, and every implement used can take almost as long as the cheesemaking itself. One of many points which arose in relation to marketing was that because of short shelf-life and the need for refrigerated transport, many soft cheeses are not widely distributed, but are sold only from the farms or locally; another was that, in spite of the popularity of grilled goats' cheese in restaurants and pecorino (sheep's cheese) for sprinkling, strong prejudice still exists in favour of cows' cheese. Although the best known traditional cheeses are cows', sheep's cheeses have a much longer history in this country: cows did not overtake sheep for dairying until the sixteenth century, when they prevailed because of their higher yield and because their milk has larger fat globules and thus is easier to separate for butter.

After cows' cheeses became the norm, the cheese eaten by most people was made partly or entirely of skimmed milk: the whole-milk cheeses which we now take for granted were luxuries for the better-off. Good low-fat cheeses are difficult to make, because as well as contributing to texture fat plays a major part in the development of flavour. However, three very low-fat traditional varieties plus one or two others are included here and I hope will encourage further experiment, not perhaps with skimmed but low-fat milk: Thelma Adams's Caerphilly, Caws Cenarth, made with morning milk only, is relatively low in fat yet tastes deliciously full and buttery.

For reasons of gastronomy as well as health, we also need a

wider range of organic cheeses. The difference between organically and conventionally raised animal foods of all kinds, including milk, is startling: organic milk has almost as much flavour again as unpasteurized compared to pasteurized. Until relatively recently, because there were so few of them, makers of organic cheese tended to concentrate on the ever-popular, long-matured Cheddar types, hence the depressingly narrow selection that used to be found in organic shops. This is rapidly changing. When the first edition of the book appeared, there were no organic blue cheeses and only one organic white mould-ripened cheese: now we have half a dozen organic white mould-rinded cheeses, two organic cream cheeses and seven semi-soft organic cheeses including two blues, with (at the time of going to press) a washed-rind one to be launched very soon. However, there are still very few organic sheep's cheeses and only one maker of organic goats' cheese (in Ireland).

While we need many more hand-made cheeses of every kind, one of our most conspicuous lacks is of washed-rind cheeses, organic or not. This perhaps is a matter of tradition, but competition from the creamery-made versions in the supermarkets has also discouraged makers from committing themselves to the popular traditional so-called 'territorials'. As a result, the authentic, crumbly Lancashire made with a double curd has become a rarity, only two people are still making unpasteurized Caerphilly, no unpasteurized Stilton is yet made (though Randolph Hodgson of Neal's Yard Dairy is working on this), and until recently there was no unpasteurized Red Leicester, which in its pasteurized form generally tastes of little more than the annatto used to colour it orange. Now, however, a cheese which does not qualify because it is made in Somerset but is otherwise similar is produced, and is delicious; another pasteurized but still very acceptable version is made in Lancashire. Excellent Cheshire and Single and Double Gloucester are made, but not enough, and only two people are currently making

Dunlop-style cheese (one of which, called Sweetmilk, is organic: see page 287).

Since by definition handmade or farmhouse cheeses cannot be made on a large scale, more cheese means more cheesemakers. At this stage I should perhaps define what I mean by handmade or farmhouse cheesemakers, since neither term always applies literally. Whereas some small-scale makers do in truth carry out every operation, even milling, by hand, others use machinery for part of or occasionally almost the whole process. To some makers, the *sine qua non* of making cheese is using the milk from their own herd or flock; others buy it in, either for lack of labour or because they work with relatively large quantities. I have included several creameries, all small by commercial standards but larger than the term 'farmhouse' might be supposed to imply, because they share the artisan maker's aim – namely, first-class quality; profit, beyond the need for viability, is incidental. First-class cheese, as with any other product, demands first-class material: the taste and quality of milk depends on the soil, standards of hygiene and husbandry, and the breed of animal, which is why I have commented on the type of country, the farms, and the livestock, as well as the cheesemakers themselves and their craft.

This kind of cheesemaking demands experience and judgement which have to be exercised on a daily basis rather than relying simply on technical expertise. Until now, cheesemakers learnt from their mothers or other cheesemakers, books, experiments with bucket and ladle in the kitchen, or were taught at agricultural colleges. However, because of the small number of applicants, courses adapted to small-scale hand- as opposed to larger-scale creamery cheesemaking at the colleges have become few and far between. The Specialist Cheesemakers' Association, which was formed in 1989 initially to give support to makers using unpasteurized milk, now offers grants towards training and can be consulted by members on any aspect of cheesemaking and related problems. These facilities have helped to recruit new entrants to the field: another boost to small-scale cheesemaking comes from the progress made in this country by the Slow Food movement, one of the aims of which is to preserve traditional foods and if necessary rescue them from extinction. Three leading Somerset makers of unpasteurized Cheddar have already joined to form a 'Praesidium', aimed at promoting their product not only in Britain but Europe: I sincerely hope, and shall do all I can to ensure, that others will follow their example.

MILK, CHEESE, AND MICROBES

One of the cheesemakers whom I visited remarked, 'Cheesemaking is almost farming bacteria'. In fact, this was an understatement: he might more accurately have missed out the 'almost' and (since he makes blue cheese) have added 'and moulds'. If this sounds unattractive, it is worth remembering that the world is densely populated with microbes of many kinds: as well as the fact that they may be in food and drink, they inhabit the soil, air, our own intestines, and the stomachs of ruminant animals, who are not nourished by protein directly derived from the herbage they eat but from bacteria which feed on it in their stomachs.

The milk of carefully fed, healthy animals is sterile in the udder but picks up bacteria on the teats, from the surrounding atmosphere after milking, and later from the vessels in which it is transported. Some of the bacteria, far from being undesirable, play a crucial part in the development of flavour in the cheese; others are pathogenic. Milk is tested regularly: routine tests do not discriminate between the different kinds of bacteria, but with due precautions the total number can be kept far below the level at which they represent any possible threat to human health. The

Specialist Cheesemakers' Association recommends a count only a tenth as high as the authorized maximum: with milk of this standard, and provided that it is maintained at this standard before use, pasteurization is unnecessary. It is also unnecessary for long-matured cheeses in which bacterial activity is much reduced; in addition there is an argument to the effect that the favourable bacteria in untreated milk act as a natural control over pathogens. On the other hand, pasteurization is essential in places where there is any risk of tuberculosis, which cannot be detected by the usual means, or if there is doubt about hygiene during transport. Some artisan makers who buy rather than produce their own milk pasteurize simply because it has been transported; the creameries invariably do so because their milk is not only transported but also comes from different sources. It should be stressed, however, that it is by no means the guarantee of safety that it is often taken to be because undesirable bacteria may enter the milk during processing. Therefore, *pregnant women and others who are immuno-compromised should not eat any cheese, whether pasteurized or not, which has been matured for less than four months* if they wish to be sure of avoiding listeria.

The 'real' cheese lamented by Patrick Rance differs from pasteurized cheese in having 'depth', by which it is meant that the taste is complex rather than simple, i.e. made up of a variety of different flavours. These develop as a result of the wide variety of bacteria naturally present in untreated milk, which cannot be, or up until now have not been, precisely reproduced by artificial means. However, as well as Real Cheeses there are a number of extremely good, or even excellent pasteurized ones: these include blues and washed-rind cheeses, where mould contributes as much as bacteria, others in which local factors combined with consummate cheesemaking seem to override the effect of pasteurization, and several made with a starter preparation containing a larger number of bacterial strains than is usual at present. Starters of this kind are now used by some of the larger creameries, with noticeable results, and offer the prospect of considerable improvement in the overall standard of pasteurized cheeses in the future.

BSE, as is well known, is caused by a mutant protein rather than an organism. It dogged me throughout my research for this book; at the time, there was much concern lest it should be found in milk as well as meat, but it never has been. It has undoubtedly played a leading part in the enormous growth of the organic sector over the past few years: to this extent, one can say that some good has come out of it. The same, however, does not apply to foot-and-mouth, which has had a devastating effect on farmers and very nearly spelt the end for at least two makers of unpasteurized traditional cheeses, one of whom, Jonathan Crump (see page 52), literally sat out a siege by DEFRA officials.

CHEESEMAKING

The basic ingredients of cheese are milk, rennet, and salt. Starter has also been almost universally used in the last fifty years; before that, makers relied on the natural bacteria in the milk. Similarly, blue mould (*Penicillium roqueforti*) for blue cheese and white penicillin mould, which produces a white rind, are now usually inoculated into the milk but originally occurred naturally: the blue entered through cracks in the rind, as the odd thread of accidental green or blue mould sometimes invades non-blue cheeses; also, a species of bacterium which intensifies flavour, *Brevibacterium lineus*, is either rubbed directly over the surface of the cheese or grows on the rinds of washed-rind cheeses, giving them a characteristic orange or pinkish glow.

The composition of *milk* varies enormously: sheep's, goats' and buffaloes' milk is more homogeneous than cows'; sheep's and buffaloes' are higher in fat and more concentrated. Milk at the beginning and end of lactation is creamier than in the middle. Fat content is also influenced by feeding: a cow's morning milk may contain substantially less cream than in the evening, after she has been grazing all day. Fat can also be reduced, the proportion of saturated fats reduced, or the proportion of protein increased with certain concentrates. Increased protein is clearly of interest to cheesemakers, but those whom I asked about feeds were certainly not manipulating their milk in this way.

Starter inoculates the milk with several strains of lactic acid-producing bacteria, which may be introduced directly into the milk or via a culture. Milk contains about five per cent milk-sugars called lactose (the lactose is the reason milk rises when it boils). The bacteria feed on the lactose and produce acid: as they reproduce, the acidity of the milk or curd rises. If left for twenty-four hours or more, the milk can be curdled by the acid alone, as for fresh, so-called 'lactic' cheeses such as Highland crowdie; with rennet, it sets more firmly in only thirty to fifty minutes.

Traditional *rennet*, called chymosin, is an enzyme derived from a suckling calf's stomach; alternatives are a genetically engineered copy (Chymosin), which is approved by the Vegetarian Society, or extracts from moulds or plants. Partly because of BSE and vegetarianism, most makers favour mould extract, although purists and those whose cheeses need long maturing still prefer to use the traditional version.

Salt, the last ingredient to be added, is needed for flavour. It also has the effect of drawing out moisture and inhibiting bacterial action.

Broadly defined techniques for making the different types of cheeses have evolved over the centuries, but as every maker adapts them to suit his or her own circumstances, there are in effect as many methods as there are makers (although some may be similar). With any method, the art of making good cheese is to balance the rate of bacterial growth with the action of the setting enzyme on the curd. To reproduce, bacteria need food, water, warmth, and a particular level of pH (acidity): different conditions favour different kinds of bacteria. Once the starter bacteria are added, everything the cheesemaker does will affect their behaviour: depending on the type of starter used, their activity will rise faster or more steadily and then drop towards the end of the make. At this stage, the cheesemaker will texture the curd for hard or semi-hard cheeses by cutting, breaking, or piling it in blocks; for soft cheeses, in contrast, it will be transferred to moulds with as little disturbance as possible. Salt will be added or the cheeses brined after moulding, or both; finally, depending on the type of cheese and the maker's method, the curd may be milled before moulding and pressing.

During ripening or maturing, a series of complex chemical reactions takes place. The bodies of the dead bacteria release enzymes which act as catalysts to give flavour. Fats and proteins break down, which also adds to the flavour, and further contributions to both flavour and texture are made by yeasts and moulds, either from the atmosphere or deliberately introduced. Mould-ripened cheeses soften because enzymes produced by the mould contribute to the breakdown of proteins and to the increase in pH, which draws calcium from the body of the cheese to the surface.

Temperature and humidity throughout the maturing period, and for the rest of a cheese's life, are as important to its eventual quality as the skill of the maker at an earlier stage. The moisture balance within the cheese affects the reactions taking place, which in turn, again, affect both texture and flavour. Cheeses exude moisture through the rind: a humid atmosphere or covering them with lard or wax are ways of preventing them from dehydrating. The reason for the traditional practice of wrapping cheeses in cloths is that the cloth absorbs and to some extent regulates moisture loss.

In most cases, I have described the individual cheesemakers' procedures with the entries, sometimes briefly, sometimes in more detail: the following, however, is a summary of the main basic methods.

The simplest method is that used for soft or unpressed cheese, which includes *fresh and white-rind varieties*; for convenience, I have referred to it as the *Coulommiers* method, although similar methods are just as traditional to Britain. The aim is to keep as much moisture as possible in the curd, which is therefore not cut at all, or only slightly. Rather than whey (the liquid part of the milk) being drawn off before moulding, the cheeses are left to drain in the moulds, with no pressure other than their own weight; this is called 'free-draining'. Fresh cheeses, as a general rule, should be eaten as soon as possible. For the white mould-ripened type, the penicillin which forms the rind is added, usually at the beginning with the starter or rennet, and the cheeses are packaged when the rind has developed, usually after ten to sixteen days; a further maturing period, varying from two to six weeks, is needed before the cheeses are ripe.

A moist curd is also needed for *semi-soft cheeses*, which are sometimes lightly pressed, and as a rule are matured for two to three months. This category includes *washed-rind cheeses*, which may be washed with cider or perry, wine, or brine, and those smeared with *B. linens* mould. Smearing or washing encourages micro-organisms to reproduce on the surface, thus giving rise to a second ripening process, which takes place from the outside inwards: water is not used because of its impurities, but the kind of liquid is relatively unimportant except insofar as it influences the species of microbe involved (salt, although discouraging to many, is tolerated by others). Washed-rind cheeses are the kind which proverbially smell of old socks; however, while the point of them is that they should be distinctive, the smell may be stronger and quite different from the taste.

Blue cheeses, most of which are also semi-soft, are not only inoculated with the mould but are also pierced to introduce extra air into the cheese as a way of controlling maturing. Stilton is matured for five to six weeks before piercing and allowed to develop a rind, whereas cheeses made by the Roquefort method are pierced at two to five days old and air excluded by wrapping them in foil when the blue has developed sufficiently. As mould flourishes in a high-acid environment, the curd is drained naturally and sometimes left with the whey for an extended period.

For *Cheddar*, the curd is cut very small and heated, or 'scalded', to about 40–41°C/104–106°F, both of which help to expel moisture and give the cheese a firm, hard texture; during scalding, the curd is stirred continuously to ensure even distribution of heat. It is then drained and textured by being cut into blocks and piled at the sides of the vat. Traditionally, the cheeses are finished by rubbing them with lard and wrapping them in cloth; maturing may be for as long as one to two years. Double Gloucester is made similarly but scalded to a lower temperature and matured more quickly.

Caerphilly is scalded, textured by cutting rather than blocking and piling, and brined; traditionally, it is eaten after only a few weeks, but Neal's Yard Dairy mature Duckett's for up to three months and Patrice Savage-Onstwedder (page 172) keeps hers for eight or longer.

North of England cheeses, such as Cheshire, Lancashire, and white Wensleydale, have a light, flaky, or crumbly texture and are often classified as *semi-hard*. The curd is cut, broken, or crumbled instead of being blocked and piled, as for Cheddar; the curd for Lancashire, the crumbliest, is traditionally made with a mixture of fresh and the previous day's, plus sometimes two-day-old curd. Maturing times vary from a few weeks to six months.

BUYING, KEEPING, AND SERVING CHEESES

Most of the cheeses included in this book are sold only at specialist shops or cheese-counters, where they will be freshly sliced to your order. Several people whose judgement I respect will say that pre-slicing makes no difference to the taste, and I would agree that the effect is less noticeable with some than others: some in fact are made with pre-slicing and supermarket sales in mind. Similarly, many cheesemakers welcome vacuum-packing because it increases shelf-life and helps the cheese to survive the wrong storage conditions. However, I maintain that unpasteurized cheese with a range of flavours will start to lose its subtlety and aroma from the moment of cutting, and that to be enjoyed at its best it should not be sliced until purchase. For the same reason, you should eat it as soon as possible: buy only as much as you think you will need and use any left over for cooking.

If a cheese has to be kept after it is purchased, or sent by post, a small whole one is a good idea; however, for immediate eating a slice from a large one is almost always a better choice because it will have been matured for longer and consequently have developed deeper flavours.

Most cheese-shops will encourage you to taste before buying. This not only enables you to try new cheeses but is also useful because one of the attractions of artisan products is that results vary. Apart from maturity, cheeses will differ according to the weather or time of year when they were made, or even the field in which the animals grazed, so the one that you thought you wanted may not in fact be as good as another on this particular occasion. As with fruit and vegetables, be flexible: buy according to judgement rather than plan.

Just as there are not enough cheeses or makers, so there is a lack of good cheese-shops. A few of the makers included here sell to supermarkets: according to one school of thought, there should be many more, but an opposing faction feels that this would be un-desirable because it would threaten specialist cheese-shops. The fate of other independent shops gives substance to this fear; on the other hand, as Eurwen Richards points out, supermarkets can and do offer sales outlets in places where specialist shops would be out of the question. In general, various considerations, including care of the cheeses and the issue of pre-packing, small output, and the variable nature of specialist cheeses, make it questionable whether supermarkets will want to compete seriously in this area. As Eurwen says, 'Selling is possibly a greater problem with small-scale manufacturing than the making!'

Some cheeses from the north of England and Scotland are at present almost or completely unobtainable in the south; similarly, one of the Irish cheeses included cannot be bought in Britain. In cool weather, however, most cheeses can be sent by rail or post: contact the makers, but leave plenty of time, since small producers do not always have matured spare cheeses immediately available.

If cheese has to be kept, the best conditions for it are those in which it has been matured: for hard, semi-hard, and most semi-soft cheeses, these are 8–13°C/46–55°F, with eighty-five per cent or higher humidity. For most people, with no cellar and only a cen-trally heated house or refrigerator to choose from, this presents a problem. Both central heating and refrigeration are drying: keep the cheese wrapped in the waxed paper in which it was (or should have been) sold and, to increase humidity but maintain the circula-tion of air, place it in a loose-fitting, unsealed food-bag. It also helps to cover the cut surfaces of whole cheeses with clingfilm if you can make it stick without covering the rind. Then put it in a cool room or the boot of the car (this is Neal's Yard Dairy's suggestion); in hot weather, you will probably have to resort to the refrigerator. The garden or windowsill is not a good idea, since animals like cheese too. Soft cheeses should be wrapped similarly and kept chilled.

Most makers recommend chilling blue cheeses. Be particularly careful to wrap blue cheeses all over as mould spores spread readily not only to other cheeses but also to anything else near. If other cheeses develop mould on cut surfaces, just trim it off: the rest of the cheese will be unaffected.

I do not recommend freezing for preference, but many small, fresh sheep's and goats' cheeses and some white mould-ripened and blue cheeses, including Stilton, do in fact freeze satisfactorily. Defrost the cheese in the refrigerator and then leave it at room temperature for one to two hours before serving. Eat mould-ripened cheeses promptly, as ripening will be quicker than usual thereafter. It is, however, a mistake to try to ripen immature ones by this means: they must be ready to eat before freezing.

A large number of cheeses is not needed to make up a cheese-board: what matters are quality and the relation of the cheeses to each other. A selection of three is quite enough: four gives an opportunity to include one which is particularly good just then but does not balance the rest quite as effectively as another. Generally speaking, cheeses which contrast in strength, taste and texture, preferably from different types of animal, will set each other off to advantage and create a satisfying whole. For example, you might choose Beenleigh Blue (sheep's), Ragstone (white-rind goats'), and Lincolnshire Poacher or Staffordshire Organic (Cheddar-type); a fourth could be Wigmore (semi-soft sheep's), Celtic Promise (washed-rind), or Lancashire (crumbly). A wonderful selection of Irish cheeses would be Mine-Gabhar (effectually organic white-rind goats'), Cashel Blue (cows'), and Gabriel (hard cows'), with Durrus or Gubbeen (semi-soft cows', rind smeared with *Brevibacterium linens*) as a fourth. Another approach might be to choose at least two cheeses of different types and strengths but with background tastes in common, thus creating an underlying harmony against which their other characteristics can be better appreciated. This is often achieved with cheeses from the same area, or even the same farm: a very successful cheeseboard along these lines could be made up with St Cuthbert's Cave (mild but distinctive semi-soft cows'), mature Berwick Edge (hard and as strong as a blue), both from North Doddington Farm in Northumberland, with Innes Button (light, fresh goats') as a contrast. A similar example, this time of cheeses from different farms but adjacent areas, might be Bonnet (hard goats'), Lanark or Dunsyre Blue, and Crannog or Criffel. The better you know the cheeses, the more interesting and subtle the effects you can achieve: the possibilities are endless.

If you do not want to buy three cheeses, two, or even just one, if it is really good, is enough. A well balanced board of three or four does not need additions, but with only one or two contrast can be supplied or flavours followed through with fruit, nuts, or salad vegetables. Where applicable, I have given particular suggestions, sometimes from the makers themselves, with the entries: more general ones include apples, notably crisp, sharp/sweet James Grieve or Falstaff, with Cheddar or Cheddar-style cheeses; pears, grapes, or figs with blues or hard sheep's cheeses; strawberries with mild, soft goats' cheeses, and plum or cherry tomatoes and/or olives with almost any goats' cheese. An alternative to fresh fruit is fruit 'cheese', which is boiled down to a solid consistency and made with half as much sugar as jam. Walnuts are often served with blue cheeses; pecans are delicious with salty ones such as Isle of Mull; hazelnuts bring out sweet, earthy, nutty or mushroom-like tones. Mellow or earthy-tasting cheeses are also excellent with asparagus; an ideal accompaniment to every kind of cheese is organic celery, which is as different from the conventionally grown version as handmade from creamery Lancashire. Salad leaves, whether as garnishes or part of a composed salad, should be bitter, or at least not sweet, e.g. chicory, endive, batavia, sorrel, lamb's lettuce, or any sort of red lettuce; celeriac tops are strong but interesting with mild Cheddars; the sharpness of watercress matches Stilton and other blue cheeses; mizuna or rocket contrasts pleasingly with mild sheep's or goats' cheeses.

Cheese served before the sweet means that you can continue to drink the main course wine and do not have to adapt from a sweet to savoury taste: three or more cheeses served at this stage are not only better without extras such as fruit but can probably also be eaten without bread or biscuits. Otherwise, I favour bread rather than biscuits partly because most of the biscuits around are so disappointing. The ideal bread for most cheeses is sourdough, but rye, wholemeal, and rough, gritty Irish soda bread go especially well with soft and semi-soft cheeses; so, in a different way, does very crisp, light French bread. Like other accompaniments to particular cheeses, flavoured breads are mentioned in the text. The only biscuits that I have come across which seem to me worthy of good cheese are: Clarke's thin oatmeal biscuits, handmade and a true luxury; Millers Damzel Original Wheat Wafers (only the plain version does not contain hydrogenated vegetable oil), Paxton & Whitfield's Plain Wheat or Mixed Seed Biscuits, or the Organic Oatcakes; and the rather more substantial Duchy Originals. Carr's plain water biscuits make a crisp, light foil to soft cheeses; Marks & Spencer's cheese digestives work particularly well with mellow cheeses.

Whether with bread or biscuits, butter (if any) should be unsalted, or only lightly salted: salty butter clashes with the flavour of cheese. Several of the cheesemakers make either ordinary or whey-butter, including the Keens, Applebys, and Bill Hogan: whey-butter is deliciously sweet and especially good with cheese because it has a more delicate, slightly less rich texture than usual, but it melts at a relatively low temperature and therefore should not be left in a hot room for long or used for pastry.

Cheeses which have been kept chilled should be taken out of the refrigerator one and a half to two hours before serving, since, as with red wine, cold deadens flavour; it also hardens soft cheeses so that white mould-ripened types will not flow. The only rinds meant to be eaten, and treated accordingly, are the white mould kind; others, if you want to eat them, should be washed. Divide cheese so that everybody has an equal share of the inside and outside: with round cheeses, this means cutting them in wedges, like a cake; cheese bought in slices should be cut lengthwise rather than across. Tall truckles are easier to serve if sliced horizontally before serving (some cheesemakers sell half-cheeses sliced in this way); the cut surface must then be covered with clingfilm or closely wrapped with cheese-paper before storage.

COOKING WITH CHEESE

When cheese is heated to a certain point, it coagulates in the same way as meat and forms lumps as dense and resilient, and reputedly indigestible, as chewing-gum: it is therefore essential to avoid over-cooking. If it does not melt sufficiently, you can always return it to the heat, but once coagulated it is beyond rescue. Apart from this, its behaviour when heated depends on the structure of the milk and the way the cheese was made. Cows' milk, with relatively large fat globules, will spread and may leach some of the fat; goats' and sheep's milk, which is more homogeneous, will break down less easily. This is one of the reasons for the popularity of goats' cheeses for grilling; it also means that sheep's cheeses in sauces and fillings need more heat than cows' before they will melt and amalgamate. Cheeses heated to a high temperature when they are made, which shrinks and hardens the curd particles, may similarly remain firm: an extreme example is halloumi, which can be fried without a protective coating.

Just as the taste of cheese is deadened by cold, it also changes when hot; however, whereas the effect of cold is consistent, that of heat is very variable. Goats' cheeses generally become sweeter; skim-milk or very low-fat cheeses tend to lose their flavour. Otherwise, no easily defined rule applies: some cheeses become bland, some taste more intense. When you have a cheese which you have not used for cooking before, and for which no recipes are given here, toast a small piece before proceeding, but bear in mind that even if it seems to keep its flavour, the taste may not be strong enough to make itself felt in a sauce.

THE RECIPES

You may feel that cooking with expensive, handmade cheeses is extravagant, but the maxim holds: you cannot produce a first-class result without first-class ingredients. There is also the fact that left-over pieces of cheese will deteriorate. However, on the assumption that you will buy the cheeses primarily for eating rather than cooking, I have balanced the recipes in favour of quick, simple dishes; in choosing them, I have also tried to give an idea of the enormous scope of cheese cookery. Blue cheese in particular can be used to give zest to meat dishes; soft cheese adds a creamy consistency to soups, can be served with fruit as a healthier alternative to cream, and used as the basis of salad dressing instead of mayonnaise. As the fact that fruit goes well with cheese suggests, the options are not limited to savoury dishes: you can use cheeses to make delicious sweets and even excellent cakes.

Unless otherwise stated, large eggs the equivalent of size 2, olive oil (not extra virgin), unsalted butter, freshly ground black pepper, and Maldon sea-salt should be used throughout. Full instructions have been given with every recipe except for the following, which occur repeatedly.

Short Pastry

Making pastry is actually very easy if you bear three points in mind: it must be kept cool, worked as little as possible, and mixed with as little water as possible. The fat should not be taken from the refrigerator until directly before use: if the dough becomes sticky, either because of a warm kitchen or through overworking, a lot of extra flour will be needed for rolling out. The same will apply if it is too wet; in either case, the proportion of fat will be reduced, with the result that the pastry will be tough. Overworking, besides generating heat, develops the gluten in the flour, which is desirable for bread or pasta but, again, will make for tough pastry.

The pastry can be kept in the refrigerator, rolled or unrolled, for three days before baking; it also freezes well. The quantity given is enough to line a 22-cm/8½-inch tart tin or dish.

> 200g/7oz plain flour, white, wholemeal, or a mixture, plus extra for
>   rolling
> salt
> 50g/1¾oz each butter and lard *or* 100g/3½oz butter (for vegetarians)

Blend the flour with a pinch of salt. Add and cut the fat into it as finely as possible with a sharp knife; then rub it with your fingertips until the mixture is like fine breadcrumbs. Make a well in the centre, add a scant 2 tablespoonsful of iced or very cold water, and draw the ingredients into a ball of dough, gradually adding just as much more water as is needed to take up all the flour. Leave the dough to rest for 15–20 minutes in the refrigerator. Dust the rolling-pin and board with flour and roll out the dough to 4–5mm/just under ¼ inch thick. Place the dough over the tart tin or dish and press it loosely and gently into the edges: it should fit closely without being stretched. Trim it generously to allow for slight shrinkage; if you are using a dish, stamp it round the rim.

Baking blind, which partly cooks the pastry, will ensure that it stays crisp under a liquid filling. Cover the pastry closely, including the rim, with cooking foil; to prevent it from rising, weigh it down with baking beans if they are available. Bake in a pre-heated oven at 200°C/400°F/Gas 6, for 10–12 minutes; remove the foil and bake for a further 5 minutes or until the pastry starts to colour.

Puff Pastry

Puff pastry takes a little time to make because, in order to produce the layers which make it puff up, you have to chill it at intervals. The following is not the classic method but the one which I find quickest and easiest. Like short pastry, it can be kept chilled for up to three days and freezes well.

> 200g/7oz plain white flour plus extra for rolling
> salt
> 200g/7oz butter straight from the refrigerator
> a few drops of lemon juice
> 1 small free-range egg for glazing (optional)

Mix the flour with a little salt. Cut 150g/5$\frac{1}{4}$oz of the butter into thin slices and, unless the kitchen is very cool, return it to the refrigerator until needed. Cut the rest into the flour as for short pastry; then rub with your fingertips until it has disappeared. Make a well in the centre and add the lemon juice and 3 tablespoonsful of iced or very cold water; mould the ingredients into a dough, adding more water as necessary. Sprinkle the rolling-pin and board with flour, set the sliced butter to hand, and roll the dough into an oblong 5mm/$\frac{1}{4}$-inch thick. Distribute half the butter over it, leaving a margin of at least 3cm/over 1 inch round the edges. Fold over the top third of the pastry and cover with the bottom third, as if folding writing-paper to fit into an envelope. Seal the edges all round and roll it out again. Add the rest of the butter, fold, and seal as before. Sprinkle the dough lightly with flour, cover it with cling-film, and put it into the refrigerator for 30–45 minutes or until it becomes firm and cool but not hard. Re-roll and fold the pastry twice more. Return it to the refrigerator and repeat the process. To use the pastry, roll it out to 5–6mm/about ¼-inch thick and follow the directions given with the recipe. If you are making a pie, trim it very generously to allow for shrinkage. Brush it with egg if you wish and bake it at 220°C/425°F/Gas 7.

 ## Stock

Making stock is perceived as taking a great deal of time; however, I have tested all the recipes in this book with chicken stock con-sisting simply of a free-range chicken carcass, 1.4–1.5 litres/2½–2¾ pints of water, and 4 or 5 peppercorns (no salt), covered and sim-mered for 3½–4 hours. Often, the chicken was pot-roasted with herbs and garlic, and sometimes wine or a couple of teaspoonsful of sherry vinegar, which help, but a plain roasted carcass will do perfectly well. The stock should be strained promptly and chilled before use so that you can skim off the fat. It will keep in the refrigerator for three days and for an extra day if reheated and simmered for 15 minutes.

Vegetarians may have their own preferences, but mushrooms are a good basis for a vegetable stock sympathetic to cheese. For flavour as well as convenience, I suggest dried porcini (but not chanterelles): any mushroom stalks or skins which may be available are a useful addition.

Vegetable Stock
10g/¼ oz porcini, soaked for 20 minutes in 300ml/½ pint hot water
2 medium onions (about 300g/10½oz together), peeled and sliced

2 medium carrots (about 200g/7oz together), peeled and sliced
mushroom stalks and skins if available, washed
a sprig of rosemary
5 peppercorns
2 tsp sherry vinegar
700ml/1¼pints water

Put the ingredients, including the porcini liquid, into a large saucepan. Bring to the boil, cover, and simmer for 25 minutes. Strain and use the same day.

Grilling Cheeses

Toast made in a toaster tends to be moist and leathery: to give the cheese a really crisp base, the bread must be dried in the oven. This is less of a nuisance than it sounds because it can be prepared twenty-four hours or more in advance. Cut the crusts from the bread and bake it at 200°C/400°F/Gas 6 for 10–12 minutes or until it turns pale gold; if baked far ahead of time, store the toast in a tin or wrapped in foil.

Before adding the cheese, sprinkle the bread with a little oil for goats' or sheep's cheeses or butter it thinly for cows'; if the cheese is very mild, add just a few grains of salt and a little pepper. With goats' cheeses, you can also rub the bread with a clove of garlic. Even with cows' cheeses, which (unless made into rarebit) will spread, make sure that the cheese covers it completely: any exposed edges will burn. As goats' and sheep's cheeses will not release fat, moisten the top of the cheese with a little more oil. Place the bread under a fairly hot grill until the cheese bubbles slightly and begins to colour: do not let it become very brown. Serve the grilled cheese alone or with celery, tomatoes, or bitter leaves.

Frying Cheeses in Breadcrumbs

This is a rich but delicious way of serving soft mould-ripened cheeses; you can also roll fresh goats' cheeses into balls and fry them by the same method. It is essential that the cheese should be hardened in the refrigerator before being cut and coated; it is equally important that the oil should be hot enough to brown and crisp the outside before the cheese has had time to melt and escape. The oil should be sunflower or olive: olive is expensive and gives a slightly less crisp result but better flavour. Avoid groundnut oil, which sometimes produces a bitter taint. Serve the cheese with a salad of cherry tomatoes and bitter leaves.

For 3–4 as a first course

25g/1oz white flour
1 medium free-range egg, beaten
40–50g/1¹/₂–1³/₄oz fresh fine brown or white breadcrumbs
salt and pepper
150–160g/5¹/₄–5¹/₂oz cheese
oil for frying
fat or sugar thermometer *or* a few small squares of stale bread

Sprinkle the flour over a large plate, pour the egg into a saucer or small bowl, and spread the breadcrumbs over another plate. Season the flour and egg moderately with salt and pepper. Take the cheese out of the refrigerator and cut it into 1.5-cm/¹/₂-inch squares (do not cut off the rind, which will add to the flavour). Coat the cheese, first with the flour, then with the egg, then the breadcrumbs: shake off any surplus but be particularly careful to ensure that the cheese is completely coated on all sides. Return the cheese to the refrigerator until you are ready to start frying.

Line a plate with absorbent paper to drain surplus fat from the cheese after it has cooked. Use a small, heavy pan for frying: pour in at least 3.5cm/1$\frac{1}{4}$ inches of oil. Place over fairly high heat until the oil has reached 180°C/350°F. If you do not have a thermometer, slide in cubes of bread: the oil is hot enough when they turn golden in about 40 seconds. Reduce the heat slightly to maintain the temperature and gently lower in a few pieces of cheese. Do not drop them in, since they might splash (be careful: hot oil burns badly and ignites easily). Add only as many as will fit into the pan without touching. Cook the cheese until just golden, then remove it instantly; drain it on the paper. Serve the first batch before you fry the next.

 ## Fruit Cheeses

Fruit cheese is so called because of its stiff consistency: people with fruit in their gardens used to make and eat it, not necessarily with but instead of cheese. This version goes particularly well with strong Cheddar and Single Gloucester.

Apple Cheese
1kg/2lb 4oz Bramley apples
5 cloves
5cm/2-inch stick cinnamon
about 425g/15oz granulated or caster sugar

Wash and chop but do not peel the apples, and put them into a large saucepan with the cores, spices, and 450ml/16fl oz of water. Bring the water slowly to the boil, stir, skim, and simmer for 1 hour, until the apples are very soft. Sieve them and weigh the purée; return it to a heavy-bottomed pan, preferably non-stick, and add half the purée's weight of sugar. Set the pan over low heat, stir until the sugar has melted, and boil it gently for another hour or until stiff and jelly-like. Lightly butter a shallow mould; pour in the cheese and leave it to cool.

Using this basic recipe, you can also make Plum and Apple Cheese, which tones well with mellow cheeses, notably Double Gloucester and Cheshire, or Pear and Apple Cheese, which is especially recommended with hard goats' cheeses. For the Plum and Apple Cheese, use 500g/1lb 2oz each Bramley apples and red plums (washed and diced), the same quantities of cloves and cinnamon as for Apple Cheese, and about 300g/10½oz granulated or caster sugar. For the Pear and Apple Cheese, use 500g/1lb 2oz each Bramley apples and Conference pears (chopped fairly small) and about 375g/13oz pectin sugar.

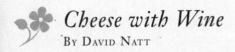

Cheese with Wine
By David Natt

The combination of cheese with wine has changed from 1960s cliché to 1990s conundrum. Successful matching requires a little careful thought. To guide your choices, you will need to consider the ways in which both sides of the partnership are constituted in order to get the chemistry right.

In the brief examples given here, I am envisaging cheese being served before dessert as part of an evening meal. It is always worth seeing how the red wine you have been drinking carries through into the cheese course, but I would recommend serving a sweet white wine simultaneously – either a semi-sweet Riesling or Chenin Blanc to herald the dessert wine to come or bringing a suitable dessert wine with good acidity forward in the meal.

FRESH SOFT GOATS' OR SHEEP'S CHEESES

The light, chalky texture of goats' cheeses, such as Ragstone, or a sheep's cheese such as Wigmore, suggests a lightish wine. Soft cheeses have fat which is 'free' or not bound into the structure of the cheese. This protects against tannins in the wine, but it also acts as a barrier against the perception of flavour. If a wine is to cut through, it must have enough acidity. Sauvignon Blanc is a classic partner but is out of place after a red wine. A degree of sweetness in the wine will not go amiss. Semi-sweet Vouvray or German Riesling Spatlese or Auslese work very well and provide a natural bridge into a sweeter dessert wine.

MOULD-RIPENED CHEESES

Mould-ripened cheeses, such as Bath Soft or Burland Green, coat the mouth and demand copious acidity (or alcohol) to cut through them. The persistent cabbage flavour of ripe examples plays havoc with the complex finish on mature red wines (though 'farmyardy' Burgundy is better than cedary claret). The clean apple flavours of Chenin Blanc blend much better, or the piercing acidity of a semi-sweet German Riesling also cuts through refreshingly and is capable of taking the overlay of cheese flavour on the finish. If red wine is essential, then a young, uncomplicated wine with bracing fruit and plenty of acidity works best.

WASHED-RIND CHEESES

Creamily textured, with pungent aromas and complex, persistent flavours, washed-rind cheeses such as Tornegus are a challenge to match. Red wines need to be very young and straightforward, and even then are likely to fade badly as tannins essential to their structure are stripped away. Young red Burgundy can become pleasantly rose-scented (if rather watery), but on the whole white wines have a better chance of success. The star turn here is good quality Alsace Gewurztraminer. Its weight of flavour and floral high notes seem well suited to such cheese, forming an interesting mixture of the slightly fetid and the scented. A semi-sweet Riesling with sufficient body can work similarly.

CHEDDAR AND CHEDDAR-STYLE

The high acidity of a mature farmhouse Cheddar or Cheddar-style cheese will eviscerate any wine where acidity is not a linchpin of its constitution. A mature claret becomes a pointless companion, despite the traditional association. Younger reds are rather cowed by the cheese but do co-exist better, provided they are not particularly tannic, since there will be little ameliorative free protein or fat in the cheese, but plenty of Umami or 'savour' to react adversely. A crisp, dry white will seem thin (as well as misplaced at this stage in a meal). The required weight needs to come from sugar. What you are looking for in many ways is the vinous equivalent of sweet pickle. Is it such a sacrilege to suggest a sweet Chenin Blanc – right in terms of acidity, sweetness, and body, and the wine world's flavour equivalent to cider, a traditionally British Cheddar accompaniment? Other rich sweet wines with good acidity can also work successfully.

BLUE CHEESES

You are not yet at the port stage of the meal, so that familiar companion is not available. A good Stilton will certainly finish off your red for you if that is what you are intent on: its combination of salt, acidity, savour, and crumbly/creamy texture simultaneously point up tannins, take out fruit acids and block flavours. A Sauternes, however, is as much at home in this environment as with blue Wensleydale or Roquefort. Other sweet wines with good acidity also work well, especially if they are already or can be botrytis-affected, when they seem to exhibit a particular affinity to the tang of blue mould. Sweet Chenin Blanc and Riesling seem good choices once more.

The Real Cheese Companion

CHAPTER 1

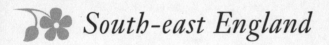 *South-east England*

VILLAGE MAID

WIELD WOOD FARM

EASTSIDE CHEESE CO.

HURST FARM CHEESES

OLD PLAW HATCH ORGANIC

SUSSEX HIGH WEALD DAIRY PRODUCTS

GREENACRES FARM

NUT KNOWLE FARM CHEESES

THE TRADITIONAL CHEESE DAIRY

CHILDWICKBURY GOATS

Village Maid

Anne and Andy Wigmore, The Cottage, Basingstoke
Road, Riseley, Reading, Berkshire RG7 1QD.
Tel: 0118 9884564

Anne Wigmore is unique among the cheesemakers in Britain in coming, not from a farming background but from the other, more modern arm of cheesemaking, the laboratory – and stands as proof of just how valuable an intimate knowledge of the relevant chemistry and microbiology can be. After studying the digestive processes of ruminants and spending several years making experimental cheeses for scientific purposes, she did not set out to revive an old recipe but aimed to create an entirely new cheese unlike any which at that time were produced in Britain. Even for her, however, perfecting it took time; perhaps because she had a very clear idea of what she wanted, she did not feel that she had completely mastered it (her word) for seven years. This was Spenwood, a hard, full-flavoured sheep's cheese: several other cheeses of this type are now made but, despite Olivia Mills and the British Sheep Dairying Association (page 9), still not nearly enough. Her next cheese was a hard Guernsey cheese, Wellington, so named because the milk originally came from the Duke of Wellington's estate, Stratfield Saye, which is just up the road; the cheeses were also matured in the Duke's cellar. The two hard cheeses were followed by Wigmore, a semi-soft sheep's cheese which remains unique in this country, and a soft Guernsey cheese, Waterloo. When I went to see them, they were still making Wellington, but they have now decided to discontinue it in favour of twice as much Waterloo. Particularly in view of the general lack of soft cheeses, this is excellent news with regard to Waterloo; however, I regret Wellington, which was distinguished for its clean, crisp tang and quite exceptional toasting properties.

When Anne started, Andy worked as a journalist, but as the cheese business gathered momentum he abandoned writing and joined her; they now work together, helped by three assistants who are employed on a part-time basis so that, like Anne herself, they can combine cheesemaking with looking after their children. The milk for the sheep's cheeses comes from two farms, one in Northamptonshire and one near Stratford-upon-Avon. The Stratfield Saye milk dried up, so to speak, when the estate was inherited by a new heir who decided to convert it entirely to arable land and sell the cows. Their milk now comes from two specific farms nearby, and as they need only take it when they want it, they find that the arrangement suits them very well: unlike many cheesemakers, they can go away for holidays whenever they wish.

It so happened that I visited them on the very first day of the new delivery: normally, although they have two vats, they make only one cheese at a time, but on this occasion, partly because they were anxious to test the new milk, they were making both Wellington and Waterloo. When I arrived, Andy was piling the blocks of curd for Wellington, which was a Cheddar-style cheese, while Anne was using a hose to wash the curds, i.e. replace some of the whey with water, for Waterloo. This is a process typically used for Gouda which reduces acidity and helps to give the cheese a mild, sweet flavour; she also uses it for her semi-soft sheep's cheese, Wigmore.

WATERLOO

Silver Medal, British Cheese Awards 1997 and 2002
A semi-soft cows' cheese; full-fat, unpasteurized milk; vegetarian rennet.
900g/2lb rounds

Waterloo is luscious and creamy, with the sweetness of the rich milk and undertones of herbs and grass. If allowed to mature for an extended time (as on occasion at Neal's Yard), it becomes firm and buttery, rather like a milder version of Durrus or Gubbeen (pages 151 and 157). If you have any left over, fry it in egg and bread-crumbs (page xxix) and serve with redcurrant jelly.

Waterloo is made according to the very simple Coulommiers method, by which the curds are ladled into moulds without prior draining, so that the whey, or in this case whey and water, pours out in a stream; no pressure is applied except by piling the moulds. Anne stacks them in piles of three for the first hour; they are then turned, remoulded, and stacked in sixes. A point about which she is especially particular, because of its effect not only on taste but also on moisture content and ripening, is salting: like a few but increasing number of other makers, she favours both a light dry salting and brining, which is partly why Waterloo is notable for a consistently creamy texture all the way through. It is matured for four weeks and remains creamy for a further two to two and a half; by ten, it will have become buttery.

WIGMORE

Gold Medal, British Cheese Awards 1996, 1997 and 2002
A semi-soft sheep's cheese; unpasteurized milk; vegetarian rennet.
450g/1lb or 1.4–1.8kg/3–4lb rounds

Wigmore is fairly firm when young but flows slightly when older (the Wigmores mature it for two to three months). Although creamy, the texture has the lightness characteristic of soft sheep's cheeses; the balance of flavours changes according to season but includes grass, herbs, and flowers. The overall impression is subtle, cool, and refreshing: the cheese does not clamour for attention, but once tried becomes compulsive. The three Gold Medals at the British Cheese Awards are absolutely justified.

SPENWOOD

A hard sheep's cheese; unpasteurized milk; vegetarian rennet.
2.3kg/5lb truckles

When matured for six months, Spenwood is relatively moist and mild, with a delicate but distinctive grassy tang; as is characteristic of all the Wigmores' cheeses, the flavour is precisely balanced between salty and sharp. At this age, it is ripe for the table: at eight to ten months, it becomes harder, drier, and stronger, not unlike a soft-tasting pecorino, and is ideal for sprinkling over risotto or pasta.

 ## Tagliatelle with Spenwood and Spring Vegetables

Use young beans: old ones have tough skins which it is preferable to remove after cooking. Similarly, as old peas can take a long time to cook, I recommend frozen (if you use fresh ones, boil them separately). As the egg is not cooked sufficiently to set, take care to use one with the Lion brand (indicating that it is free of salmonella).

Cooking time: about 30 minutes
For 2–3

125g/4¹/₂oz frozen or young fresh broad beans, weighed after
    podding
salt
150g/5¹/₄oz frozen peas
100g/3¹/₂oz baby spinach, washed
250g/9oz fresh tagliatelle, plain or flavoured with garlic and herbs
25g/1oz butter
1 tbsp oil
200g/7oz baby or very young leeks, chopped into 1cm/¹/₂-inch slices,
    washed, and left to dry

1 medium shallot (about 50g/1¾oz), peeled and finely chopped

3 cloves garlic, peeled and finely chopped

2 tsp flour

2 tsp Dijon mustard

2 tsp white wine vinegar

pepper

1 large free-range egg yolk, beaten

2 tbsp double cream

140g/5oz Spenwood (8–10 months old), finely grated

Boil the beans in 600ml/1 pint slightly salted water for 9–10 minutes or until just tender. Add the peas and spinach, stirring to ensure that the spinach is submerged; bring the water back to the boil and cook for a bare 2 minutes (no longer). Drain the vegetables over a bowl; reserve the cooking liquor. Cover the vegetables to keep them warm.

Set a large pan of water to boil for the tagliatelle. Melt the butter in the oil over medium heat and fry the leeks and shallot for about 1½ minutes. Add the garlic and continue to fry for another 2–3 minutes or until the leeks are soft and the shallot starts to change colour; turn constantly, since leeks burn easily. Stir in the flour off the heat. When it is thoroughly incorporated, pour in 300ml/½ pint of the vegetable liquor (do not throw away the rest), return the pan to the heat, and stir until the sauce thickens. Add the mustard, vinegar, and a moderate seasoning of salt and pepper; reduce the heat to low and simmer for 3–4 minutes, stirring constantly. Remove the pan from the heat.

While the sauce simmers, cook the tagliatelle. Check that the water is boiling: add a little salt and the pasta, bring the water back to the boil, stir, and boil briskly for 2–3 minutes or according to the instructions on the packet, until the pasta is *al dente*. Drain at once and return it to the hot pan.

While the pasta cooks, gradually add about a tablespoonful of the remaining vegetable liquor (which should still be fairly hot) to the egg yolk, beating continuously with a fork; continue beating until it is smooth and set it aside. Add the cream to the sauce and bring it to the boil. Stir in the peas, beans, and spinach, return the sauce to the boil, and add all but about 3 tablespoonsful of the cheese. Remove the pan from the heat and stir in the egg yolk. Continue stirring until the mixture thickens; if necessary, return the pan to low heat for a moment but do not allow it to boil or the egg may curdle. Toss the sauce with the tagliatelle and serve immediately with the rest of the cheese sprinkled on top.

Wield Wood Farm

CHRISTINE NEWENS, WIELD WOOD FARM, UPPER WIELD, ALRESFORD, HANTS SO24 9RU.
TEL: 01420 563151/564182

The revival of sheep dairy-farming in Britain is largely the achievement of the late Olivia Mills: with Robin Congdon (page 107), she led the way in raising sheep for milking; she was also the founder and secretary of the British Sheep Dairying Association and author of the remarkably downright but often wryly funny *Practical Sheep Dairying*, which covers not only raising sheep but also how to make it pay. Almost everyone planning to milk sheep, from the Whites in Cornwall (page 115) to Allan Brown in Wigtownshire (page 275), went to her for advice. To stimulate new ideas in a field which it was part of her life's work to turn into a profitable industry, she used to take members of the Association abroad every spring: the year the first edition of this book went to press, a group which included the Hardys and Mary Holbrook (pages 21 and 66) went to Bulgaria.

Innovation in the dairy sector, as well as cheesemaking and her 200-ha/500-acre farm near the perhaps rather too pretty village of Preston Candover, were all part of her inheritance. The farm was bought by her father, who, with Hosier (the inventor of the Hosier bale), pioneered machine-milking for cows; her mother taught her to make cheese – and be mistress of it. No cheesemaking routine, Olivia declared, should be onerous to the maker: 'Never let your cheese rule you.' On the other hand, she agreed that cheesemakers should take the trouble to learn about the chemistry involved even if in practice they work by judgement and eye. A point which she was especially anxious that I should emphasize was that, like Mark Hardy's (page 21), any kind of sheep's cheese should be accompanied by ricotta (which is made from the whey): 'Ricotta represents profit.' Very sadly, she died in September 2002, but Christine, who has acted as farm manager and cheesemaker at Wield Wood for the past twenty years, is continuing the production of Walda exactly as before: the only difference from the customers' point of view is that it is now sold at most of the Hampshire farmers' markets, notably Winchester, as well as in shops.

WALDA

A hard or semi-hard sheep's cheese, according to maturity; thermized milk; vegetarian rennet. 1–2kg/2lb 4oz–4lb 6oz

The young cheese is moist and very mild, tasting gently of the Sussex grass but with a slight peppery aftertaste; the more mature cheese is drier and harder, with a distinctive tang and quite a strong aftertaste. It is sold plain or with caraway or green peppercorns: the latter is especially recommended.

The recipe for Walda is very simple. The milk is heated to 57–58°C/135–136°F, i.e. thermized, which does not kill all the bacteria present but destroys some pathogens and reduces the likelihood of off-flavours 'blowing' caused by gas-producing organisms; it is then cooled to 29°C/84°F before starter and rennet are added. When the curd has set, it is drained, cut, and left to rest for about another half-hour before being salted and moulded; salting (dry) follows after unmoulding the next day. The maturing time is three months to a year: if you want a mature cheese, which is especially suitable for cooking, it can be ordered from the farm.

 ## Walda and Anchovy Salad

This is delicious but potent: serve it with rough, crusty bread. If possible, wash the salad leaves an hour or so before the meal to give them plenty of time to dry.

For 4

1 clove garlic, peeled and chopped
4 tbsp virgin olive oil
1 tbsp red wine vinegar
salt and pepper
175–225g/6–8oz mixed curly endive and non-sweet salad leaves, such
    as lamb's lettuce, baby spinach, red chard leaves, mizuna or rocket,
    washed and allowed to dry
175g/6oz Walda (plain)
12–16 anchovy fillets, rinsed
85g/3oz (20–24) black olives, pitted if you wish
about 16 basil leaves, washed and allowed to dry

Crush the garlic in a mortar. Add the oil, vinegar, a very little salt, and a moderate seasoning of pepper, and beat until homogeneous. Arrange the salad leaves on the serving plates. Thinly slice or (if very mature) crumble the Walda over the leaves, then add the anchovy fillets and olives. Tear the basil leaves into two or three pieces and scatter them over the top. Beat the dressing again with a fork and pour it over the salad directly before serving.

 Eastside Cheese Co.
PAT ROBINSON, EAST LODGE, TANDRIDGE HILL LANE, GODSTONE, SURREY RH9 8DD. TEL: 01883 743617

The founder of the Eastside Cheese Company was James Aldridge, who died unexpectedly two years ago in very sad circumstances. He leaves a gap in the British cheese world that no one else can fill. To an extent that was perhaps not recognized until towards the end of his life, the current revival of Real Cheese in Britain is largely due to him. Randolph Hodgson of Neal's Yard Dairy has done more than anyone else to ensure that it receives the attention that it deserves, but James was the *éminence grise* behind the scenes: by maturing, experimenting and instructing others, he played a crucial role in improving its quality and extending its range. In accordance with his feeling about unpasteurized milk, a James Aldridge Memorial Trophy, donated by HRH The Prince of Wales, is now presented annually for the best unpasteurized British cheese: the first, in 2001, was won by Kevin and Alison Blunt for Golden Cross (page 30).

He started out in the building trade, where he would probably have stayed if he had not been forced to change his occupation because of an injury. His first idea was to open a sandwich shop, but he was deflected by Pat, who was at that time working in a store selling cheap ham and cheese near Southampton. Although the cheese was by no means of the type that he spent nearly twenty years promoting, it roused his curiosity: the first 'real' cheese he tasted, and continued to love all his life, was Duckett's Caerphilly (page 92). He opened James's of Beckenham in 1981 and, along with the usual blocks of creamery-made Cheddar, sold the unpasteurized, farmhouse-made cheeses for which the shop became known. As Neal's Yard Dairy does now, he collected them from the farms himself, and to minimize travelling would take as many as the makers were prepared to sell, whether they were ripe or not, which led him into maturing. The expertise which this demands increasingly engrossed him; it also led him to develop his first washed-rind cheese, Tornegus, based on Duckett's Caerphilly. After eight years, having become far more interested in this side of his business than retailing, he sold the shop to set up as a wholesaler-cum-maturer, in the style of French *affineurs*.

Thereafter, he worked from home maturing, rind-washing and making his own cheeses in a dairy which was in effect a laboratory. Of the numerous cheeses he produced at one time or another, one that I particularly remember is a hard goats' cheese called Gruff, which was mild but at the same time powerful, sweet yet smoky, and cool and refreshing on the tongue, others were a combined sheep's and goats' cheese of extraordinary richness and subtlety and a marvellously sweet sheep's Wensleydale, as well as Lord of the Hundreds (page 38) and St Francis (page 198). His attitude to cheesemaking was like that of the developmental chef: once a recipe had been perfected, his interest in it receded and he progressed to the next. Certainly, when he started experimenting, not all his ideas were successful, but for James learning was the whole point of the exercise: he did not mind if a recipe turned out less well than he had hoped so long as he was able to find out why.

The need for both instruction and recipe development was shown by the number of cheesemakers who applied to him when they had problems or wanted to launch a new cheese. Usually, he went to them, partly because they might not be able to leave their animals, but mainly in order to assess their working environment. All his services were given for love: he never asked anyone for payment, even for expenses (which were usually minimal: rather than staying in a hotel when he was working away from home, he would sleep in his van).

His definition of Real Cheese did not change over the years: to him, the particular joy of it was the taste of the ripened milk unfolding in successive layers of flavour on the tongue. This cuts out pasteurization: if you pointed out that a few good pasteurized cheeses are nevertheless made, he would reply that they might perhaps be good, but never very good (though he did concede that this might be less true of blue cheeses). Multiple starters were therefore of no interest to him either: he felt that if you wanted to add flavour to a cheese, you might as well do so directly. He was also one of the few people I have met who stated flatly that there is no substitute for animal rennet, which he used for all his own cheeses (though his washed-rind ones, made by others, were vegetarian). One of his concerns about the present revival was that success may tempt makers to increase output at the expense of quality: in particular, he worried about hygiene, since the more people involved in any operation, the harder it becomes to maintain impeccable standards.

Towards the end of his life, he cut down on experimental cheesemaking and began to write. He passed on the recipe for St Francis some years ago to Ruth Lawrence at Womerton Farm, Shropshire (page 197); his partner, Pat Robinson, continues to make Tornegus, which is washed with local Kentish wine, lemon verbena, and mint. His second washed-rind cheese, based on a Gouda-style cheese called Teifi made by John and Patrice Savage-Onstwedder (page 172), is now made by the Savage-Onstwedders themselves.

TORNEGUS

A washed-rind cows' cheese; full-fat, unpasteurized milk; vegetarian rennet. 2 kg/4lb 6oz drums

The name is derived from the Somerset word 'tor' (the original cheese is made in Somerset) and 'negus' to signify flavoured wine. The cheese has a silky feel and almost semi-soft texture: when moderately ripe, it has a spicy flavour, but it becomes fruitier and more powerful as it matures, although the taste is not as pungent as the smell may suggest.

 ## *Hurst Farm Cheeses*

VICTORIA TAGG, HURST FARM, DAIRY LANE, CROCKHAM HILL, KENT TN8 6RA. TEL: 01732 866 516

Like Joe Schneider (page 44) and Charlie Westhead (page 190), Victoria came to cheesemaking by accident. Her mother runs a farm in Kent, near where James Aldridge lived, and hired a farm manager from South Africa who was in fact a cheesemaker and announced that they ought to make cheese. The Taggs agreed, and equipped a dairy for him. He made about a dozen Gouda-style cheeses and then decided that Britain was not where he wanted to be, and departed for Canada. As the Taggs knew Pat and James, they went to James, explaining that they had an expensively equipped dairy but no cheese, and he gave them a recipe which he had christened 'Snow Hill Wensleydale' (see page 16: Wensleydale, one has to remember, was originally a sheep's cheese). By this time, James was already ill: he did not live long enough to help Victoria with the cheesemaking, but she did a three-day course at

Roseneath College and, as her cheese demonstrates, has managed admirably on her own. Her milk comes from a farm near Portsmouth; she named the cheese Crockendale because she lives at Crockham Hill and the recipe was for Wensleydale.

CROCKENDALE

Hard sheep's cheese; full-fat, unpasteurized milk; vegetarian rennet.
2.5–2.75kg/5lb–5lb 4oz rounds

This is a wonderful example of the sort of multi-flavoured cheese that James loved. At first, it produces a mild, milky, slightly caramel-like taste; later, the mildness gathers momentum in the mouth and a peppery flavour develops, not strong, but sufficiently positive to be interesting. The texture is moist enough not to seem dry, but slightly crumbly, with a satisfying, nutty feel. I think it is delicious.

At the moment, Victoria only makes the cheese once a week (she will make it more often, she says, when her children are older). The milk is heated to 24°C/75°F, starter added, and milk heated on to 29°C/84°F over thirty minutes. A few minutes later the rennet is added and the curd left to set for about forty minutes. It is then cut, stirred briefly, and left to stand for half an hour. Thereafter, it is reheated to 30°C/86°F, pitched, drained, bundled up in muslin sheets, and set with a slight weight over it. After another half hour it is unwrapped, the curd broken, and the cheese re-bundled: this is repeated until the correct acidity is reached. At that point, the curd is milled, salted and moulded. The next day the cheese is put under a press, and the day after that brined. Maturing time is about four months.

Old Plaw Hatch Organic

Philip Donker (Cheesemaker), Old Plaw Hatch Farm,
Sharpthorne, East Grinstead, West Sussex
RH19 4JL. Tel: 01342 810857

Old Plaw Hatch Farm is an old, probably very old foundation: according to a former director, Andrew Carnegie, there has probably been a farm on the site since medieval times, when it marked one of the entrances to Ashdown Forest ('Hatch' means gate: the forest used to be a royal hunting preserve). It is not merely organic but biodynamic: biodynamism, which was first propounded by Rudolf Steiner in 1924, extends the organic principle to self-sufficiency, or near self-sufficiency (a ten per cent margin to allow for temporary problems is permitted) in order to avoid exploitation of the environment and ensure infinite sustainability. Thus Old Plaw Hatch grows all its own hay, wheat, and oats for animal feed and the plants from which its own range of homeopathic medicines is made. A few years ago, it went into partnership with another biodynamic farm about 10km/6 miles away, and, to raise capital towards extending their activities, the two farms have turned themselves into a co-operative. As such, they sold shares during their first year to 120 people, mostly local residents, who include a merchant banker, a vice-president of an American bank, two managing directors, a lecturer in agriculture, and a journalist. All of them value the chance to play a part in producing their own food; they can visit the farms whenever they like, attend Open Days and other events, and the farms benefit from their financial and other expertise.

The second farm, Tablehurst, specializes in meat: last year, it won first prize at the Organic Food Awards for its Sussex beef. It also produces Welsh and Dorset lamb, Sandy and Black pork, and chicken. Plaw Hatch offers a wide selection of exceptionally excellent fruit and vegetables (the raspberries are especially recommended), plus eggs, milk, two cheeses, yoghurt, and beef from a dual-purpose herd of dark red Dutch MRI (Meuse-Rhine-IJsell) cows, whose milk is more concentrated than Friesian and has smaller fat globules, which makes it especially suitable for cheese. For some years, only a hard, Cheddar-style cheese was made, but Philip Donker has developed a second, semi-soft one loosely modelled on German Tilsit.

OLD PLAW HATCH ORGANIC

Bronze Medal British Cheese Awards 2001 and 2002
A hard, Cheddar-style cows' cheese; full-fat, thermized milk; vegetarian
rennet. 5kg/11lb truckles

The smooth, silky, slightly elastic texture of the cheese is slightly reminiscent of Gouda, although it is not made by the Gouda method; the taste is full and rounded, with grassy and herbal flavours and a well developed Cheddar-like tang. It comes in different strengths according to maturity: all go especially well with wholemeal bread and apples or apple cheese (page xxx); the mature version is also excellent for cooking.

This description of making the cheese was written before Philip took over, when the cheesemaker was Rachel Webb. For two years during the interim, the cheese was made by Joe Schneider (page 44): by now, certain changes have been introduced, notably that the cheese is bound with cloth, in the traditional Cheddar manner, rather than the rind being rubbed with oil. Also, the mature version is sold at six to eight months; there is also an extra mature version aged ten to twelve months. The milk is first heated to 63°C/145°F, i.e. thermized, to kill organisms likely to sour or give it off-flavours; it is then cooled to 35°C/95°F and starter added, followed by rennet thirty-five minutes later. When the curd has set, it is cut into 1cm/^{1}/$_2$ -inch squares, stirred for fifteen minutes, left to rest, and stirred and scalded to 38°C/100°F for another fifteen minutes. After a brief rest, the whey is run off and as much liquid as possible is drained from the curd by a repeated process of pressing in a cheesecloth, turning, and cutting. The next stage is milling and salting, followed by moulding in tall truckle moulds and pressing for thirty-six hours. Finally, the cheeses are brined and oiled with sunflower oil to inhibit the growth of mould on the surface. For the next two to three weeks they are turned and oiled every day, and thereafter once a week or fortnight, depending on their age and the weather, for three or five months.

 ## Plaw Hatch Scones

Cheese scones have always seemed to me rather a problem, since you have to use quite a lot of cheese to achieve a perceptible taste: however, the more you use, the more danger there is of the scones ending up solid and heavy. Old Plaw Hatch Organic and Westcombe Cheddar (page 89) can be used interchangeably.

I have given only a small proportion of wholemeal flour partly for the sake of lightness and partly because the taste competes with that of the cheese.

Cooking-time: about 12 minutes
Makes 8–10 large scones

175g/6oz plain, preferably strong organic white flour
75g/3oz plain organic wholemeal flour
4 tsp bicarbonate of soda
Pinch of Maldon or other sea salt
Generous grinding of pepper
1oz/25g unsalted, preferably organic butter

140–145g/4½oz mature Old Plaw Hatch Organic or Westcombe
  Cheddar, finely grated
2 tsp Dijon mustard
7–8 tbsp buttermilk

Pre-heat the oven to 200°C/400°F/Gas 6 (it is important that the oven should be heated by the time the scones are ready to bake). Lightly butter or oil a largish baking sheet.

Stir together the flours, bicarbonate of soda, salt and pepper, and rub in the butter with your fingertips until it disappears. Stir in 125g of the cheese. Keep the remaining 15–20g to sprinkle over the tops of the scones.

Make a well in the centre of the mixture, add the mustard and 7 tbsp of the buttermilk, and fold the dry ingredients into the liquid to make a fairly soft dough. Handle it very gently, and work it as little as possible. If all the flour is not taken up, add a little more buttermilk. Either mould it into slightly flattened balls or roll it out to about 2cm/¾inch thick and cut it into rounds. The scones tend to rise slightly better when moulded but rolling produces a marginally tidier result. Sprinkle the top of each one with a little cheese, place them close together on the baking sheet, and put them immediately into the oven. (Placing them close together on the sheet encourages them to rise upwards rather than spreading outwards.) Bake for 11–12 minutes or until well browned and serve while still hot.

SUSSEX DEW-POND

A washed-rind cows' cheese; full-fat, unpasteurized milk; vegetarian rennet

Like Old Plaw Hatch Organic, the cheese has a full, well-rounded flavour and quite a strong tang. The sample I tried was moist and elastic but somewhat harder than semi-soft, as it is meant to be: however, it is a new cheese still under development and I am sure that Philip will soften it up, so to speak, in the future. It is also made smoked or with peppercorns: both versions seemed to me successful, especially the smoked, which has a much softer, more melting texture than the original.

Sussex High Weald Dairy Products
MARK HARDY, PUTLANDS FARM, DUDDLESWELL, UCKFIELD, EAST SUSSEX TN22 3BJ. TEL: 01825 712647

Putlands Farm is in an idyllic situation on the edge of a plateau in the middle of the Ashdown Forest, with views over a richly wooded valley and rolling hills; in the foreground is an artificial lake created for ornamental and conservation purposes by Mark's father. The Hardys senior, who bought the farm on their return from Kenya, did not originally envisage cheesemaking, but decided to rear sheep because they had limited acreage. At first, the success of the cheese prompted them to rent extra land and increase their flock until they were grazing and milking 300, but at this point they accepted that they could not keep up with Mark's needs and he began to buy in extra milk. They have now reduced their flock to forty and he buys milk from seven neighbouring farms – and still complains that there is never enough, especially in winter. The lack of sheep's milk was his main reason for enlarging his range with a cows' cheese, Ashdown Foresters, which in my view is the subtlest and most interesting of all his products.

His cheesemaking began as a result of an agreement to supply milk to a cheesemaker who planned to make halloumi for the Cypriot community in London but then withdrew: unwilling to abandon the idea, Mark went to Cyprus to learn how to make it and began to produce it himself. Initially, it sold well; after two or three years, however, the Cypriots in Cyprus started exporting a cheap cows' milk substitute which spoiled his market and forced him to diversify. First, he developed Duddleswell, a full-flavoured hard cheese which might be described as the sheep's equivalent to Cheddar; next came a soft cheese, Sussex Slipcote, made to a traditional local recipe. From the beginning, he had utilized the whey left over from cheese for ricotta; now, besides Ashdown Foresters, he makes feta, fromage frais, yoghurt, and a second-hand sheep's cheese, Sussex Pecorino (organic). He also makes a fresh, low-fat soft cows' cheese with a slight flavour of herbs and a texture like thick cream, which can be used as a base for dips, fillings, and stuffings or sweetened and served as an accompaniment to some soft fruits (not strawberries). As much of the sheep's milk as is available is organic; the cows' cheeses are made with organic milk from a farm at Horsted Keynes, near Haywards Heath, where at the time of writing (2003) Mark is converting a grain store into a new dairy. When I first met him, five years ago, he and his cheesemaker, Colin Brinkworth, processed 400–900 litres/88–198 gallons of milk a day (the variation reflected the seasonality of sheep's milk at that time): the figure has now risen to a consistent 1,200–1,300 litres/275 gallons a day.

DUDDLESWELL

Silver Medal, British Cheese Awards 1995 and 2001
A hard sheep's cheese; pasteurized milk, sometimes organic; vegetarian rennet. 2kg/4lb 6oz rounds

Duddleswell has a short, slightly fudgy texture and a rich, sweet, faintly caramel-like taste with undertones of butter and grass.

The milk is heated to 32°C/90°F, starter is added, and the milk left to ripen for an hour before renneting. When the curd has formed, after about fifty minutes, it is cut into 1-cm/$\frac{1}{2}$-inch cubes and scalded to 38°C/100°F over a further forty-five minutes. It is then drained and Cheddared twice, i.e. cut into blocks and piled at the sides of the vat. As soon as it has reached the correct acidity, probably after another forty-five minutes, it is milled, very lightly seasoned with sea-salt, moulded, and pressed for forty-eight hours, with turning after twenty-four; finally, it is brined for a further twenty-four and matured for a minimum of two months.

SUSSEX SLIPCOTE

Silver Medal, British Cheese Awards 1996
A fresh sheep's cheese; 19% fat, pasteurized milk; vegetarian rennet.
115g/4oz rounds or 1kg/2lb 4oz rolls

Sussex Slipcote is made according to a recipe dating back to the sixteenth century (before sheep's cheese had been eclipsed by cows'). Originally, the name was used for cheeses which had been matured for at least two weeks, until they 'slipped' off their 'coats' because they became soft and runny under the rind. The Sussex High Weald version, however, is a soft cheese with the mousse-like texture typical of fresh sheep's cheese; the taste is mild and flowery, with a faint lemon-like tang. It comes plain, coated with crushed peppercorns, or flavoured with garlic and herbs.

The milk is heated to 32°C/90°F, starter and rennet are added together, and the curd is left in an incubator for twenty-four hours. The excess whey is skimmed from the top and the curd is salted and flavoured before being put into moulds to drain naturally for twenty-four to thirty hours. The cheeses can be eaten directly but will keep (chilled) for up to a month.

HALLOUMI

A semi-hard fresh sheep's cheese; organic milk; vegetarian rennet.
8cm/3¼-inch blocks

Halloumi has a dense, toffee-like texture: its particular characteristic is that, because it has already been cooking in boiling whey, it does not melt when heated and can be fried or grilled like tofu or meat. Chiefly because of heating to a high temperature, it is too bland to eat without accompaniments or some form of flavouring; as is traditional, Mark uses mint.

Partly because of its texture, proper halloumi must be made with sheep's milk, which is heated to 32°C/90°F. Rennet is added, and the curd is left to set for an hour (no starter is used). The curd is then cut, scalded slightly, pressed into shallow moulds, and stacked for another hour to extract the whey. When the whey has run off, it is heated to 85°C/185°F and the cheese cut into blocks which are thrown into the hot liquid and allowed to stew, literally in their own juice. Finally, the blocks are brined and dusted with mint.

To serve, season the cheese with coarse pepper and just a grain or two of salt, dry-fry or grill it until golden on both sides (do not add oil), and drizzle very generously with lemon juice. For a simple but delicious salad, serve it on top of a mixture of hot and bitter salad leaves.

RICOTTA

A soft, fresh, cooked sheep's whey cheese; vegetarian rennet.
Blocks of various weights

Ricotta is very mild and intended primarily for cooking with added flavouring; however, it can also be served on the cheeseboard or used as a spread. Most versions are of a creamy consistency, but Mark's is drained to a block for vacuum-packing: this means that it is ideal when a stiff filling is needed but may need moistening for other purposes. For the table, it combines the mousse-like quality characteristic of fresh sheep's-milk products with the nutty texture of the cooked curds. There are various ways of flavouring it: two good ones are with chives and fromage frais or sage.

To make the ricotta, the whey is heated to 85°C/185°F, the acidity adjusted if necessary, and the cheese scooped out as soon as it floats to the surface; it is then lightly salted and drained in shallow moulds.

FETA

A hard Greek-style sheep's cheese preserved in brine; pasteurized milk, sometimes organic; vegetarian rennet. Blocks of various weights

Although feta, like halloumi and ricotta, is now often made with cows' milk, it was originally a sheep's cheese. It is salty, as the brine suggests, but also sharp and fresh-tasting: to modify the saltiness, soak the cheese for a couple of hours in cold water. There is no better way of eating it than simply to toast it, when it melts as smoothly as cream and needs no addition except perhaps a few drops of lemon juice.

Starter and rennet are added to the milk simultaneously, as for Sussex Slipcote; when the curd has set, it is lightly scalded, scooped into moulds, and left to drain, with turning at intervals, for two or three days. It is then immersed in brine for a minimum of two months.

FROMAGE FRAIS

A soft fresh sheep's cheese; 9% fat, unpasteurized milk; vegetarian rennet.
175g/6oz cartons (plain) or 90g/3¼oz tubs (flavoured)

The unflavoured version is fairly sharp and is intended for cooking, when its sharpness comes into its own: I have found no other cheese which gives the same tang and intensity of flavour. For eating *per se*, it is flavoured with fruit, including orange, lemon, and raspberry.

Although simple enough now, the recipe for the cheese took Mark and Colin over a year and a half to develop. The milk is heated to 82–85°C/180–185°F, and then cooled to 45°C/113°F before starter is added. After renneting, the curds (which are not drained) are kept at 45°C/113°F for twenty-four hours.

 ## Putlands Farm Sticky Lemon Pudding

In this recipe, the cheese is used instead of eggs, which gives a much more concentrated flavour: by replacing it with three medium-sized eggs, you can turn it into an excellent moist cake. To accompany the pudding, serve either the lemon or raspberry fromage frais or the plain cheese flavoured to taste.

Cooking time: 35–40 minutes
For 6

200g/7oz butter
250g/9oz caster sugar
175g/6oz Sussex High Weald Dairy sheep's fromage frais
1 small lemon, preferably organic
1 tbsp brandy

125g/4¹/₂oz finely ground self-raising wholemeal flour
¹/₂tsp bicarbonate of soda
50g/1³/₄oz ground almonds

Set the oven to 180°C/350°F/Gas 4; grease a 22cm/8¹/₂-inch souf-flé dish. Beat the butter and sugar to a cream; add the fromage frais and beat until smooth. Wash and finely grate the lemon zest into the mixture; squeeze and stir in 2 tablespoonsful of the juice and the brandy. Sift together the flour, bicarbonate of soda, and almonds; add to the mixture and stir thoroughly. Turn it into the dish and bake for 35–40 minutes, until the pudding has risen and turned golden brown. Serve hot.

ASHDOWN FORESTERS (ORGANIC)

Bronze Medal, British Cheese Awards 1996 and 1997; Winner of the Organic Food Awards 1997
A hard cows' cheese; full-fat, pasteurized milk; vegetarian rennet.
1.5kg/3lb 5oz and 3.5kg/7lb 11oz truckles

The cheese has a wonderfully smooth, creamy feel and, although pasteurized, a spectrum of gentle flavours: in particular, a freshness reminiscent of tart apples is offset by the rich taste of the Guernsey milk. Altogether, it is subtle and delicious.

Starter is added and the milk left to ripen for an hour. When ready, it is heated to 32°C/90°F before renneting and the curd left to set for another hour. It is then scalded slowly to 40°C/104°F, scooped into basket moulds, kept at 20°C/68°F for twenty-four hours, and turned at intervals. Finally, the cheeses are brined for a further twenty-four hours and matured for six to eight weeks.

Greenacres Farm

KEVIN AND ALISON BLUNT, GREENACRES FARM,
WHITESMITH, EAST SUSSEX BN8 6JA.
TEL: 01825 872380

Rather than setting out to make cheese, the Blunts were handed it
on a plate, so to speak. Their original ambition was simply to farm:
when they bought Greenacres, which has only 2.4ha/6 acres, they
planned to specialize in free-range hens, but bought a bonus of
four goats for Kevin, who up until then had worked chiefly with
cows. However, as in the case of the Jenners (page 32), the goats
completely captivated them, and now (including kids) they have
220, as well as 1,000 hens. At first, they sold only eggs and milk, but
as the milk yield rose, they began, almost inevitably, to experiment
with cheese. An expatriate French neighbour, Regis Dussatre, who
also kept goats and made two cheeses, Chabis and Dussatre,
decided to sell up and return to France. As a result, they were not
only able to buy his milking parlour and some of his goats and
equipment, but they also inherited his recipes and outlets, including Neal's Yard Dairy and James Aldridge's shop at Beckenham.
Since then, they have continued Chabis, turned Dussatre into
Golden Cross (named after the nearest village), and added a third,
triumphant cheese to their range, Flower Marie, made to a recipe
devised for them by James.

Lacking the space to raise sheep themselves, they buy in the
milk for Flower Marie from Dorset (when they started making it,
none was available locally, perhaps partly because of Mark Hardy:
see previous entry). The goats, who are mainly Saanens but with
a few British Alpines and Toggenburgs, produce between 400
and 700 litres/100 and 150 gallons a day; milking takes five hours.
The Blunts acknowledge that if they settled for fewer goats and
bought in extra milk, they could make more cheese, which would

almost certainly pay, but their love of the goats is overriding, so instead they have reduced the number of hens (which peaked a few years ago at 2,000). They have two herds, divided into spring and autumn kidding, so that the supply of milk, although uneven, is continuous.

I visited them in the spring kidding season and watched a mother giving birth as easily and calmly as if she did it every morning. At that time of year Kevin keeps them in, but they are let out during the day in summer; however, he says that if there is the slightest nip in the air they never stay out for more than half an hour, and they always return at the first drop of rain or at dusk. During very hot weather, he has tried to induce them to go out in the evenings instead of the heat of the day, but without success.

On the other side of the yard is the dairy, which has a hot-room or incubator as well as a drying room equipped on the same principle as the Jenners' (page 32) but with an ordinary freezer unit and fan. In the cheesemaking room, my attention was caught by the Blunts' moulds, which are fitted with trays above for the surplus curd as a way to save the labour of refilling: some came from Dussatre but the rest they had to buy from France, since, like other items of cheesemaking equipment, they are not made in this country.

CHABIS

Bronze Medal, British Cheese Awards 1997
An unpressed goats' cheese with a white mould rind; full-fat, unpasteurized milk; vegetarian rennet. 90–100g/3¼–3½oz rounds

The Blunts sell Chabis when it is one week old, but some cheese-shops mature it on for a further three to four weeks. When young, it is mild, but at four weeks it has developed a gentle but distinctive tang.

To make Chabis, the morning and evening milk are mixed, heated to 20°C/68°F, and starter, rennet, and penicillin for the rind added simultaneously. The curd is left in the incubator for twenty-four hours before being ladled into the moulds, with the surplus in the trays. The cheeses are turned after ten to twelve hours, and after another twelve hours are moved to the drying room. They are salted the next day, kept for a further one to two days, and then transferred to the maturing room for five to six days while the rind starts to develop. From this point, they can be eaten or left to mature for longer according to taste.

GOLDEN CROSS AND LAUGHTON LOG

Bronze Medal, British Cheese Awards 1996 and 1997 (Golden Cross);
Gold Medal, 2001 (Golden Cross) and the 2001 James Aldridge
Memorial Trophy for the Best Unpasteurized British Cheese,
donated by HRH The Prince of Wales
An unpressed goats' cheese log with a white mould rind; full-fat,
unpasteurized milk; vegetarian rennet. Golden Cross: 225g/8oz;
Laughton Log: 1kg/2lb 4oz

The two cheeses differ only in size. On both, the white penicillin rind is grown over a charcoal (as opposed to ash) coating: the charcoal adds considerably to the taste. In particular, they are notable for their fine, silky texture and in being among the very few British goats' cheeses which are moderately strong: partly for this reason, they are outstanding for grilling.

Golden Cross and Laughton Log are made in a similar way to Chabis, but are dusted with charcoal and packaged to prevent the rind from becoming crusty after it dries. The maturing time at the Blunts' is three to four weeks, but Neal's Yard Dairy mature them on for another four to six: when I tried to buy one directly after it had been delivered, I was firmly told to come back after a month.

FLOWER MARIE

Bronze Medal, British Cheese Awards 1996; Silver Medal, 2001
An unpressed white mould rind sheep's cheese; unpasteurized milk;
vegetarian rennet. 200g/7oz or 600g/1lb 5oz squares

The name is appropriate since the cheese has a blossom-like lightness and sweetness; as well as flowers, the flavours include herbs, summer grass, and cream. The texture is soft, sometimes molten under the rind, but the longer the cheese is matured, the firmer it becomes, with a correspondingly deeper, richer taste.

The milk, which all comes from the same farm, is delivered frozen. After defrosting, it is heated to 20°C/68°F and starter, rennet, and penicillin added together, as for the other cheeses. The curd is ladled into square moulds and left to drain for one to one and a half hours; it is then turned at intervals for the rest of the day, i.e. for the next twelve to fourteen hours. In the evening, the cheeses are unmoulded and left to drain again, brined, and dried in the drying room for one to two days. Finally, they go to the maturing room, where they are turned after five or six days, with care being taken at this stage not to disturb the growth of the rind by touching them (Kevin turns them like a cake, with a tray on top of them). They are wrapped a day or two later and can be eaten thereafter at any time over the next six weeks.

Nut Knowle Farm Cheeses

LYN AND JENNY JENNER, NUT KNOWLE FARM, WORLD'S
END, GUN HILL, HORAM, EAST SUSSEX TN21 0LA.
TEL: 01825 872214

In an earlier existence, the Jenners lived in a large house in
Woodmancote, near Brighton; they then spent twenty years at
Nut Knowle Farm at the foot of the Sussex Downs. Now, because
of the M23 and road improvements around Brighton, they have
moved to World's End, near Horam, which – at least when I went
there, on a dark, damp January day – seemed aptly named. From
London, you approach via the A22, which could hardly be more of
a contrast to the motorway; you turn off down a small side road
and into a deeply rutted track leading past a farm on which there
was no sign of people or animals and a pond so covered with weed
that it was scarcely identifiable as such. You drive on, past another
farm, and on, the track (labelled 'footpath') becoming ever more
liquid with rich, sticky, almost black mud. Their house, which at
that time they had only just finished renovating, similarly rose
from what might have been primeval slime – the combined result,
I gathered, of contractors' vehicles, cows, and an overflow from
their pond.

In their Woodmancote days, Lyn was a successful dealer in
antique silver, flying to sales all over the world and working with
'women who wore leather and men who wore mink'. Then one day
they were held at gunpoint and robbed. Lyn is dismissive about
this experience, saying only that it was 'unpleasant': one of their
reactions, however, was to buy two German shepherd dogs.
Although the dogs were in fact as gentle as possible, they fright-
ened the milkman, who refused to deliver.

The Jenners therefore tried a carton of goats' milk, liked it, and
after visiting various goatkeepers and viewing a number of goats

with increasing excitement and enthusiasm, bought their first goat, a British Toggenburg called Treacle. As Treacle was lonely by herself, their next step was to find her a companion, Honey; Honey was followed by Sweetie, then Toffee, until the herd had increased to fourteen. They then accepted that their lives had changed, moved to Woodmancote, and began to make cheese, experimentally at first, but later with the same flair and professionalism as had distinguished them in the silver business.

They now have 400 Toggenburgs, British Alpines, and Saanens, with names beginning with the appropriate letter of the alphabet, like car registration numbers, according to year of birth. For the same reasons as others with large herds, they keep their goats indoors: Lyn remarked, rather despondingly, that if let out they will eat literally anything, making the production of a cheese with consistent flavour impossible. They live in open sheds carpeted with straw so sweet-smelling that it would be worthy of a scent and are fed on barley and hay grown on the farm plus a compound feed specially mixed to the Jenners' requirements.

Lyn is even more emphatic than Charles Westhead (page 190) about the importance of not disturbing the milk, which is pumped directly from the milking parlour to a tank above the cheesemaking room so that it need not be pumped again but runs into the vats by force of gravity. To offset the effects of differing weather conditions on the cheeses before they are matured, the dairy also includes a drying room, where the air is filtered by a sterilizing fan. Lyn and Jenny make ten different cheeses: one, however, is still at the experimental stage and three are aimed chiefly at the catering trade, including an ash-covered, pyramid-shaped cheese which is served on British Airways. Of the remaining six, three are made to their own recipes, one is French, one Swiss, and one, St George, made to a recipe which they bought when they first started cheesemaking. Another, Caprini, is marinated in rapeseed oil and comes in various flavours, including peppers with herbs, chillies, and spices; wild nettle and garlic; and lemon and black olives.

ST GEORGE

A Camembert-style goats' cheese; full-fat, unpasteurized milk except by request; vegetarian rennet. 150g/5¼oz or 280g/10oz rounds (boxed)

When ripe, St George is flowing and creamy, with a very crisp white mould rind. The taste is of herbs, earth, and mushrooms, quite strong and distinctive but with scarcely any hint of goat as such: the goat simply adds intensity to the other flavours. Altogether, interesting and delicious, but hard to come by: if you find it, snap it up at once.

For all the cheeses listed, the milk is heated to 18°C/64°F before the starter is added. For St George, penicillin for the rind is also added, and the temperature is increased to 25°C/77°F before the addition of rennet. The curd is left to set for an hour, then cut very small, drained, and poured into moulds. The cheeses are salted and turned twice, once as they are moulded and again when the moulds have been piled; after unmoulding, they are diced and matured for two weeks. They can be kept (chilled) for up to a month.

SUSSEX YEOMAN

A hard, washed-rind goats' cheese; full-fat, unpasteurized milk except by request; vegetarian rennet. 2kg/4lb 6oz truckles

Sussex Yeoman has a pleasantly fudge-like texture and nutty taste overlaid by a tang just strong enough to hold its own against a medium Cheddar.

Rennet is added when the milk has been heated to 32°C/90°F. After an hour, the curd is cut very small and left for a further half-hour. It is then scalded over thirty minutes to 38°C/100°F, ladled into moulds, and turned within ten minutes; this is followed by pressing with a pound-for-pound weight overnight. Next day it is removed from the press and brined over the following night; finally, it is drained for a further twenty-four hours and the rind washed with water. During the two months the cheese is left to mature, it is turned once a week 'and loved'; the rind is scrubbed before each despatch. If stored at around 10°C/50°F, it will keep for some time.

WEALDEN

A semi-hard, black-rind goats' cheese; full-fat, unpasteurized milk except by request; vegetarian rennet. 200g/7oz or 450g/1lb truckles

Like St George, this is an unusual, quite strong cheese but with very little taste of goat: instead, it has a cool herbal tang with earthy undertones. One example that I tried was slightly blued, which added an extra dimension to the taste.

For this cheese, the Jenners use a vat which can be tipped so that the whey drains from the top. Rennet is added when the milk is at 28°C/82°F and the curd left overnight. Next day the whey is tipped off and the curd transferred to moulds, which are turned after six to ten hours; the following day the cheeses are unmoulded and salted. They are then left for a period in the drying room before being matured for a month.

The Traditional Cheese Dairy

MIKE AND KAREN TURNER IN ASSOCIATION WITH CLIFF
AND JULIA DYBALL, THE OLD FACTORY BUILDING,
BATTENHURST ROAD, STONEGATE, EAST SUSSEX.
TEL: 01580 201610

The Old Factory Building, deep in the Sussex countryside, used to
be the egg-sorting station for Stonegate Farm Eggs. When Mike
took it over, it was simply a shell of four walls and a roof: in effect,
therefore, he has been able to start from scratch in designing a
purist but perfect hand-cheesemaker's dairy, forward-looking
rather than merely up-to-date in terms of hygienic arrangements
yet without a single labour-saving device. The cheesemaking room
contains a large but not unmanageably large vat, plus a smaller,
covered one for experimenting; on the wall hang a shining harp (a
frame with vertical wires) for cutting the curd, a curd shovel for
piling it, a stirring paddle, and rake. The only other items are a
chemical air-sterilizer, which looks rather like an old-fashioned
electric fire, and the sink, which is supplied with purified water so
that when the floor is washed or the vat rinsed after disinfecting
there is no risk of contamination by tap-water.

The Old Factory Building is his second attempt to create a
dairy: when I went to see him, it had been in use for only a month,
prior to which he had been out of production for nearly a year
because an extremely rare but disastrous infection had forced him
to abandon the first. This was in a former stables and at first had
seemed ideal; however, for a reason which for some time no one
could identify, all the cheeses blew, i.e. burst their rinds. The cause
was finally established as hetero-fermentative *lactobacilli*, a bacteria
allied to the sort used for starter, which had originally entered the
building in the horses' feed. Since there was no way of eradicating
it, he was obliged to close down, thus losing his investment in the

premises and £50,000 in cheese. All he says now is: 'Well, yes – it was expensive, but it was all part of the learning process. None of us had ever come across it before.'

A dairy farmer's son, Mike started his career trying to sell his father's milk in bags, American-style, which at the time seemed a bright idea; as the bags leaked, the enterprise was doomed to failure, but he was constantly asked by would-be customers for cheese. This led first to wholesaling, which he still does, and then to the desire to make cheese as well. A cheesemaker called David Doble, who made a cheese called Castle Hill, lived in the same village: just as he and David had agreed to go into partnership, David's circumstances changed and he moved to Surrey. Mike therefore developed his own adaptation of the cheese, Myrtle Grove, which he says 'was never as good as it should have been ... because of the learning curve'.

A few years later he met James Aldridge (page 12), who was just beginning a period of intensive study and experiment. Between them, they turned Myrtle Grove into Olde Sussex, which has been a bestseller for nearly a decade; Mike then introduced a smoked version, Goodwood, and a variation flavoured with cider, garlic, and herbs.

He and James also began to develop a hard sheep's cheese, Lord of the Hundreds, made to a recipe of James's, which took them a long time to perfect but was finally launched in 1994. Two years later, it won the Supreme Championship at the London International Cheese Fair, which particularly pleased him because, far from being specially made for the occasion (as cheeses often are), it was not even carefully chosen, but simply pulled from the racks at the last minute: thus, as he says, it genuinely represented the quality of the cheeses actually on sale. He now produces a smoked version called Danegate Gold, which is notable for being smoked twice, and has adapted the recipe to make an interesting, slightly peppery-tasting goats' cheese, Skeete.

OLDE SUSSEX

Silver Medal, British Cheese Awards 2001 and 2002
A hard cows' cheese; full-fat, unpasteurized milk; vegetarian rennet.
4kg/8lb 13oz wheels

Olde Sussex is surprisingly different from David Doble's adaptation of the original Castle Hill, which had a smoky tang: Mike's, in contrast, is deliciously light, refreshing, and summery, with a slightly crumbly texture and an unusual, lemon-like taste.

LORD OF THE HUNDREDS

Silver Medal, British Cheese Awards 2001 and 2002
A hard, slightly grainy sheep's cheese; unpasteurized milk; vegetarian
rennet. 3.6kg/8lb squares

The particular quality of the cheese is the salty/sweet balance of flavour: the taste is distinctly smoky but the smokiness does not overwhelm its rich, nutty undertones and the sweetness characteristic of sheep's milk. The maturing time is four to six months: at four months, the cheese is relatively soft-tasting, but at six has become strong enough for sprinkling on soups and pasta and flavouring other dishes in the same way as pecorino.

The Lord's Fish Soufflé

Cooking time: 50–60 minutes
For 2–3 as a main course or 4–5 as a first course

250g/9oz cod, washed, skinned, and boned
150ml/¼ pint or a little more dry white wine
salt and pepper
1 tbsp oil

2 cloves garlic, peeled and finely chopped
15g/^{1}/$_2$oz white flour
100ml/3^1/$_2$fl oz whipping cream
2 large free-range egg yolks, beaten
100g/3^1/$_2$oz Lord of the Hundreds, finely grated
1 tbsp basil, washed and finely shredded
4 large free-range egg whites

Place the fish on a piece of cooking foil large enough to wrap into a parcel, pour about half the wine over it, and season moderately with salt and pepper. Wrap and bake the fish in a pre-heated oven at 180°C/350°F/Gas 4 for 15–20 minutes or until it is opaque all the way through and can be flaked easily with a fork. Leave it in its liquor to cool.

Warm the oil over fairly low heat and fry the garlic until it begins to show signs of changing colour: it should not be allowed to brown. Remove the pan from the heat at once and stir in the flour. Drain the fish liquor into the pan, return it to low heat, and stir until the sauce starts to thicken. Pour in the rest of the wine and the cream. Season with 1 teaspoonful of salt and a moderate grinding of pepper, simmer gently for 3–4 minutes, and allow to cool. Stir in the egg yolks. Flake the fish finely, checking for bones, and add it to the pan; stir in the cheese and basil. The mixture should be of soft dropping consistency: if it seems stiff, add a little more wine.

Heat the oven to 200°C/400°F/Gas 6; butter an 18cm/7-inch soufflé dish. Add a generous pinch of salt to the egg whites and whisk until they are opaque, close-textured, and stiff enough to hold their shape. Fold them into the fish mixture gently but swiftly: it is more important to mix them quickly, retaining as much air as possible, than to ensure that every lump of white is dissolved. Turn the mixture into the soufflé dish and bake in the middle of the oven,

without opening the door while it is baking, for 35 minutes or until
it has risen and turned golden: if a skewer inserted into the middle
does not come out clean, bake it for a few minutes more. Serve
immediately.

 Childwickbury Goats

ELIZABETH AND DAVID HARRIS, CHILDWICKBURY ESTATE,
ST ALBANS, HERTFORDSHIRE AL3 6JX.
TEL: 01727 841151

Almost everyone I have met who keeps goats and makes cheese
claims that they never really intended to – the goats simply took
over. This is certainly true of Elizabeth and David Harris.
Elizabeth has a degree in animal nutrition and used to be an envir-
onmental scientist; David ran a landscaping business. As he needed
space on which to keep machinery, they bought a plot of land on
the Childwickbury estate near St Albans, where they lived. When
a small farm on the estate came up for sale, they decided to buy it
and live the Good Life, supporting themselves on their own produce. To start with, they kept ducks, chickens, geese, and pigs as
well as goats – but the goats took over: 'All the rest had to go.'

Initially, idealistically, they let the goats run everywhere, but this
turned out to be unsustainable. 'They ate the wrong things, they
got sick, the milk was interrupted': now, therefore, they keep them
in a huge barn and feed them throughout the year on hay. However,
the Harrises have ensured that they have continuous outdoor access
with a grass play area and toys, plus a fallen oak tree to climb over
(Elizabeth told me this on the day when it was announced that
farmers could be prosecuted for not providing balls for pigs to play
with). The sexes also have freedom to mingle: unusually among

goat-keepers, they leave their billy-goats with the females for most of the year. This means that kidding and hence the milk is staggered, which removes the problem of lack of milk in the winter.

Now, after eight years, they have a mixed-breed herd of 110: to begin with, it consisted of pedigree Toggenburgs (brown), Saanens (white), and British Alpines (black and white), chosen by Elizabeth on the basis of their milk records; by now, however, many of the goats are crosses. As their output is limited, the only shop that the Harrises supply is Neal's Yard Dairy; otherwise, they sell at St Albans market and the local farmers' markets, where they need only take as much cheese as they like.

Although the question was clearly unnecessary, I asked if they did in fact feel that they had found the Good Life. 'We made much more money landscaping, but – yes, very much so! This is fantastic....'

CHILDWICKBURY

A fresh goats' cheese; full-fat, pasteurized milk; vegetarian rennet.
200g/7oz rounds

It may be the goats' Hay diet, the fact that the milk is used immediately after milking, Elizabeth's magical touch as a cheesemaker, or the fact that every stage of the cheesemaking process is carried out by hand: whatever the reason, the cheese is completely wonderful. It is light, firm yet mousse-like, and above all creamy, with a sweet, delicate, creamy flavour and no perceptible taste of goat at all. Whether or not it is pasteurized seems irrelevant: it is perfect just as it is.

VERULAMIUM

A soft, white mould-ripened goats' cheese; full-fat, pasteurized milk;
vegetarian rennet. 200g/7oz rounds

Elizabeth was asked to make this by Neal's Yard Dairy and had to
learn specially. It too is deliciously sweet and creamy, with a slightly
cheesier flavour than Childwickbury and just a gentle hint of goat.
It did not seem to me quite so outstanding, but that is probably a
matter of personal taste (it could also have been due to the particular samples that I tried).

When the Harrises first tried cheesemaking, they used the milk
unpasteurized as soon as it left the udder; now they pasteurize but
Elizabeth still believes that using the milk absolutely fresh is vital to
the quality of the cheese. Any which is not needed for that day's
cheesemaking is frozen in small blocks so that it defrosts quickly:
Elizabeth puts two into the pasteurizer every day to cool the milk,
which at that stage is still warm. It is then heated to 72°C for fifteen
seconds before being cooled to 34°C, when the starter is added,
plus a solution of *penicillium candida* for Verulamium. Renneting follows thirty minutes later, after which the milk is left to stand for
three quarters of an hour to three hours depending on the weather
(setting takes much longer in the winter). Once set, the curd is
simply ladled into moulds, without prior cutting, and left to drain
overnight. The cheeses are turned in the morning and finally salted
six to twenty-four hours after turning, again depending on the time
of year. Childwickbury is ready for sale twenty-four hours after salting and Verulamium left to ripen for ten to fourteen days at 8°C.

CHAPTER 2

South-west England

Daylesford Creamery

Smart's Gloucester Cheese

Wick Court Gloucester Cheeses

Charles Martell

Cerney Cheeses

Sleight Farm

Park Farm Cheeses

Exmoor Blue Cheeses

Dorset Blue Cheese Company

J. A. & E. Montgomery Ltd

S. A. & G. H. Keen

Westcombe Dairy

Chris Duckett at Westcombe Dairy

The Lubborn Creamery

J. G. Quicke and Partners

Ticklemore Cheese

Sharpham Creamery

Tala

Lynher Dairies

Menallack Farm

Daylesford Creamery

JOE SCHNEIDER, NEW FARM, DAYLESFORD, MORETON-IN-
MARSH, GLOUCESTERSHIRE GL56 0YG.
TEL: 01608 658005; FAX: 01608 658009

The first time I visited Daylesford was just after Joe had moved there, before the dairy or the huge Cotswold barn which has been turned into a shop had been converted. The buildings stood empty and silent, the site is isolated, and a fine rain was falling: altogether, it seemed damp, muddy, desolate and depressing.

Now, only a year later, the contrast is so great that if I had not recognized the road leading to it and the view from the drive as you approach, I would not have identified it as the same place. A spacious car-park in front of the farm buildings was full of large cars, the buildings looked trim and spruce, with all the woodwork painted a restful lichen green, the mud had been replaced by tidy paving-stones, and there were people everywhere. The centre of activity was the shop, which will surely be the model for all organic farm-shops of the twenty-first century. Daylesford is owned by the Bamford family who live at Wootton, an organic estate in Staffordshire, where they raise the meat for sale here and in due course at a second shop to be opened nearby, in Moreton-in-Marsh. The vegetables, however, are grown at Daylesford by a 'fantastic' market gardener called Ben Raskin, and bottles of sauces and cordials, jams, honey, and preserves, bread, muffins, pasties, cakes, and various salads are all specially made, the bread and pasties by a baker who has been lured from Anton Edelmann at the Savoy. I cannot answer for other items, but a banana muffin that I took home was memorable: wonderfully crusty on the outside (admittedly, I heated it up) and as light as a cloud within. I could have eaten it on the spot because one end of the barn is furnished as a restaurant where you can have lunch or tea, and there are more tables in an upstairs gallery.

After looking round Joe's dairy, Randolph Hodgson of Neal's Yard described it as 'a cheesemaker's dream'. Even allowing for the fact that Joe has two assistants, and that they are now making two very different cheeses, it is enormous. Everything in it is to Joe's specification. The expanse of floor is covered with large honey-coloured tiles: a smooth floor, he observed, would have been easier to clean but more slippery, and he opted against slipping. There are three cheese-presses, one thirty or forty years old, beautifully restored, and the others copies of it custom-made in Holland. The vats, also from Holland, are of warm, highly polished teak rather than the usual soulless stainless steel. The milk is pumped into them directly from the milking-parlour, which is just twenty-five yards away.

Although he now has a reputation as one of the finest organic cheesemakers in Europe, Joe did not set out to be a cheesemaker but, rather like Charles Westhead and Mike Allwood, fell into it more or less by accident, in his case as a result of a chance meeting – or, to go back a little further, as a result of meeting his wife. He was born in New York State and went to Holland because his wife had been offered a job there by her employers, the electronics company, Philips. Up until then, he had no idea what he wanted to do with his life: then he met a Turk who taught him to make feta. Over the next few years he travelled round France and Belgium learning how to make a wide variety of cheeses; he started out in Britain at Old Plaw Hatch Farm in Sussex (page 17) making a hard cheese of the same type as Daylesford, though with a very different flavour. Recently, to perfect his second Daylesford cheese, he went back to France to study the making of Pont l'Evêque. This second cheese is the more welcome because so far very few British cheesemakers have attempted cheeses of this sort: to encourage more of them to try was one of James Aldridge's particular missions.

DAYLESFORD CHEDDAR

Gold Medal and the Patrick Rance Memorial Trophy for the Best British
Cheese at the 2002 British Cheese Awards; Joe Schneider also won the
Cheese Person of the Year award
A hard cows' cheese; full-fat, unpasteurized organic milk;
traditional rennet.
10kg/22lb, 2.5kg/5lb 8oz, and 454g/1lb truckles.

Every now and again you encounter a cheese in which a number of flavours, although perceptible, combine to form a whole which is more than the sum of its parts. Daylesford is one of these. The taste is a medley of warm, soft flavours which include milk, fresh hay and clover, with spicy undercurrents and a hint of smokiness. Rather than being strong, the tang is simply the tip of a pyramid of flavours. The texture is smooth, but like velvet rather than silk in that it has just enough grain or pile to make itself felt against the tongue.

This is Joe's own description of how the cheese is made:

The morning is spent ripening the milk and cutting the curd... The curd is cut using mechanical knives but as the day progresses, the handwork becomes more strenuous. The whey is drained, and the curd is allowed to mat at the bottom of the vat. We then cut it into blocks, and Cheddar it on a table, which means regular flipping and stacking of the blocks on top of each other until the curd is smooth and mellow. We then mill it into smaller pieces and salt by hand. Each mould is then filled by hand and placed on the press overnight. The next day all the cheeses are turned out and dipped in hot water to help form a good rind. They then return to the press and are put under gradually increased pressure for the next two days. Then they are taken out and bandaged, ready for the ripening room. In this room temperature and humidity are controlled to match the conditions of a traditional cave or cellar and the cheeses are regularly turned. The rinds start to develop a smooth coat of blue-green-grey mould, which is kept in check by frequent rubbing of the cheese. Then the ageing process begins...

He goes on to describe how he makes his second cheese, Penyston, which at the time of going to press I haven't been able to try because none is yet available: however, I am told that it is soft and creamy, with a 'divine aroma'.

The milk is ripened overnight, warmed in a traditional round vat, allowed to set, and cut by hand using a special knife. It is then given time to mature, and gently turned over in the whey by hand every fifteen minutes or so. The curds and whey are poured into perforated moulds and put into a warm room to drain. They are turned frequently. Two days later they are sorted by hand and put into the cellar. There, the cheesemakers frequently rub and brush the coats with a light brine, to develop the right flora for Penyston's special texture, smell, and flavour.

 ## Smart's Gloucester Cheese

DIANA SMART, OLD LEY FARM, CHURCHAM,
GLOUCESTERSHIRE GL2 8AR. TEL: 01452 750225

Diana Smart did not start making cheese until she was over sixty. For her, cheesemaking was the fulfilment of a wish which had grown over twenty years of living at Old Ley Farm; when she finally began, her aim was, as it still is, to make Gloucester cheese as authentically as possible.

In this, her first and remaining problem was the type of milk. The old Gloucester cattle, who are dark chestnut red with a white stripe down their backs and magnificent horns, are now very rare, and indeed might be extinct were it not for Charles Martell and the other members of the Gloucester Cattle Society (see page 54); she nevertheless acquired a couple of cows in the hope of gradually building up a herd. Unfortunately, the cows have not obliged, having produced only one female calf to date: all the rest have been male or the twins of males (which means that they are sterile), so that most of the milk for the cheese comes from four dozen Holsteins.

Like most cheesemakers, she uses commercial starter, saying that she does not dare to make her own, and the milk is piped from the milking parlour to the dairy; otherwise she makes few concessions to modern practices. Her recipes and some of her equipment, including a hand-operated Victorian mill, came from two old ladies, the Misses Smith, who used to make cheese between Cam and Berkeley in the Severn valley. She abandoned an acidometer when she found that the readings always coincided with her own judgement, and uses pieces of old sheet instead of cheesecloths (boiled and therefore perfectly sterile). She beamed with approval when I said that I had noted 'Moulds lined with old boiled sheets'.

She makes her three cheeses twice a week: Double Gloucester on Tuesdays and Single Gloucester or Harefield, her newest cheese, on Thursdays. Formerly, she was helped by her son Jamie, but he died suddenly and she now works with an assistant called Gary.

SMART'S DOUBLE GLOUCESTER

Silver Medal, British Cheese Awards 1994; Bronze Medal, 1997
A hard cows' cheese; full-fat, unpasteurized milk; vegetarian rennet.
1.4–1.6kg/3–3½lb and 3.2–3.6kg/7–8lb truckles

'Rich', 'mellow', 'powerful', 'earthy, almost smoky' are some of the adjectives used to describe Diana's cheese in my notes. The texture is slightly crumblier than Cheddar, becoming crumblier with maturity. In the early eighteenth century, Gloucester cheeses were celebrated, along with Cheddar, as the finest in England: if this is anything like the historical version, one can understand why.

The milk (morning and evening) is heated to 30°C/86°F; just before it reaches this temperature, Diana adds starter and annatto, the dye traditionally used to give the cheese its rosy colour. The rennet is added after about half an hour, when she judges that the acidity has risen sufficiently, and the milk is left to set for an hour and a quarter. Gary then cuts the curd, scalds it to 38°C/100°F over forty minutes, stirring continuously with a (new) hay-rake, and continues to stir for a further twenty minutes. The curd is left to rest before the whey is drained off, to be fed in the old-fashioned manner to the pigs, including an enormous Tamworth sow and an old but splendid Gloucester Old Spot boar. While the whey drains, Gary and Diana have lunch; after lunch, they cut the curd into squares and pile and turn it a total of five times to drain it further. At this point, Diana tests it between her teeth to see if it 'squeaks', which denotes that it is ready for milling. To mill it, she divides it into three and peels it apart in layers, when it looks rather like mattress stuffing; afterwards, the milled curd resembles wood chippings. Salt is then carefully rubbed in by hand, which takes some time; finally, the cheeses are moulded and pressed for forty-eight hours, with turning after twenty-four. The maturing time is at least six months.

Trout and Double Gloucester Fish Cakes

It is better to bake than boil the potato because (as one would expect) baking gives a lighter, drier result, which is especially advantageous for fish cakes made with cheese. The cakes can be made a day in advance.

Cooking time: 1 hour (potato only)
Makes 8 cakes

200g/7oz (1 small) baking potato, e.g. Cara, Marfona, Kerr's Pink, washed
240g/8¹/₂oz trout, filleted, skinned, and boned
salt and pepper
1 tsp green peppercorns, crushed
1 small onion (70g/2¹/₂oz), peeled and very finely chopped
115g/4oz mature Smart's or Appleby's Double Gloucester, finely grated
25g/1oz white flour
1 large free-range egg, beaten
55g/2oz fresh, finely grated breadcrumbs
oil for frying

Prick the potato and bake it at 200°C/400°F/Gas 6 for 1 hour, until it is soft all the way through. When it is cool enough to handle, scoop out the inside or peel it, removing the hardened flesh next to the skin.

Check the fish for bones, wash, and season it lightly with salt and pepper. Wrap it in a parcel of cooking foil and bake it at the same heat as the potato for 10–12 minutes or until the fish is pale and flakes easily with a fork. Thoroughly drain the parcel and mash the fish with the potato, green peppercorns, and ¹/₂ tea-spoonful of salt. Stir in the onion and cheese.

Spread the flour over a large plate, turn the egg into a small bowl, and spread the breadcrumbs over a second plate; season the flour and egg moderately with salt and pepper. Form the fish mixture into cakes, coat all over with the flour, egg, and breadcrumbs, and fry them briskly until golden.

SINGLE GLOUCESTER

Bronze Medal, British Cheese Awards 1997; Silver Medal 2001
A hard cow's cheese; low-fat, unpasteurized milk; vegetarian rennet.
675–900g/1½–2lb, 1.4–1.6kg/3–3½ lb, and 3.2–3.6kg/7–8lb truckles

Single Gloucester cheeses were originally more economic than Double Gloucester because they matured quickly and were often made with a proportion of skimmed milk. Smart's Single Gloucester is of particular interest now as one of only three surviving examples of traditional handmade skim-milk cheeses of this type. The fact that it loses its flavour when hot perhaps partly explains why in the past cooked cheese dishes did not play a major part in the national diet. It has a deliciously light texture and beautifully balanced taste, with a cool, clean tang and grassy sub-flavours. It is not as strong as Harefield (below), but proves that low-fat cheeses can compete with whole-milk ones on perfectly equal terms.

The morning milk is separated and added to the previous evening's whole milk; it is then heated as for Double Gloucester. Relatively little starter is used; rennet is added half an hour after the starter and the milk left to set. After an hour and a half, the curd is cut, scalded to 34.5°C/94°F over thirty minutes, with continuous stirring, and allowed to settle before the whey is run off. The curd is then cut into sixteen squares, turned (but not piled), and left to rest for twenty minutes before being cut into sixty-four squares and turned again. Further cutting follows; finally, the curd is salted as

for Double Gloucester, milled, pressed, and matured for three to
four months.

HAREFIELD

*Bronze Medal, British Cheese Awards 1995; Silver Medal, 1996 and
1997*
A hard cows' cheese; low-fat, unpasteurized milk; vegetarian rennet.
2.7–3.2kg/6–7lb truckles

Harefield is made in a similar way to Single Gloucester but
matured for at least a year. The long maturing gives it a hard, dry
texture and a tang as salty/sharp as Parmesan but with a grassy
rather than smoky taste. Perhaps even more than Single Gloucester,
it shows how excellent low-fat cheeses can be.

Wick Court Gloucester Cheeses

JONATHAN CRUMP, WICK COURT, ARLINGHAM,
GLOUCESTERSHIRE GL2 7JJ. TEL: 01452 740117

As you approach Wick Court, which stands on a flat peninsula of
land in a bend of the Severn, the silhouette of the house seems for-
midably tall, stretching far above the surrounding trees. Once, a
huge oak towered above the drive near the gate, and another, with
wide, sweeping branches, shaded the parkland behind the house:
however, although both are still alive, they are 400 or more years
old and all the major branches have broken off, leaving gigantic,
gnarled trunks topped with only a hairline of shorter, sprouting
branches. Just past the first is what looks like a pond, generously
populated with ducks and elegant Brecon Buff and Buff Back

geese; there are also rare-breed Silver Spangled Hamburg chickens wandering about. In fact, the pond is part of a moat, which was probably built less for defensive reasons than as a status symbol or, perhaps, for a supply of water or fish.

There has been a house on the site since the twelfth or thirteenth centuries, but the original structure was replaced in the fourteenth and restyled and extended in the 1660s. That cheese was made on the adjoining farm over the centuries, presumably (this being Gloucestershire) from Gloucester cattle, seems fairly certain: the seventeenth-century version of the house included a dairy, and the sales details compiled just before the First World War listed a cheese-room on the first floor. When the war was over, the house and farm were bought by a gentleman farmer called Robert Dowdeswell, who had four daughters and a son; after he died, the son and daughters continued to run the farm and built up a herd of Gloucester cattle. They were known in the area as being very reclusive: a neighbour said that he had never been invited beyond their garden gate – evidently because he was a bachelor and the Misses Dowdeswell were spinsters.* It is also alleged that unexpected visitors were liable to be greeted by one of the sisters, Alex, carrying a shotgun.

As time went by, the Dowdeswells' herd of Gloucesters became the object of much speculation and interest. Like other old, traditional breeds, Gloucester cattle were increasingly rare: by 1950, only fifty cows, in two herds, remained – one of these herds being theirs. A few years later, the other herd was sold: when Alex and her sister Ella, who to judge from photographs were by then at least sixty, decided to put their herd up for sale as well, it was feared that pure-bred Gloucesters might become extinct. However,

* See Charles Martell (contributor), *Tales of Gloucesters*, The Gloucester Cattle Society 2001, page 15.

at this point Charles Martell (see page 56) and other enthusiasts formed the Gloucester Cattle Society, which ensured that, to use Charles' own words, 'the Gloucester breed climbed slowly and painfully from near oblivion'.*

It was for the sake of the cows rather than in order to make cheese (which he had never attempted before he arrived) that Jonathan took over the farm at Wick Court, which for him, as the home of the Dowdeswells' herd, had taken on almost iconic status. He does not live in the house: after the last Miss Dowdeswell died, it passed to a trust and both house and farm lay empty for some years. Eventually, the property was leased to a charity, Farms for City Children, which arranges for parties of inner-city primary-school children to spend a week helping on a farm and learning how to look after animals. On the day of our visit, the yard seemed very full of children, but in fact there were fewer than usual – only sixteen rather than up to thirty-six: this was because of the BBC, who that week were making an educational film at the farm, *Let's Make a Story* (which was screened in March 2003).

No one could be better qualified to teach children how to handle and understand animals than Jonathan, who has been crazy about them since he was a child. He kept ducks and chickens in his parents' back garden, owned his first sheep at the age of twelve, and his first cow, a black Irish Kerry, at eighteen. Before taking over the farm at Wick Court, he spent four years working at the Cotswold Farm Park, which specializes in rare-breed animals. Besides the ducks, geese, chickens, and his herd of Gloucesters, which currently numbers thirty-five, his stock at the Court includes a flock of fifty Jacob, Castlemilk Moorit, and Cotswold breeds of sheep and eight pedigree Gloucester Old Spot pigs,

* See Charles Martell (contributor), *Tales of Gloucesters*, The Gloucester Cattle Society 2001, page 18.

plus two Tamworths. He almost lost his Gloucesters over the foot-and-mouth crisis: when we went out into the field behind the house to look at them, the nearest one turned tail and fled as soon as she caught sight of me. Jonathan grinned and said, 'It's because you're carrying a notebook. She thinks you're a Ministry official.'

WICK COURT SINGLE GLOUCESTER

A hard cows' cheese; full-fat, unpasteurized milk; vegetarian rennet.
3.6-4.5kg/8-10lb truckles

Jonathan has been making cheese for five years, learning from books, a cheesemaking instructor called Val Bines, Charles Martell (page 56), whom he says has been very helpful and, perhaps above all, experience. When I tried his cheeses about three years ago, I was impressed by the taste but noted that the texture was heavy. I have tried them again, not only now but last autumn (2002) and am amazed: besides a remarkable spectrum of sub-flavours, perhaps because some of his pasture has been permanent for over half a century, I found that both had a remarkably light, smooth, silken texture. Can this be due to Charles Martell's influence, I wonder? The Single Gloucester has an almost apple-like freshness with sub-flavours of grass and herbs and a surprisingly positive (rather than strong) tang.

WICK COURT DOUBLE GLOUCESTER

A hard cows' cheese; full-fat unpasteurized milk; vegetarian rennet.
3.6-4.5kg/8-10lb truckles

If anything, the texture of the piece I tried was even smoother and more seductive than the Single. The flavour is sweet, rich and smoky, with a hint of hay. Where the Single Gloucester would be perfect with a Chardonnay, the Double calls for a warm, full-blooded claret.

In the winter, Jonathan makes the cheese twice a week; in summer, it may be three times. As his milking-parlour is very small, he milks the cows three at a time. His dairy is puritanically plain and clean (the children are not allowed inside but can watch the cheesemaking from the door). The milk is heated to 30°C before the starter is added and left to ripen for an hour. After renneting, Jonathan leaves the curd for another forty-five minutes to set; he then cuts and heats it to 35°C for Single Gloucester and 37.5°C for Double. This is followed by stirring for twenty minutes, leaving it to stand for a further twenty minutes, draining, and cutting it into blocks, which are turned until the correct acidity has been reached. Finally, it is milled, salted with two per cent of salt, moulded, and pressed for two days. The Single Gloucester is matured for three months, the Double Gloucester for two.

Charles Martell

CHARLES MARTELL, LAUREL FARM, DYMOCK,
GLOUCESTERSHIRE GL18 2DP. TEL: 01531 890637

Laurel farmhouse is full of prints and pictures: in the time he never has, i.e. very occasionally, Charles paints, and in another life might have been an artist. He is a consummate cheesemaker: even cheese, however, is subservient to his passionate commitment to Gloucester cattle. When he moved to Laurel Farm in 1972, there were only sixty-eight Gloucesters in the world: he bought as many as he could find, revived the Gloucester Cattle Society, of which he is patron, and started making cheese as a way of publicizing his cause rather than for its own sake. The number of registered female cattle has now risen to about 700 and his own herd, which has been more co-operative than Diana Smart's two cows, has grown to thirty (including three bulls). Recently, he also took up the cause of Gloucester cheese: although, as Diana's case illustrates, it is at present impracticable to insist that it should be made of Gloucester milk, he has established that the name Single Gloucester can be applied only to cheeses made in Gloucestershire.

His great regret as a cheesemaker is that, with only twenty-five Gloucesters and 22ha/55 acres, he cannot produce enough milk for an economic quantity of cheese. He does not split his herd for winter milking: some of his cheeses are made from his own milk while it is available and the rest (Friesian) is bought from a neighbouring farm, which he feels obliged to pasteurize because it has travelled. However, like Paddy Berridge, Mary Burns (pages 131 and 142), and a few others, his skill is such that without being told, I do not believe that anybody would know. This is not to say that if you tried them side by side, the difference between the pasteurized and unpasteurized versions of his cheeses would be unnoticeable, but in comparing them you would also have to allow for the fact that the cows came from different farms with different grazing and that one herd was of Gloucesters and the other of Friesians.

SINGLE GLOUCESTER

Gold Medal, British Cheese Awards 1996; Silver Medal, 1997;
Gold Medal 2001; Bronze Medal 2002
A hard cows' cheese; full-fat, pasteurized and unpasteurized milk;
vegetarian rennet. 3.6–4.5kg/8–10lb truckles

Charles's Single Gloucester is as traditional as Diana's but totally different because it is made with whole-milk and is notable for its creamy texture and rich taste. The texture is miraculous: although technically hard, the cheese melts in the mouth like mousse or ice-cream. The taste is full of nuances, fresh but without a trace of sharpness, sweet and sunny without being flowery, and above all buttery.

Charles's three hard cheeses are all made by a similar method to Single Gloucester. The milk is heated or cooled, depending on whether it was pasteurized, to 32°C/90°F before the addition of starter; renneting follows after forty-five minutes. When the curd has set, after about another thirty minutes, it is cut and scalded for half an hour to a temperature which depends on the weather. It is then drained, milled, salted, and moulded; finally, the cheeses are pressed for two to three days and matured for up to two months.

HEREFORD HOP

A hard cows' cheese coated with toasted hops; full-fat, usually pasteurized milk; vegetarian rennet. 3.6–4.5kg/8–10lb rounds

The cheese is smooth, moist, and creamy, with a soft but distinctive flowery rather than hop-like taste. It gains rather than loses flavour when heated and is delicious toasted.

Hereford Hop is pressed longer and heated to a higher temperature than Single Gloucester. It is matured in a crust of toasted hops: Charles says that he is not sure precisely how this affects the cheese, but, flavour aside, it presumably helps to keep it moist and contributes to its rich, creamy character.

Hereford Hop Chive and Bacon Creams

Cooking time: 12–14 minutes (excluding bacon)
For 5–6

5–6 rashers streaky unsmoked bacon (l each), baked brown and crisp
1–1¹/₂ tbsp chives, washed, dried, and snipped finely
4 large free-range egg yolks
salt and pepper
270ml/¹/₂ pint less 2 tbsp milk
2 tbsp whipping or thin double cream
100g/3¹/₂oz Hereford Hop, cleared of any fragments of rind and
    finely grated

Pre-heat the oven to 190°C/375°F/Gas 5. Lightly butter five or six ramekin or similar baking dishes. Break the rashers of bacon into fragments and spread them over the bottoms. Sprinkle with the chives. Season the yolks lightly with salt and moderately with pepper, beat until smooth and homogeneous with a fork, and gradually stir in the milk and cream. Stir in the cheese. Ladle the mixture into the dishes, set the dishes in a bain-marie, and bake for 12–14 minutes or until firm and just showing signs of turning golden.

STINKING BISHOP

Gold Medal, British Cheese Awards 1994; Bronze Medal, 1996; Gold Medal and trophy for the Best Export Cheese, British Cheese Awards 2001 and 2002
A semi-soft cows' cheese; full-fat, usually pasteurized milk; vegetarian rennet. 1.5–1.8kg/3lb 5oz–4lb rounds

Like the French Epoisses, the cheese smells – slightly or strongly according to ripeness – of old socks. The smell is more potent than the taste, which is utterly different and totally delicious, but impossible to describe except by saying that it is the essence of cheese. I am told that at the 1996 Besançon cheese fair, the French refused to believe that it was not made in France.

Instead of being drained, milled, and salted, the curds are washed in perry and ladled directly into moulds; to increase moisture content and encourage bacterial activity, salt is not added until the cheeses are turned out.

MAY HILL GREEN

Bronze Medal, British Cheese Awards 2001 and 2002

May Hill Green is identical to Stinking Bishop except that it is not rind-washed, i.e. it lacks the Stink: instead, the surface of the cheese is covered with chopped nettles.

STARVALL ROYAL

Gold Medal and trophy for the Best New Cheese, British Cheese Awards 2001

Starvall Royal is Stinking Bishop made with the unpasteurized milk of HRH The Prince of Wales's own organic herd of Ayrshire plus a few Gloucester cattle at Highgrove House. At present, it is made only in small quantities and not for sale.

Stinking Bishop Fritters with Cider

Allow thirty minutes to an hour for the batter to stand. The cheese should be kept chilled until just before use so that it is firm when added to the batter. Serve with apple chutney or pear and apple cheese (page xxxi).

125g/4¹/₂oz white flour
salt and pepper
1 large free-range egg
125ml/4fl oz strong cider
1 large free-range egg white
about 50g/1³/₄oz Stinking Bishop per head, chilled, rind removed,
  and cut into 1.5cm/¹/₂-inch squares
sunflower oil for frying

Sift the flour with the salt and pepper, make a well in the middle, and add the egg plus a little of the cider. Stir the flour into the liquids, working towards the outside: add more cider as needed until all the flour is taken up. Beat the mixture against the side of the bowl until no pockets of flour are left; then stir in the rest of the cider to make a thick paste. Leave the batter to rest for 30–60 minutes.

Set a plate lined with absorbent paper ready to draw excess oil from the fritters as they come out of the pan. Whisk the egg white until it is opaque and stiff enough to stand in peaks; fold it lightly into the batter. Gently stir in the pieces of cheese. Pour enough oil into a wok or frying pan to cover the bottom fairly generously; allow it to warm for a moment or two over medium heat, and fry the pieces of cheese to a deep gold on each side. Do not fry more at a time than will fit into the pan without touching. Drain the fritters on the paper and serve immediately.

DOUBLE BERKELEY

A hard cows' cheese marbled with annatto; full-fat, pasteurized and unpasteurized milk; vegetarian rennet. 3.6–4.5kg/8–10lb truckles

Like Single Gloucester, the texture is wonderfully light, delicate, and melting; the taste is mellow and very buttery but, again, surprisingly fresh. The overall effect is milder but richer than a matured Double Gloucester, as is consistent with history, since the Vale of Berkeley was considered a particularly rich grazing area. Double Berkeley is made in almost exactly the same way as Single Gloucester but annatto is added with the starter.

Cerney Cheeses

LADY ANGUS, CHEESEMAKER: MARION CONISBEE-SMITH, CHAPEL FARM, NORTH CERNEY, CIRENCESTER, GLOUCESTERSHIRE GL7 7DE. TEL: 01285 831312

Originally, Cerney cheeses were made to a French recipe (as they still are) in the quintessentially English surroundings of a Cotswold country house. The house, redesigned by Decimus Burton in 1791, is situated deep in the hollow of a wold, surrounded on three sides by steeply wooded hillsides and a lawn which slopes upwards towards the main garden; in front, the former deer-park stretches down to the pond which in earlier times supplied the household with ice. The garden is best known for roses, but also remarkable for herbs, of which there are forty varieties, and a seriously gastronomic selection of fruit and vegetables.

Lady Angus was taught to make cheese by a farmer's wife at Valencay, near Tours; Marion Conisbee-Smith, who has managed the dairy for the past fifteen years, still uses the same basic recipe and goes to Valencay every year to buy the mixture of oak ash and salt with which the cheeses are coated. Even so, the English version differs from the French: for one thing, it tastes much less of goat. According to Marion, one reason for this is that, unlike the British, French goatkeepers do not segregate their male and female animals but keep them all together, which is said to give the milk a more distinctive taste. Lyn Jenner (page 32) explained why at the 1995 Goat Conference: 'If you put your male into the milking herd, this can cause tainted milk, because they spray everything in sight, including the goats' udders. Some won't agree with this, but it is certainly my experience.' (*Goat News*, Winter 1995)

The milk was produced on the premises in the early days but is now bought from neighbouring farms. Marion used to make all the cheese in the former butler's pantry at Cerney House; a few years ago, however, the ground floor of a nearby farmhouse was converted into a new, much larger and better equipped dairy. Recently, as she now has the use of land for grazing, she bought two Gloucester cows from Jonanthan Crump (page 52), and plans in due course to make, not Double or Single Gloucester, but one of the soft cheeses which used to be made in the area. At present, she is experimenting with her Gloucester milk and scouring old books and the local libraries for recipes.

CERNEY

Silver Medal, British Cheese Awards 1996; aged Cerney, Gold Medal, trophy for the Best Soft White Cheese, and Supreme Champion British Cheese Awards 2001; Gold Medal, 2002
A fresh goats' cheese coated with ash; full-fat, unpasteurized milk; vegetarian rennet. 250g/9oz truncated pyramid

The taste is full and rich, with flavours of cream, herbs, and nuts but only the mildest tinge of goat; the texture is similarly nutty, and much firmer and more concentrated than is usual for a fresh cheese.

The cheese is made over a period of five days. On the first morning, the milk is warmed to blood-heat and starter and rennet are added together; the starter, which is homemade, is part of the Valencay recipe. The following morning, the curd is ladled into cloths and left to drain for a further twenty-four hours; on the third morning, Marion transfers it to moulds, pressing it down fairly firmly, and sprinkles the top with the mixture of ash and salt. On the fourth day, the cheeses are unmoulded and the rest of the surface is salted; they are then left for a final day to dry. They can be eaten immediately or kept (chilled) for up to a month.

Cerney Chicken in Pastry

Cooking time: 25 minutes
For 6

2 tbsp oil
3 cloves garlic, peeled and finely chopped
1 tbsp rosemary, washed and very finely snipped
6 small chicken breasts, skinned and boned *or* 6 small, thinly cut pork
    escalopes
salt and pepper
flour for dusting
1 quantity puff pastry (page xxvi)
150g/5¼oz Cerney
1 small egg, beaten *or* milk for glazing

Warm the oil over medium heat and fry the garlic until it starts to change colour; add the rosemary, turn, and remove the pan from the heat.

Beat the meat with a pestle to tenderize and thin it, and season each breast or escalope moderately with salt and a little more generously with pepper. Dust the rolling-pin and board with flour, roll out the pastry very thinly, and cut it into squares about 5cm/2 inches larger than the width of the meat.

Set the oven to 200°C/400°F/Gas 6. Thoroughly mix the cheese with the rosemary, garlic, and oil; place a sixth of the mixture (about 1 tablespoonful) in a strip down the shorter side of each piece of meat, roll up the pieces (pork makes tidier rolls than chicken) and set each roll on one side of a square of pastry, leaving a margin of about 2.5cm/1 inch from each end. Moisten the edges, fold them over, and seal them securely. Trim or fold back the ends as for a parcel; brush with the beaten egg or milk and make two or three slashes across the top. Bake for 25 minutes or until the pastry is pale gold.

CERNEY BANON

Bronze Medal, British Cheese Awards 2002
A fresh goats' cheese washed in Marc de Bourgogne and wrapped in vine leaves; full-fat, unpasteurized milk; vegetarian rennet. 160g/5½ oz rounds

Marion matures the cheeses in the refrigerator for a week before delivery to the shops; at this age, they merely have a mild, faintly vinous taste. However, if kept refrigerated for a further two weeks, they develop a wonderfully deep, rich, nutty flavour – without, however, the pungent aroma of the usual kind of washed-rind cheese. At this age, they are delicious: if you buy one, find out how old it is and if necessary give it extra time to ripen.

CERNEY STARTER

A fresh goats' cheese; full-fat, unpasteurized milk; vegetarian rennet. 50g/1¾oz buttons

Cerney Starter is primarily intended for grilling: each button is of a thickness and size to be cooked directly as an individual portion.

As is needed for grilling, the texture is relatively dry; the flavour is fresher and more delicate than the other Cerney cheeses. The Starters are usually sold frozen: allow one and a half to two hours for defrosting.

Lady Angus suggests grilling the buttons with a little thick honey: set the cheese on croutons, add honey, pepper, and olive oil, place them under a hot grill to brown them lightly, and serve them with bitter leaves. Alternatively, grill them with fruit and apple or red-currant jelly or sugar plus a tablespoonful of Jersey cream on top. Good combinations are Cerney Starter and grapes with pear and apple jelly or black cherries with demerara sugar.

Sleight Farm

MARY HOLBROOK; CHEESEMAKER: PHYLLIS TEALL, SLEIGHT FARM, TIMSBURY, BATH, AVON BA3 1HN. TEL: 01761 470620

Sleight Farm is on a hill with a view stretching over Bristol and the Severn Bridge to South Wales on the one hand and Salisbury Plain on the other: much of it was blotted out by rain when we arrived, and when we left it was dark, but the vista of lights across Bristol was dramatic and gave an exhilarating sense of space. The farm is one of the few that I have visited outside the organic movement which is still mixed, with a beef herd and pigs as well as goats and, at that time, sheep for cheese (Old Ley, where the Smarts keep pigs, chickens, and sheep for lamb is another: page 47).

Mary used to be an archaeologist and then became a museum curator. She originally started making cheese because she had two goats who gave more milk than she could drink. She now has ninety, all bred on the farm, and is renowned throughout the cheese world for the exquisite cheeses and her profound knowledge of cheesemaking, gained from a combination of personal experience and observation of practices in France and other countries, notably Portugal. The quality of her cheeses is probably mainly due to individual judgement and skill, but other factors include a traditional, near-organic approach to farming and her similarly traditional cheesemaking methods. At the time of our visit, the exceptionally dry summer had impelled the Holbrooks to use artificial fertilizer for the first time in five year; normally, they do not need it, since they have rich clay soil and abundant supplies of pig manure. There is no question of keeping the goats permanently indoors, although Mary never lets them out until the dew has dried as a precaution against worms; she has also given up producing winter milk, which is less stressful for the animals and gives her a rest.

In the dairy, she uses very little starter and rennet, and no starter at all for her latest cheese, Tilleys, which is also remarkable for being made with an enzyme derived from cardoons instead of a conventional type of rennet, according to an old Portuguese custom. The cardoons are infused in water and the infusion added to the milk directly after milking, when the milk is at a certain temperature: exactly the right temperature is vital if it is to work. Like James Montgomery and a few others, she uses traditional, i.e. animal, rennet for her other two cheeses. Until very recently, she made a total of seven, three goat and four sheep: very sadly, indeed from a personal point almost tragically, she has now sold her flock. I say tragically because, although I always maintain that I have no favourite cheese, her two soft, white mould-ripened sheep's cheeses would be very strong contenders if I had. I always looked forward to them as particular treats at around Easter, when they were available again after the winter. However, all is not quite lost, since she is passing on her techniques and as much as she can of her expertise to Dave and James Bartlett, who keep a flock of organic sheep near Shepton Mallet and hope to start production later this year.

SLEIGHT

A fresh goats' cheese; full-fat, unpasteurized milk; traditional rennet.
115g/4oz logs; seasonal: March–November

All Mary's cheeses have a warm, nutty, slightly mushroom-like taste: Sleight is distinctive but delicate, with a notably fine, creamy texture. It is sold plain or coated with pepper, rosemary, or garlic and herbs.

TYMSBORO'

Gold Medal, British Cheese Awards 1997
An unpressed goats' cheese coated with ash under a penicillin rind; full-fat, unpasteurized milk; traditional rennet. 225g/8oz truncated pyramids; seasonal: March–November

The rind may be tinged greenish-grey rather than white: the green is an invading strain of penicillin, as edible as the white and welcomed by Mary because it adds to the flavour. Directly underneath the rind, the cheese will have ripened to a cream; the middle is compact but quite wonderfully light and smooth. The taste is deep, rich, nutty, and sweet/sharp, with hints of earth, mushrooms, and herbs which vary with the season; without being strong, it has a pronounced tang, although of cheese rather than goat.

TILLEYS

A compact goats' cheese, hard or semi-hard according to maturity; full-fat,
unpasteurized milk; extract of cardoon. About 1.2kg/2lb 11oz rounds;
seasonal: March–November

The texture is fudgy when young but becomes harder as it ages,
with a few small holes; the taste is salty/sweet with suggestions of
nuts and earth and a definite tinge of artichoke. In particular, it is
absolutely excellent toasted.

Warm Salad of Tilleys with Hazelnuts

You can either grill the cheese on slices of baked bread or fry it in
egg and breadcrumbs: the second looks more elegant but I recommend the first because the flavour of the cheese is more intense if
it is left in one piece.

For 2

40g/1^1/$_2$oz whole (unskinned) hazelnuts
100g/3^1/$_2$oz Tilleys
2 half-slices of baked bread drizzled with oil and lightly seasoned
   with salt and pepper for grilling (page xxviii) *or* 25g/1oz flour,
   1 small free-range egg, and 25–40g/1–1^1/$_2$oz fresh breadcrumbs,
   plus oil for frying
2 tbsp virgin olive oil
^{1}/$_2$ tbsp red wine vinegar
salt and pepper
mixed sharp or bitter, or non-sweet salad leaves (batavia, spinach,
   oakleaf or lambs' lettuce, land- or watercress, sorrel, rocket,
   mizuna), washed and dried

Crisp the nuts by toasting them in a moderate oven for 4–5 minutes or toss them in hot oil (but do not use the oil in which you plan to fry the cheese).

If you are grilling the cheese, place it on the bread in thick slices, trimming the bread if necessary so that none of it is exposed (if uncovered it will burn). If you are frying the cheese, cut it into squares and coat them with flour, egg, and breadcrumbs (page xxix).

Beat together the oil, vinegar, and a slight seasoning of salt and pepper; toss the salad leaves with the dressing and arrange them round the edge of the serving plates. If you are grilling the cheese, place the bread slices under a hot grill until they turn golden; for frying, line a dish with absorbent paper to drain off surplus fat, fry the cheese squares until golden, and blot on the paper. Place the cheese in the centre of the salad plates, sprinkle with the nuts, and serve.

Park Farm Cheeses

GRAHAM AND GABRIELLE PADFIELD, CHEESEMAKER:
PETER HUMPHRIES, PARK FARM, KELSTON, BATH, AVON
BA1 9AG. TEL: 01225 424139

Although one tends to associate Camembert-style cheeses with France, the Padfields' first two cheeses, Bath Soft and York, are in fact revivals of traditional British recipes. Cheeses of this type used to be made in many parts of the country but did not become nationally known because of transport and storage problems (as still applies in the case of many fresh cheeses). I tried Bath Soft as soon as I saw it on sale, strikingly packaged in plain cream and black, and found that although it was perfectly ripe, with a soft, flowing texture, it had absolutely no taste at all. Another was the same: the entry in my tasting notebook ends plaintively: 'Why does anybody bother to make this cheese?' A year later, I tried it again – and was stunned: not only was it even softer and creamier but it was also brimming with sweet, summery, yet surprisingly intense flavours. After sampling several more equally triumphant examples, I could hardly wait to find out how they had brought about such a transformation. The answer is simple: experience.

Graham is a third-generation farmer, but no one in his family had ever made cheese before: he turned to it because of the milk quota, which prevented him from expanding quantitatively. Feeling that it was futile to compete in the Cheddar market, he looked through old books on cheesemaking and settled on Bath Soft as the obvious choice (Kelston is only 6km/4 miles from Bath). He and Gabrielle started by experimenting in the kitchen, like others new to cheesemaking, but with consistent lack of success: the cheeses remained obstinately hard and unripe. After some time, they gave up, but a few weeks later came across a couple of cheeses which they had forgotten and which, to their astonishment, turned out to be delicious: they still had to find out why, but the knowledge that the recipe could be made to work was enough to encourage them to persist.

Graham equipped a dairy (which by now has cost £20,000), enlisted Peter's help, and began to make the cheese on a regular basis, although for the first year only once a fortnight. At this stage, they had by no means mastered it: as well as lack of taste, it went through a phase of being bitter. Graham, who is not given to complacency or sales' talk, said, 'Frankly, it was horrible – almost inedible. I can't think why anybody bought it.' Fortunately, however, they did, so that he and Peter now make cheese every day and have introduced three more cheeses, Kelston Park (named after the neighbouring stately home), Bath Triple Cream Cheese, and Bath Blue. In addition, the farm has been fully organic since Christmas 2002.

There are several points of interest about their cheesemaking process. One is that they use only evening milk, which is considerably richer than the morning's. Their method is basically the Coulommiers process: as is a common practice in France, they add the rennet in buckets rather than a vat, because the curd for soft cheeses should not be stirred but if left to set in a vat varies slightly according to whether it is at the edge or in the middle. Also, the cheese is salted by rubbing the dry salt over the surface after moulding, which delays the inhibiting effect of salt on bacterial activity and probably increases flavour.

BATH SOFT

A Camembert-type soft cows' cheese; full-fat, unpasteurized evening milk; vegetarian rennet. 10cm/4-inch squares (about 280g/10oz)

Bath Soft is gloriously rich, flowing, and creamy, with a widely mixed bouquet of sweet, flowery flavours, sometimes cooler, sometimes warmer and more vibrant, depending on the season. Eating it is pure luxury. A 1906 recipe quoted on the label says that the cheese 'will demonstrate its ripeness by spreading on bread as butter does': a good alternative to bread is very crisp oatcakes, such as Clarke's (page xxii).

The milk (Friesian) is left to stand overnight, warmed, and then starter and penicillin for the rind are added together. Before renneting, it is run into a total of twenty buckets, to each of which the rennet is added individually: when the curd is firm enough to 'break over the finger', usually in forty to forty-five minutes, it is cut once vertically with a knife, left to stand for twenty minutes, and poured into moulds, which, according to tradition, are square. The cheeses are then left in a warm place until the next morning, when they are turned out and set on racks in the maturing room.

They are matured for three weeks, with wrapping after two to prevent the escape of moisture, and remain at a more or less perfect stage of ripeness for a further three to four weeks.

KELSTON PARK

Bronze Medal, British Cheese Awards 1997 and 2001
A Camembert-type soft cows' cheese; full-fat, unpasteurized evening milk;
vegetarian rennet. 675g/1½ lb rounds

The new cheese is larger than Bath Soft, which gives it stronger, more intense flavours. It is made in much the same way, but is poured into round rather than square moulds.

Exmoor Blue Cheeses

IAN AND RUBY ARNETT, WILLETT FARM, LYDEARD ST
LAWRENCE, NEAR TAUNTON, SOMERSET TA4 3QB.
TEL: 01984 667328

Exmoor Blue Cheeses was founded by Alan Duffield, who moved to the West Country after a career with ICI and started out farming sheep on the moors. He continued for some years but eventually gave up the sheep in order to take over the dairy at Willett Farm, in the valley between the Quantock and Brendon hills. For the past four years, the cheese has been made by Ian, working first with Alan and subsequently with Sandra White. Just before Christmas 2002 he and his wife Ruby bought the business.

When Alan first arrived at the dairy, only one cheese was made, a hard sheep's cheese called Coleford Blue: by using not only sheep's but goats', Jersey, and buffalo milk and adapting the recipe to soft as well as hard cheeses, he extended the range to nine, of which Ian and Ruby are still making seven. The Jersey milk is brought and quality-tested from local farms by Milk Link, the sheep's comes from Nether Stowey, four or five miles away, the goats' from Norsworthy Goats, near Crediton in Devon, and the buffalo from a herd called the Blissful Buffaloes near Holsworthy, Devon.

This is the original Willett Farm recipe. Initially, it is fairly simple, but the final stages stretch over a number of days. The milk is warmed slightly before starter is added, then heated to 31°C/88°F before the addition of rennet and *Penicillium roqueforti* for the blue. When the curd has set, which takes one and a quarter to one and a half hours according to the weather, it is cut coarsely in two directions with long flat knives. For the soft cheeses, it is moulded without draining; for the firm, it is heated a few degrees, drained, and turned until it is dry before the moulds are filled. After moulding, the cheeses are finished for the day except for turning in the evening.

The next morning, they are all turned again, and the soft cheeses are brined; on the third day, the soft cheeses are aerated by piercing. Thereafter, all the cheeses are taken to the maturing room where they are sprayed with white penicillin for the rinds: this shows less on the soft, more quickly matured cheeses, but gives a definite gloss to the firmer ones. The hard cheeses are left to drain for three days before brining, brined for two, and drained for another two before piercing; finally, they are drained for a further five days before being set to mature in rooms, which, to encourage mould, are kept at a humidity of around ninety-five per cent. Although they do not become exceptionally blue on the inside, the mould on the surface develops, not into a mere crust or moss but a veritable garden, with long, fine dark grey fronds reaching into the air. (The fronds brush off immediately: there is no trace of them once the cheeses are moved.) Maturing times are three to seven weeks for Baby Brendon and the soft cheeses and two to three for the hard.

EXMOOR JERSEY BLUE

A semi-soft blue Jersey cheese; 35% fat, unpasteurized milk; vegetarian rennet. 500g/1lb 2oz and 1.2kg/2lb 10oz truckles

Jersey Blue is the most popular of the Exmoor Blue cheeses: it is fairly firm-textured, with the sweet, buttery taste of the rich milk and gentle herbal undertones. The blue is just strong enough to be piquant without overwhelming the background flavours of the cheese.

Butternut Squash and Tomato Soup with Jersey Blue

This is a thick, glowing orange soup with a mellow flavour which matches the character of the cheese. As only a little cheese is needed, it is an excellent way of using up a small piece. It can be prepared in advance.

Cooking time: 55–65 minutes
For 3–4

2 small or 1 large onion/s (about 200g/7oz), peeled and finely chopped
6 cloves garlic, peeled and chopped
700g/1lb 9oz ripe tomatoes, peeled, chopped, and the cores removed
salt and pepper
$^3/_4$–1 tsp caster sugar
$^1/_2$ butternut squash (about 350g/12oz when prepared), peeled, the
    seeds and pulp removed, and chopped into 1.5cm/$^1/_2$-inch squares
4 tbsp double cream
70g/2$^1/_2$oz Exmoor Jersey Blue, coarsely grated or finely chopped

Pre-heat the oven to 190°C/375°F/Gas 5. Spread the onions and garlic over the bottom of a medium-sized baking dish; cover with the tomatoes. Season the tomatoes fairly generously with salt and pepper and sprinkle them with the sugar. Bake for 45–50 minutes, until they look slightly dry and shrivelled.

Transfer the contents of the baking dish to a saucepan, add 400ml/14fl oz water and the squash, and simmer for 10–15 minutes or until the squash is tender; liquidize until the soup is very smooth. If you are making it ahead of time, keep it chilled until needed.

When you are ready to serve, bring the soup to a simmer over low heat; simmer for 3–4 minutes, thinning with a little more water if necessary, and stir in the cream. Sprinkle the cheese into the bowls after serving.

PARTRIDGES

A semi-soft blue Jersey cheese; full-fat, unpasteurized milk; vegetarian rennet. 1kg/1lb 5oz drums

The blue is strong but the cheese itself deliciously rich and sweet, with a luscious, creamy texture. The name originates from the fact that it was originally made specially for Partridges of Sloane Street; now, however, it is widely sold.

SOMERSET BLUE

A firm Jersey cheese with a predominantly white mould rind; 40% fat, unpasteurized milk; vegetarian rennet. 2–2.5kg/4lb 6oz–5lb 8oz

Having been matured for longer, Somerset Blue is bluer and stronger than Exmoor Jersey; however, it has a similarly rich, buttery taste with a hint of herbs. It can be kept at 4°C/39°F for up to two months.

BABY BRENDON

A soft goats' cheese; full-fat, unpasteurized milk; vegetarian rennet.
About 400g/14oz rounds

Baby Brendon is unusual in that it is one of the very few goats'
cheeses made in Britain which actually tastes of goat. However, it
is also quite exceptionally sweet, with background flavours of herbs
and a strong infusion of flowers. If kept, it becomes harder, with a
slight grain, but retains its sweetness.

BLISSFUL BUFFALO

A blue buffalo cheese; full-fat, unpasteurized milk; vegetarian rennet.
115g/4oz, 225g/8oz, 450g/1lb, and 900g/2lb rounds; 1.8kg/4lb rounds

Buffalo milk is even richer than sheep's milk (eight per cent as
opposed to six per cent fat). This is reflected in the rich, creamy
texture of the cheese; like fresh sheep's cheeses, however, it is also
wonderfully smooth and light. The taste, similarly, is sweet and
creamy, with nuances of grass and flowers to which the blue adds
just the right amount of zest to be interesting but not overwhelming. This is a delightful cheese: as well as on the cheeseboard, it is
particularly good with plums and pears.

Dorset Blue Cheese Company

MICHAEL DAVIES, WOODBRIDGE FARM, STOCK GAYLARD,
STURMINSTER NEWTON, DORSET DT10 2BD.
TEL: 01963 23216; FAX: 01963 23063

Michael says that he had wanted to make cheese ever since taking
a cheesemaking course as a student. For a long time he had been

deterred by the fact that he lives in Cheddar country: cheese and Cheddar seemed synonymous and, like Graham Padfield (page 70), he did not feel that he could compete with the 'big boys' (although in Dorset, Woodbridge Farm is only about 16km/10 miles from the Keens). However, as a dairy farmer producing only liquid milk before the introduction of the quota, when the milk lake was deepening and the butter mountain soaring, he began to ask himself seriously whether there was any point in what he was doing. While he was in this state of uncertainty, his attention was drawn to a case involving the sale of second-grade Stiltons as Dorset Blue Vinneys.

Blue Vinney was a local hand-skimmed-milk cheese which had not been produced on a significant scale since the war, although Patrick Rance discovered several farms where it was still being made in very small quantities. The blue in the authentic cheese, so the story goes, was encouraged by maturing it with mouldy boots or old harnesses; the Stiltons were bought from Leicestershire and disguised by being left in a Dorset cellar to acquire a little genuine local mould. To Michael, the fact that there was clearly a demand for Blue Vinney was decisive. He found a number of recipes at the Ministry of Agriculture, Fisheries and Food office in Dorchester and for the next two months experimented in his garage every Saturday, using cut-off pipes instead of moulds (as is practised regularly by at least two Irish cheesemakers) and maturing the cheeses in his larder, where, predictably, they turned even the cornflakes blue. Today, he employs two cheesemakers and produces 540kg/1,200lb of cheese a week.

Blue Vinny (he spells his version without the 'e') is interesting as an example of a traditional skim-milk cheese and one of the very few, possibly the only one, which was blue – the blue rectifying the hardness and lack of flavour for which many such cheeses were known; his recipe is a reminder that a crucial point about all of them was that the milk was skimmed by hand rather than machine.

If you toast the cheese, you can see that it still contains an appreciable amount of fat: Michael reckons that it is about three per cent.

DORSET BLUE VINNY

Gold Medal, British Cheese Awards 2002
A blue cows' cheese; hand-skimmed, unpasteurized milk; vegetarian rennet.
1.8–2.3kg/4–5lb cylinders and 6kg/13lb 3oz

The cheese has a nutty texture and because of its low fat content tends to crumble, particularly if, as some are, it is very blue. Even when very blue, however, it is not overwhelmingly strong, since the blue has a pleasingly soft taste which tingles rather than bites in the mouth. It keeps its flavour relatively well when heated; as the mould does not liquefy, it also retains little nutty clusters which are delicious on tomato soup or polenta. Apart from the blue, it melts smoothly, and is excellent toasted. It also freezes perfectly.

The cows (Friesian) are milked at 5 a.m. and the milk left for two and a half to three hours to allow the cream to rise before it is hand-skimmed. Unless the cheesemakers can find the time to turn it into clotted cream, the cream, sadly, is thrown away. The temperature and acidity of the milk are checked, starter and *Penicillium roqueforti* for the blue added, and the milk left for another hour before renneting. After a further one and a half hours, the curd is stirred and cut to the size of broad beans; it is then left to stand again, this time until the next morning, when it is drained and the whey fed either to the cows or the pigs. Jonathan Crump at Wick Court (page 52) is among the very few who still keep pigs to drink it, according to the custom when mixed farming was the norm.

The next stage is to texture the curd by cutting it into blocks and piling them at the end of the vat; this is followed by milling, salting, and moulding. Instead of being pressed, the cheeses are left at 15.5°C/60°F for four days, with turning every day: at this point, they look like pans of rather pale, dry scrambled egg. After four days, they are turned out and dressed with a flour paste mixed with a little more *roqueforti* so that the rinds also become blued. For the next five or six weeks, the cheeses are turned daily and some are pierced to introduce extra air: not all of them need it, but with some piercing may have to be repeated several times. Thereafter, they are matured for two and a half to five months, with turning every two or three days.

 ## Polenta with Blue Vinny and Tomatoes

The porridge for the base can be made the day before.

Cooking times: 20 or 60 minutes (porridge), according to type;
5 minutes for grilling or 16–20 for baking before serving

For 6–10

125g/4½oz polenta meal
700ml/1¼ pints milk, skimmed, semi-skimmed, or whole, *or* milk and
    water
1 tbsp cream (single or double)
salt
15g/½oz butter
about 300g/10½oz (4 fairly large) ripe tomatoes, skinned
pepper
150g/5¼oz Blue Vinny, crumbled

Put the polenta meal into a cup or funnel so that it can be poured steadily. Bring the milk (or milk and water) and cream to the boil, add ¹/₂ teaspoonful of salt and the butter, and pour in the meal gradually, stirring continuously. Reduce the heat to a simmer and continue stirring for 3–5 minutes, until the mixture thickens; simmer for an hour, stirring fairly frequently. Some brands of meal are quick-cooking and do not need simmering for as long, but in all cases I recommend at least 20 minutes. If the porridge sticks to the bottom of the pan, leave it while it cooks and soak the pan afterwards. Pour it into a lightly buttered 22cm/8¹/₂-inch tart dish and leave it to cool.

Slice the tomatoes, discarding the stalk ends, and arrange them over the top of the polenta; season with pepper and cover with a thick layer of cheese. Bake at 220°C/425°F/Gas 7 for 16–20 minutes or grill until browned.

J. A. and E. Montgomery Ltd

JAMES MONTGOMERY, MANOR FARM, NORTH CADBURY, YEOVIL, SOMERSET BA22 7DW. TEL: 01963 440243

Like the Ducketts and Keens (pages 91 and 84), the Montgomerys have made cheese for three generations. Even more than most people who work with it, James lives it and loves it; he is also exceptionally lucid about the cheesemaking process and all that precedes it, i.e. the grazing, cows, and quality of the milk. The business is a family concern shared by his mother and brother; however, it includes two farms, and his brother Archie manages the second, which is arable and not directly connected with the cheese. James, at Manor Farm, produces milk for direct sale and a new cheese called Jersey Shield from a herd of Jerseys and the Cheddar from 120 Friesians. Originally, his family made the cheese from Ayrshire milk, which has a relatively high solids content: the

Ayrshires were switched to Friesians for the sake of the increased yield but the cows are bred to give milk which as far as possible retains the Ayrshire characteristics, in particular with regard to the protein ratio. He has never standardized it with equalizing separators, as is the custom among larger cheese producers (page 97), but until recently enriched it when necessary with skim-milk powder. However, he always disliked both the necessity and the result, since the cheese became 'chippy' if too much was used, and as from this year (2003) has abandoned the practice. The farm is not organic, but the soil, which is silty clay loam, is excellent and the grazing very rich.

MONTGOMERY'S CHEDDAR

> *Gold Medal, also Best Cheddar Cheese and Best Traditional British Cheese, British Cheese Awards 1996; Gold Medal, Extra Mature Traditional Cheddar, 1997 and 2001; Silver Medal, Mature Traditional Cheddar, 2001; Gold Medal plus the Patrick Rance Memorial Trophy for the Best British Cheese, Extra Mature Traditional Cheddar, 2001; Bronze Medal, Traditional Cheddar, 2002; also, the James Aldridge Memorial Trophy for the Best Unpasteurized British Cheese, donated by HRH The Prince of Wales, 2002*
> *A hard cows' cheese; full-fat, unpasteurized milk; traditional rennet. 26kg/57lb cylinders*

At ten months old, Montgomery's Cheddar is relatively moist, with a slightly rough, granular texture; as it ages, it becomes drier and grainier. When younger, the taste is deep but soft, more delicate and feminine than Keen's or Quicke's (pages 84 and 104), with not quite such a strong tang; however, at two years old, if you are lucky enough to find some, it is as powerful as any cheese in the world. At this stage, it may have developed a few knots of blue, probably near the rind, which is a recommendation rather than otherwise. I do not suggest it as a preference for cooking because the flavour loses its subtlety. It is a cheese to savour as it stands.

The cheesemaking is carried out by a team of three, organized on a rota system to include weekends. It takes, or should take, four to four and a half hours, as measured from renneting to milling – which was the only absolute timing James would give because of the need for judgement at every stage. The evening's milk is chilled and added to the morning's while still warm from the cow; it is then heated to 35°C/95°F and Barber starter, which is incubated to a culture before use, is added: James prefers this to the usual kind straight from the packet because he finds that it makes the resulting cheese less acidic and gives a broader spectrum of flavour. When the acidity has reached the desired level, usually in about forty-five minutes, the milk is renneted. The curd, similarly, usually takes about forty-five minutes to set: cheesemaking does not proceed until it has 'a clean break'.

The next part of the process, which is carried out mechanically, is to scald it to 41°C/106°F, at the same time stirring and cutting it to the size of wheat grains. This is followed by draining, cutting a channel down the middle of it, and 'Cheddaring' (this is done by hand). The Montgomerys' method of draining is to run the curd into another vat; digging the channel and Cheddaring (i.e. cutting it into blocks and piling and re-piling) textures the curd and releases further moisture while the acidity begins to rise. When the acidity has reached the correct point, it is checked by salting, and the curd is milled with an old peg-mill which James favours because it gives an uneven result and makes for an interesting, slightly less than homogeneous texture to the cheese. A second salting follows, after which the cheeses are packed into moulds lined with linen, and pressed overnight.

The next day the cheeses are sealed by dipping in hot water, re-wrapped, and pressed for a second night. On the third day, they are rubbed with melted lard and wrapped in a final coat of muslin, which is firmly stuck to them by pressing briefly. The Montgomerys mature them for a year or longer on wood (rather than stainless steel), with turning as necessary to prevent them from sticking to the shelves.

MONTGOMERY'S JERSEY SHIELD

Bronze Medal, British Cheese Awards 2002
A hard cows' cheese; full-fat Jersey milk; traditional rennet.

Whereas Montgomery's Cheddar is universally acknowledged as perhaps the best Cheddar in the world, opinions are split over Jersey Shield. Some people, myself included, think it is utterly delicious, whereas others feel that it lacks edge: for this reason, William Oglethorpe at Neal's Yard Dairy washes the rind to turn it into Ogleshield, which is delicious in a different way. The plain, unenhanced cheese is mild, buttery and wonderfully sweet, with tastes of meadows and flowers which come all the more to the fore because of its low-key character.

 # S. A. *and* G. H. Keen

GEORGE KEEN, MOORHAYES FARM, VERRINGTON LANE,
WINCANTON, SOMERSET BA9 8IR. TEL: 01963 32286

When I visited the Keens, in April, Somerset looked as if it had just been created. The new season's grass was so short that the whole county might have been a lawn; the banks sparkled with freshly opened primroses and the hedgerows were clouded with white blackthorn blossom. Moorhayes Farm stood out against the new-ness like a symbol of continuity: the tall, gabled farmhouse is sixteenth century, and appears the more impressive as you approach because it is set back above the road on the hillside. Like the Montgomerys, the Keens are brothers whose family has made cheese on the same farm for three generations. Their grandfather came here in 1900, when everyone who farmed made cheese as a matter of course; the same dairy, traditionally placed next to the kitchen, was used until 1990. One of the old covered cheese vats now stands next to the Aga, serving a double purpose as a store-cupboard and table. A barn across the yard has been converted into a new, much larger dairy, enviably well equipped and carefully purpose-designed; nevertheless, when he moved into it, George was very worried about its effect on the cheese. One of his main concerns is that it should be 'genuinely traditional, just as it has always been. Otherwise, why do we bother to make it at all, when there are so many commercial Cheddars on the market?' He stressed that every circumstance influences it: not only the soil, grazing, cows, season, freshness of the milk, and method of making it, but also the position of the dairy, particularly the direction that it faces, which affects humidity, and the materials used for the cheesemaking equipment. In the event, he says that although the cheese has in fact changed, he thinks 'not for the worse'.

Rather like Archie Montgomery, George's brother Stephen raises cash crops; the livestock on the farm, however, now consists only of the dairy herd. George greatly regretted giving up the pigs but found that they did not pay. Despite this and his attention to every detail connected with the cheese, he regards himself as a farmer rather than cheesemaker, taking the old-fashioned view that making cheese is not a separate occupation but merely a branch of farming. 'I didn't choose to be a cheesemaker, I chose to be a farmer, and cheesemaking is part of that.' Consistent with this is his policy of never buying in milk to increase output, no matter how much demand for the cheese might rise; similarly, his commitment to his cattle, in their own right as well as in relation to the cheese, is paramount. With a few exceptions, his herd is closed, i.e. home-bred, and building it up has been his life's work; he knows all the cows personally, and his feeling for them obviously goes very deep. This was just at the time when hysteria over BSE was at its height: the aspect of it that most upset him was not the likelihood of a cull (which, as it happened, was announced that evening) but simply that he could not bear to see the cows ill. It seems that although they do not actually go mad, they become restless, neurotic, and unhappy; although he cannot be sure that they are in physical pain, he reckons that at least they must suffer from headaches.

KEEN'S CHEDDAR

Silver Medal, British Cheese Awards 1996; Gold Medal, Mature
Traditional Cheddar, 1997; Bronze Mature Traditional Cheddar, 2001
A hard cows' cheese; full-fat, unpasteurized milk; traditional rennet.
1.4kg/3lb and 29kg/64lb cylinders

The texture is moist, smooth, and surprisingly light; the taste, spicy and deep, striking the tongue at many levels, with a warm, powerful, distinctive tang. This is serious Cheddar, less sweet and summery than Montgomery's at the same age but an ideal partner to equally serious wines and, with Quicke's, probably the best Cheddar in the world for cooking.

The cheese is made by a method similar to but not quite the same as the Montgomerys': the most obvious differences are that the temperature used to warm the milk at the beginning is lower, the curd is scalded after rather than during cutting, and the cheese is pressed for an extra day. The milk arrives at the dairy at 8.30 a.m. and is warmed to 30°C/86°F. A cultured starter is added while it heats; it is renneted when it has reached the full temperature and left to set for about forty-five minutes. It is then cut to a size between a wheat-grain and a pea before being stirred and scalded to 40°C/104°F over about an hour, until the acidity has risen and the curd is 'firm and nutty: you can feel it knocking your fingers'. This means that it is ready for draining, which is carried out by running it into another vat, or 'cooler'; Cheddaring, milling, and salting follow. The cheeses are pressed for twenty-four hours, dipped in hot water (which helps the rind to form), and pressed for another twenty-four hours: they are then rubbed with lard and covered with two layers of muslin. Finally, they are pressed for a further twenty-four hours and matured for a year on wooden as opposed to stainless steel shelves, which George (like others) feels are detrimental to flavour.

 ## Westcombe Dairy

Richard Calver; Cheesemaker, Bob Bramley:
Westcombe Dairy, Lower Westcombe Farm,
Westcombe, Shepton Mallet, Somerset BA4 6ER.
Tel: 01749 831300

Last year (2002), three leading producers of unpasteurized Cheddar in the traditional Cheddar area, Keens', Montgomery's, and Westcombe Dairies, joined forces to become one of the two first Slow Food Praesidia in Britain and Ireland – the other being wild smoked salmon caught off the Irish coast. The name Slow Food might be more helpfully translated as Real Food – but would then lose its edge as the opposite to fast food. Slow Food was founded by an Italian, Carlo Petrini, because of his horror at finding that a McDonalds had opened in the Piazza di Spagna in Rome. Within three years, it had become an international movement and is now active in forty-five countries. Its basic aim is to protect traditional foods and styles of cooking, although its initiatives range from Slow Cities to an annual award to the person judged to have contributed most to biodiversity. The Praesidium scheme is designed to publicize and give practical support to artisan foods in danger of extinction (the one for Cheddar has been established in association with the famous cheese-shop and wholesaler, Neal's Yard Dairy). Each Praesidium lays down conditions which guarantee authenticity and the excellence of the product: Somerset Cheddar is made of milk produced from cheesemakers' own farms, the curd is set with animal as opposed to vegetarian rennet (which affects flavour), and Cheddaring, i.e. cutting the curd into blocks and piling it, is carried out by hand. The cheeses when they are made are bound in cloth (which regulates moisture loss and hence, again, flavour) and matured for a minimum of eleven months.

Westcombe is the newcomer in the trio of dairies, since both the Keens and Montgomerys have been making Cheddar for three generations, whereas Richard Calver, whose background is farming, only went into the cheese business five years ago. However, cheese has been made since the 1880s on the Westcombe site, with milk from the same three farms as today: indeed, Westcombe has a claim to fame as the dairy where Edith Cannon, daughter of the famous Cheddar-maker Henry Cannon, was working when she won the championship for the best cheese made in the British Empire. She subsequently went on to become the Principal of a cheese-school founded by the Bath and West and Southern Counties Society (as it was then called) at Wells.

Visiting Westcombe is three-dimensional gastronomically, so to

speak, since the site includes not only the dairy but Bay Tree preserves and James's chocolates. As you enter the yard, the smell is of
chocolate rather than cheese, and on your right you may see the
bespectacled, white-coated figure of James through the window of his
office. Thanks to extractor fans in the roof, there is no smell of cheese
in the dairy either – in contrast to the delicious aroma in the enormous,
two-storey maturing-room. Like parts of the London Library, the
floor dividing the storeys is a grille, which allows the air to circulate
evenly. The temperature here is kept at 11°C and the floor regularly
sprayed with water to keep the humidity at the desired level.

As well as Cheddar, Richard and Bob are making Westcombe
Red, a mild, annattoed hard cheese something like Red
Leicester. For this, I take a little of the credit: when I first met
Richard, before the dairy opened, I remarked that I did not
know what an unpasteurized Red Leicester would taste like and
suggested, not altogether seriously, that he should try it. They
are also experimenting with a blue cheese, but this is for the
future, not least because it will mean opening a separate dairy
(otherwise they would probably end up with blue in all their
cheeses).

WESTCOMBE DAIRY TRADITIONAL MATURE CHEDDAR

Silver Medal, British Cheese Awards 2001 and 2002
A hard cows' cheese; full-fat, unpasteurized milk; traditional rennet.
24-25kg/ 53-55lb cylinders

The taste of Westcombe falls neatly between the softer, more
flowery tones of Montgomery's and the altogether more robust
character of Keen's. The tang is prounounced but not so strong as
to cloak hints of herbs and grass. I particularly liked its texture,

although Richard worries lest it may be a little too soft. Again, it falls between Montgomery's, which is crumblier, and the more elastic, cohesive texture of Keen's. Rather than being crumbly, it melts in the mouth and seems surprisingly light and insubstantial. Possibly I was lucky, but the piece I tried had developed tiny, crunchy crystals of calcium, a sign that the cheese has been matured for a long time.

WESTCOMBE RED

A hard cows' cheese coloured with annatto; full-fat, unpasteurized milk; traditional rennet.
9-10kg/ 20-22lb rounds

I have no way of judging how like unpasteurized Red Leicester this may be, as only pasteurized versions of Leicester are available for comparison: however, one difference which almost certainly applies is that the milk is sweeter than in Leicestershire. Westcombe is mild and flowery, with hints of grass and apples and a slightly smoky aroma. At four months old it is fresh-tasting, but becomes stronger and mellower at five or six. As its popularity indicates (Richard and Bob are finding that they cannot make enough of it), it is the sort of cheese that you could happily eat every day. It is delicious toasted, which brings out the sweetness of the milk.

The milk comes from a total of 400 Friesian-Holsteins from three farms. Their pasture is particularly rich in clover, and some is permanent, probably with five or six different kinds of grass in addition to a wide variety of weeds and wild flowers. In winter they are fed silage rather than hay – not that Richard disapproves of hay: 'It's wonderful, but impossible to make decently in England!' In addition, they are given high-protein supplements of crimped wheat and soya (all their feed is GM-free).

Both the cheeses are made with a cultured starter from the same maker as James Montgomery, and as with James, a different one is used every day of the week (hence Randolph Hodgson of Neal's Yard Dairy's otherwise incomprehensible remark that he always preferred Montgomerys made on Thursdays). The Red is made in a similar way to the Cheddar but milled in a peg-mill, which shreds the curd, rather than the chip-mill used for the Cheddar, which slices it; also, it is Cheddared rather less, which means that it retains more moisture. Both cheeses are pressed from the time when they are finished until the next morning; they are then immersed in hot water to encourage the formaton of the rind, pressed again for twenty-four hours, cloth-wrapped and larded, and finally pressed for a further twenty-four hours. The Cheddar is matured for eleven to eighteen months and the Red for four or five, or occasionally six.

Chris Duckett at Westcombe Dairy

The Ducketts, like the Keens and Montgomerys, had made cheese with milk produced on their own farm for three generations: in their case, however, although their farm is only a few miles from Cheddar, the cheese in question was Caerphilly. This was typical of a pattern which emerged after the coming of steam-power and the easy transport of liquid milk. An important incentive for cheese-making had been preservation: when it became possible to sell the milk directly, many farmers both in Wales and elsewhere were happy to save themselves the work of making it into cheese. The gap in the market was filled by those on the south side of the Bristol Channel who had the advantage of richer grazing and were probably making cheese anyway.

Again like the Keens and Montgomerys, there are two Duckett brothers: Chris was primarily the cheesemaker while his brother Philip looked after the cows. When I visited them a few years ago, their mother too was still active, moulding butter with old-fashioned wooden pats in a little room just beyond the dairy. Even at that time, Chris was having trouble with his hips (both of which have now been replaced): for this reason, and because one of their staff had left, he and Philip decided to sell their herd and buy in the milk for the cheese. All did not go well: the bought milk, although from specified local herds, caused problems. When Richard came up with the offer of a share of his milk, plus the use of the dairy, Chris was only too delighted to accept: in fact, he says now that without Richard he would almost certainly have had to retire. As it is, he seems to have fallen on his feet. Westcombe is not far from his own farm, at Wedmore, where he lives (and keeps a herd of dark brown alpacas and a family of llamas), and that he has not lost his touch as a cheesemaker is shown by the fact that last year he won the championship for the best territorial cheese in Britain at the prestigious Nantwich International Cheese Show.

DUCKETT'S CAERPHILLY

A semi-hard cows' cheese; full-fat, pasteurized milk; vegetarian rennet. 990g/2lb, 1.8-2.3kg/4-5lb, and 3.6-4kg/8 lb-8lb 13oz truckles

Some of the cheeses are sold at only a week old, when they are firm and refreshing, with a gentle, lemon-like sharpness. The Westcombe site includes a shop which sells them aged about three weeks: by then they have become smooth, moist, and much sweeter, though still with a slight hint of lemon. Neal's Yard Dairy matures them for one to two months, until they have become almost semi-soft, with a deliciously smooth texture and sweet, creamy taste. Like other Caerphillies, they melt beautifully: hence presumably the popularity of Welsh rarebit.

Cheesemaking takes about four hours, starting as soon as the milk is delivered in the morning. The milk is warmed to 20°C/68°F, starter added, and the milk heated to 26°C/79°F. It is then left to ripen for about two hours before being re-heated to 32°C/90°F for renneting. When the curd has set, which takes about forty-five minutes, it is cut and scalded a few degrees higher and stirred continuously for another forty-five minutes or until Chris can tell by the 'feel', which should be smooth and elastic, that the correct acidity has been reached and it is ready for draining. After draining, instead of being piled in blocks and milled, as for Cheddar, it is swept into heaps and cut first into 5cm/2-inch, then 2.5cm/1-inch squares. This is followed by a light salting, moulding in muslin cloths, and pressing for an initial half-hour before the surfaces are salted again; finally, the cheeses are pressed for sixteen hours and brined for twenty-four.

 ## Welsh Rarebit

For 2

15g/¹/₂oz butter
3 level tsp white flour
2 tbsp strong cider
salt and pepper
1 tsp Dijon mustard
1 tbsp double cream
200g/7oz Mature Duckett's Caerphilly, finely grated
2 whole or 4 half-slices baked bread (page xxviii), sprinkled with oil
    and pepper

Melt the butter in a small pan over low heat; stir in the flour off the heat. Add the cider, return to the heat, and stir continuously until thick. Season with a pinch of salt and a generous grinding of pepper, stir in the mustard, and simmer gently, stirring often, for 2–3 minutes to ensure that the flour is cooked: by this time, the mixture will be very stiff and gluey. Stir in the cream and remove from the heat. Thoroughly stir in the cheese. Put a thick layer of the mixture on each piece of bread, making sure that the bread is entirely covered (if exposed, it will burn). Grill until the cheese is well dotted with brown: it should spread just enough to trickle over the sides of the bread.

AVALON

A semi-hard cows' cheese flavoured with caraway seeds; full-fat, pasteurized milk; vegetarian rennet. 1.8–2.5kg/4–5½lb truckles

Avalon is similar to the Duckett's Caerphilly but is matured for only seven to ten days. Not being particularly fond of caraway, I was surprised that I liked it: however, the seeds remove the sharpness characteristic of new Caerphilly and leave it with a pleasant, marshy, slightly salty rather than acid tang.

 ## Avalon and Sultana Tea Bread

I suppose you might call this a version of Welsh *bara brith* ('speckled bread'). Lovers of caraway seeds may wish to add a few more; those who do not can use plain Caerphilly. Serve it at once, preferably while it is still warm.

Cooking time: 30–40 minutes, depending on the size of loaf
Makes 1 x 600g/1lb 5oz loaf or 2 smaller loaves

150g/5^1/$_4$oz plain, preferably organic white flour

100g/3^1/$_2$oz plain, preferably organic fine wholemeal flour

1 tsp salt

1^1/$_2$ tsp bicarbonate of soda

125g/4^1/$_2$oz caster sugar

25g/1oz butter, chopped small

150g/5^1/$_4$oz Avalon, finely grated

140g/5oz sultanas

about 225ml/8fl oz strong tea

Pre-heat the oven to 180°C/350°F/Gas 4. Sift together the first four ingredients and mix them with the sugar. Rub in the butter until it has disappeared; stir in the cheese and sultanas. Add most of the tea; pour in the rest gradually until the mixture is a light but fairly soft dough. Turn the dough into a loaf tin (or tins) lined with cooking foil: the tin should not be more than two-thirds full to allow for rising. Bake the bread for 35–40 minutes until well browned for a large loaf, or 30–35 minutes for smaller ones. Serve with cottage cheese, butter, or butter and marmalade.

DUCKETT'S SMOKED CAERPHILLY AND WEDMORE

A semi-hard cows' cheese (Wedmore: with chives); full-fat, pasteurized milk; vegetarian rennet. 1.8–2.3kg/4–5lb truckles

The Smoked Caerphilly is moist, with a light texture and tiny holes. The smoking is carried out when the cheeses are only two to three days old, so that they are still slightly sharp: the taste of smoke, although pronounced, is not overwhelming and the result is surprisingly pleasing and delicate.

Wedmore is similar to Smoked Caerphilly but has a more pronounced smoky tang because of the added chives. If this sounds like overkill, it is not: although stronger than the other cheeses, the result is harmonious.

The Lubborn Creamery

James Farnham, Manor Farm, Cricket St Thomas,
Somerset
Website: www.lubborn.co.uk

When I first visited the Lubborn Creamery, the cheese was made in a converted Victorian malt-house in Crewkerne, and Piers Fieldon, who founded the company, was still Managing Director. The malt-house was tall, red-brick, proudly utilitarian, and beautiful because of it. Now James Farnham has taken over from Piers and the Creamery has been moved to new, purpose-built premises five miles outside Crewkerne, where it looks across a narrow valley to a sky-line of small, billowing hills. In front of it is an irregular row of old, magnficent beech trees, identifiable at that time of year (February) only by their silvery trunks and the pattern of their twigs. In three months' time, the woods which surround Cricket St Thomas will be afloat in a sea of bluebells. As a member of the staff remarked, they have swapped a picturesque building for picturesque surroundings – and, as she emphasized, are happy with the exchange.

The Creamery makes Bries, Camemberts and Camembert-style goat cheeses; they have also just developed a semi-soft cheese with *Brevibacterium linens* rather than penicillin mould on the rind. The cows' milk comes from twelve farms within 20km/12 miles of the Creamery, plus selected organic farms for organic Brie, and the goats' from nine farms in the area. Unlike small producers, who accept that their milk may vary and modify their procedures accordingly, Piers ensures that his products are consistent by standardizing all the cows' milk before cheesemaking begins. This is done by removing and separating a proportion of the milk, perhaps a quarter of it, concentrating the skim, and returning an appropriate amount of the concentrate to the rest (in effect, the equivalent of James Montgomery's addition of skim-milk powder: page 82). The goats' milk, which tastes stronger the more it is disturbed, is not standardized; however, mainly in the interest of flavour, Piers insists that his suppliers' goats are kept in. I asked if he thought the goats minded: given his professionalism, I feared that he would consider it a sentimental point – but not at all. He replied that when he started it had often worried him but he has since satisfied his conscience about it, using the analogy of Londoners, who live in conditions which some would find intolerable yet feel that they live full and rewarding lives. Goats, he emphasized, are sociable animals, who will be happy so long they are with the herd.

SOMERSET BRIE

Silver Medal, British Cheese Awards 1996 and 2002; Bronze Medal, 1997
A soft white mould rind cows' cheese; full-fat, pasteurized milk; vegetarian
rennet. 1.1kg/2lb 7oz or 2.5kg/5lb 8oz wheels or pre-packed slices

The cheeses have an exceptionally crisp crust and rich, flowing texture, on which you can rely, since they are not distributed for sale until they are ripe. The flavour is fresh, sweet, and creamy, mild in the smaller size but fuller in the large. Especially in view of the very reasonable price, buying half or a whole large wheel is not as extravagant as it sounds, since it can be used for a salad dressing or stuffing, or fried in breadcrumbs (page xxix).

Two enormous cylinders are used for preparing the starter. In one, the solution in which the starter is cultured is mixed, heated, and thus sterilized; the starter itself is added in the second. Under the direction of Piers's microbiologist, Matthew Organ, not only starter and penicillin for the rind but also yeasts are added to the cows' milk to aid the ripening process and promote the differences between the Bries and Camemberts; extra starter is also added to the milk for the Camemberts to produce a stronger flavour. Apart from this, all the cheeses except Taurus are made in the same way.

After the starter and other preparations are added, the milk is left to stand for forty minutes before being pumped into one of the series of vats, which stand in a row like the trucks of goods trains. It is then renneted and allowed to set: as cheesemaking is continuous throughout the day, each vat, or truck, contains milk at a different stage of setting. The cow curd is cut into 2cm/$^3/_4$-inch squares and the goat curd into smaller pieces. Thick pipes at the bottom of the vats convey both curds and whey to the curd pump, and from there the curd is taken to the belt of moulds. At the end of the belt, the moulds, still raining whey from every hole, are piled in stacks of eight to drain; after being turned several times, they are transferred to an enormous tiled draining room.

In the morning, they are turned out and salted in the salting chamber, which looks like an enormous box. To encourage the growth of an extra crisp rind, the cheeses are sprayed with a further dose of penicillin by a 'fogging' machine. They are wrapped as soon as the rind has developed, partly, to use Piers's delightful phrase, 'to avoid earthy tastes from the air', partly to retain ammonia which is given off during ripening, and, most obviously, to keep them creamy and moist. As yet, only the Camemberts are machine-wrapped, but Piers is hoping to install a machine for the goat cheeses soon (which, he was careful to emphasize, would not mean redundancies but that staff are freed for further expansion: whether in terms of quantity or new cheeses, he did not say). After wrapping, the goat cheeses are sent out at once, the Camemberts after ten to sixteen days, and the Bries after sixteen days.

Somerset Brie and Garlic Mushrooms

Either the sauce or the complete dish can be prepared a day ahead.

Cooking times: 8 minutes for the sauce, 8–10 for the mushrooms
For 4

4 large mushrooms (400–450g/14oz–1lb combined weight), peeled
   and stalks removed
salt and pepper
6 cloves garlic, peeled, 2 roughly and 4 finely chopped
15g/$^1/_2$oz butter
1 tbsp oil
1 large shallot (about 55g/2oz), peeled and finely diced
100g/3$^1/_2$oz button mushrooms, washed and diced
125ml/4fl oz dry white wine
2 tsp dill, washed, dried, and finely chopped
150g/5$^1/_4$oz Somerset Brie (with rind), chopped
40g/1$^1/_2$oz Parmesan, grated
4–5 tbsp fresh white breadcrumbs

Wash the large mushrooms and dry them with kitchen paper, squeezing out as much moisture as possible. Place gills upwards on a lightly oiled baking tray, or plate if you are preparing the dish in advance. Season moderately with salt and pepper.

Crush the roughly chopped cloves of garlic in a mortar; add and beat in the butter and set it aside. Warm the oil over fairly low heat and fry the shallot and the rest of the garlic for 1$^1/_2$–2 minutes or until soft; add the button mushrooms, season with a little salt and rather more pepper, and fry, turning often, for 3–4 minutes or until they begin to colour. Pour in the wine, raise the heat, and cook away the liquid. Remove the pan from the heat and stir in the garlic butter and dill; add and stir in the cheeses, pressing the Brie gently against the bottom of the pan until it has melted sufficiently to mix with the other ingredients. Place a quarter of the mixture on top of each mushroom. If you are making the dish in advance, allow the mushrooms to cool, cover, and chill.

Pre-heat the oven to 200°C/400°F/Gas 6. Sprinkle the mushrooms with the breadcrumbs and bake them for 10–12 minutes, until the topping is brown and crisp. Serve at once, with bread or tagliatelle lightly dusted with Sussex or other pecorino to mop up the juices.

WINDWHISTLE ORGANIC BRIE

Gold Medal and trophy for the Best Soft White Cheese, British Cheese Awards 2002
A soft, white mould-ripened cows' cheese; full-fat, pasteurized organic milk; vegetarian rennet
1.1kg/2lb 7oz or 2.5kg/5lb 8oz wheels or pre-packed slices

The taste is fresh and gentle, like Somerset Brie, but (as one might expect) somewhat stronger, with an almost perfect balance between saltiness and sweetness. Although the rind of the one I tried most recently was not quite as crisp as on the ordinary Somerset Brie, the texture of the interior was wonderful – smooth, rich, creamy, and yet surprisingly light.

The cheese is named after the hill up which you drive on the way to the Creamery.

SOMERSET CAMEMBERT

Silver Medal, British Cheese Awards 1996 and 2002
A soft white mould rind cows' cheese; full-fat, pasteurized milk; vegetarian
rennet. 220g/scant 8oz rounds

Again, the texture of the interior is deliciously rich and creamy, with the contrast of a thick, crisp rind; the taste includes a tinge of grass and a hint of mushrooms from the rind.

To make Somerset Camembert Fritters, follow the recipe on page 61. The flavour is improved slightly if you substitute red wine for cider; with red wine, serve redcurrant jelly or raspberry vinegar instead of apple chutney.

TAURUS

Semi-soft goats' cheese; full-fat, pasteurized milk; vegetarian rennet.
140g/5oz rounds

Rather than a white penicillin rind, like the other Lubborn cheeses, this one has the soft, pinkish bloom of *Brevibacterium linens*. It also has a correspondingly strong cheesey smell, but tastes relatively mild. Lubborn assures me that it is not washed-rind: nevertheless, the cheese is interesting as one of the very few utilizing *B. linens* made by a relatively large dairy in this country.

SOMERSET GOAT CHEESE OR CAPRICORN

Silver Medal, British Cheese Awards 2002.
A soft white mould rind goats' cheese; full-fat, pasteurized milk; vegetarian
rennet. 100g/3½ oz rounds

Both names apply to the same cheese, depending on where it is
bought. The cheese has a crisp rind and creamy flowing interior.
Unlike the cows' cheeses, it may not be ripe when purchased, in
which case keep it chilled for a few days. To me, this is the Mars
Bar of cheeses: small, cheap, easy to buy, and with just enough
taste of goat to be interesting.

J. G. Quicke and Partners
TOM LANGDON DAVIES, WOODLEY FARM, NEWTON
ST CYRES, EXETER EX5 5BT. TEL: 01392 851222

The Quickes have made cheese on the same farm, not just for three
generations, like the Keens and Montgomerys, but for over 450
years. During and after the Second World War there was a long
lapse, which initially was due to the ban on farmhouse cheesemaking and afterwards because, when the ban was lifted, Mary's
father agreed to sell the milk to another cheesemaker who continued in business for nearly twenty years. The present dairy was set
up by Mary's mother, Prue, in 1973, when the cheesemaker finally
emigrated to Australia. At that time, cheesemaking was still
regarded as part of the normal business of a mixed farm, as it had
always been; the success of the dairy enabled the Quickes to continue mixed farming for a few more years, but eventually, like
almost everyone outside the organic sector, they felt obliged to
specialize. However, they do not concentrate solely on the cheese;

instead of giving up their pigs, they have turned them into a second profitable enterprise (their pork is sold via Peninsula Pigs to Marks & Spencer).

The dairy herd consists of 340 pedigree Friesian–Holsteins, which is large but still not large enough: restrained from enlarging it still further by the milk quota, they buy in an extra supply of quality-tested Friesian–Holstein milk from Milk Link. Their own cows are genetically based on Ayrshires so that, like the Montgomerys', the milk has Ayrshire characteristics, including a high solids content. Their method of making Cheddar is also similar to the Montgomerys': they differ, however, in pasteurizing most of the milk, in using vegetarian rennet for some of their cheeses, and making a range of products, including not only plain but smoked and flavoured Cheddars, Double Gloucester, Red Leicester, two soft cheeses, a lactic cheese and a new cheese with added cream, Westholme (available in several flavours), a new hard goats' cheese, and whey-butter and ice-cream.

Unpasteurized cheeses are made only on particular days, when there is no mud and the milk is especially suitable; Mary, who is in charge of the cheesemaking, prefers to use traditional rennet for long-matured cheeses because she finds that the vegetarian version gives a metallic taste to those matured for more than six months. The Gloucester and Red Leicester are made in almost the same way as the Cheddar but at different acidities; the goats' cheese is also made by a similar method. The soft cheese is rich and creamy, and is ideal for cooking or making dips and pâtés; at present, because of its short shelf-life (seven to ten days), the Quickes sell it only from their farmshop.

QUICKE'S TRADITIONAL CHEDDAR

Bronze Medal for Mild Traditional Cheddar, British Cheese Awards 1996;
Silver Medal for Extra Mature Traditional Cheddar, 1997;
Gold Medal for Mature Traditional Cheddar, 2002
A hard cows' cheese; full-fat, pasteurized and unpasteurized milk;
vegetarian and traditional rennet. 25.2kg/55½ lb truckles

The texture is smooth, moist, and more compact than either
Montgomery's or Keen's; the taste is deep, clean, and true. The
strength of the cheese depends on its age, which varies from six
months for the Mild to eighteen months for the Extra Mature,
which is very powerful. After trying one sample (from Neal's Yard
Dairy) I noted: '*Really* strong ... leaves the mouth tingling'; another
time, however, when both were labelled Extra Mature, Keen's was
the stronger. Like Keen's, the cheese is superb on the table, and the
two can be used interchangeably for cooking.

 Mary Quicke's Celeriac Chowder

Mary gave me only the rough outline of this recipe, so it may not
be precisely as she intended: it is nevertheless extremely good. If
you can buy organic celeriac, use it, not only because it will probably be fresher than when conventionally grown but may also be
sold complete with leaves, which add flavour (those left over are
delicious in salads).

A vital point about celeriac is to peel it carefully, removing inlets
of skin and tough flesh under the surface, which otherwise will
remain as abrasive edges in the soup, rather like bits of core in apple
pies.

Cooking time: 40–45 minutes
For 4

1 medium onion (about 150g/5¼oz), peeled and finely chopped
15g/½oz butter
½ tbsp oil or a little more
1 small leek (85–100g/3–3½oz), finely sliced, washed, and left to dry
1 medium (250g/9oz) floury potato, e.g. Cara or Kerr's Pink, peeled
    and diced into 8mm/⅓-inch squares
1 smallish root celeriac (500g/1lb 2oz), prepared in the same way as
    the potato
salt and pepper
1 litre/1¾ pints vegetable or chicken stock (page xxvii), skimmed of
    fat
2 fronds celeriac leaves if available, washed
2 tbsp double cream
125–140g/4½–5oz Quicke's or Keen's Cheddar, finely grated

Sweat the onion in the butter and oil over low heat for 10 minutes
or until soft but not brown. Add the leek and stir-fry for 1–2 minutes: moisten with extra oil if necessary. Add the potato and
celeriac, season with 1 teaspoonful salt and a fairly generous grinding of pepper, and pour in the stock. Throw in one stem of celeriac
leaves, bring just to the boil, cover, and simmer for 25–30 minutes
or until the potato and celeriac (root) are tender.

While the soup simmers, pull 6–8 celeriac leaves from the second
stem and shred them finely. Add the cream to the soup; remove the
pan from the heat and take out the cooked stem of celeriac. Stir in
about two-thirds of the cheese and sprinkle the soup with the shredded leaves. Serve the rest of the cheese separately.

QUICKE'S TRADITIONAL OAK-SMOKED CHEDDAR

Bronze Medal, British Cheese Awards 1996; Silver Medal, 2001;
Bronze Medal, 2002
A hard cows' cheese; full-fat, pasteurized milk; vegetarian and traditional
rennet. 6.8kg/15lb truckles

As smoked cheeses go, this is one of the best: the taste of smoke, though strong, does not overwhelm that of the relatively mild, young cheese. When used for cooking, for which it is excellent, both flavours intensify.

QUICKE'S TRADITIONAL RED LEICESTER

Gold Medal, British Cheese Awards 1996; Bronze Medal, 1997
A hard cows' cheese; full-fat, pasteurized milk; vegetarian rennet.
16kg/35lb truckles

The cheese has a light, open texture and rich, buttery, but very mild flavour. Along with Butler's version, made in Lancashire, Quicke's is perhaps the best of the pasteurized so-called Red Leicesters produced (I say so-called because they are not made in Leicestershire: for this reason, the producer of the only similar unpasteurized cheese, Richard Calver of Westcombe Dairy, has avoided the name Leicester and calls his cheese Westcombe Red).

Ticklemore Cheese

Robin Congdon, Sharpham Barton, Sharpham Estate, Ashprington, near Totnes, Devon.
Tel: 01803 732737

Our visit to Robin Congdon was especially memorable not only for the location of his dairy but also because of his all-expressive way of talking about cheese, which conjures up the densely populated world of micro-organisms in the minimum of words. To reach his house, which is house and dairy combined, you go up a hill via the usual narrow, twisting West Country lane enclosed by walls or high banks. The hill is steep but not remarkable and in no way prepares you for the view of the Dart valley which suddenly spreads out before you at the top. The river winds northwards between convex slopes patchworked with woods which at that time of year were bare and dark, interspersed with fields dusted with snow: in the summer I am sure that it is very pretty, perhaps too pretty, but on a winter afternoon, with an evening mist gathering, it had the drama of a slightly blurred black and white photograph. Robin's house is almost on the summit, overlooking the river: he certainly does not make cheese for the sake of living here, but he chose the site and put up the house himself rather than moving into an existing building in a less inspirational spot.

Before becoming a cheesemaker, he had farmed on the estate (which includes four farms) and during that time started milking sheep, not with any particular aim but simply because in the 1970s nobody else had thought of it except Olivia Mills. This led to making yoghurt for Harrods, which he delivered himself: cheese was the obvious next step. Eventually, he gave up farming to concentrate on cheese: he now makes blue cows', sheep's, and goats' cheeses plus a non-blue hard and a fresh goats' cheese – and bemoans the fact that the cows' cheeses are much the most popular. With his partner, Sarie Cooper, he also runs a cheese-shop in Totnes at the bottom of the hill, the excellence of which comes as something of a surprise in such a small town (though there is no real reason why it should).

As he showed me round the dairy and explained his cheese-making processes, his descriptions were so rich in aphorisms that I can only remember a few. The most memorable was: 'Cheesemaking is almost farming bacteria', but 'There are so many generations of life in a cheese' was a close runner-up. He also stressed that cheesemaking is very much what you feel with your hands, and that it calls for judgement at all times because there are so many variables: the weather, the field in which the animals are grazing, the animals' state of mind, and luck – and, he added, a cheese needs love as well.

DEVON BLUE

Silver Medal, British Cheese Awards 1997
A blue cows' cheese; full-fat, unpasteurized milk; vegetarian rennet.
3kg/6lb 10oz cylinders

Devon Blue has a moist, slightly crumbly texture and a soft, many-tiered taste which includes flavours of grass, flowers, cream, and butter, with earthy hints. The blue is just strong enough to be lively without overwhelming the other flavours.

To make the blue cheeses, the milk is warmed, starter added, and the milk heated to 34°C/93°F before the addition of rennet and *Penicillium roqueforti* for the mould. The curd is left to set for thirty to sixty minutes, cut twice, once coarsely and once finely, with a harp (a set of vertical wires instead of a blade) and stirred at intervals for twenty to eighty minutes according to the kind of cheese. It is then left to rest and, like the Exmoor Blue cheeses (page 73), moulded without draining; instead, the cheeses are turned several times on the first day and once on the second. For two days, they are kept very warm (20–22°C/68–72°F), after which they are rubbed with salt and spiked to allow extra air to enter. When enough blue has developed, in three or four weeks, Robin wraps them in foil or plastic, according to the French rather than the Stilton method (instead of wrapping, Stilton is not pierced until it is five to six weeks old). The goats' cheese, Harbourne Blue, is matured for four months, and the cows' and sheep's cheeses, Devon and Beenleigh Blue, for six to eight.

BEENLEIGH BLUE

Gold Medal, British Cheese Awards 1996
A blue sheep's cheese; unpasteurized milk; vegetarian rennet. 2.7kg/6lb
cylinders; scarce in winter

The cheese is slightly crumbly, with tiny, bubbly holes. Cheese addicts are divided between those who prefer Beenleigh and those who prefer Harbourne: Beenleigh, being sheep, is richer and sweeter, with hints of grass and flowers and a distinct tang of the sea. As with Devon Blue, the blue, although strong, complements rather than overwhelms the other flavours.

Beenleigh Blue Pâté with Sage

For 4–6

1 fair-sized clove garlic, peeled and chopped
225g/8oz goats' curds or Perroche (page 193)
115g/4oz Beenleigh Blue, chopped
8–10 sage leaves, washed and finely chopped

Crush the garlic to a paste in a mortar. Add and mash the two cheeses; stir in the sage. Serve with pears or fresh figs.

HARBOURNE BLUE

Silver Medal, British Cheese Awards 1996 and 1997
A blue goats' cheese; full-fat, unpasteurized milk; vegetarian rennet.
2.7kg/6lb cylinders; scarce in winter

The texture is creamy and melting; the taste includes suggestions of the sea and moors. It is a wonderful cheese, but with the background of goat the blue can be very powerful. As Robin acknowledges, its strength varies considerably: more than most blues, it is better eaten last rather than first on the cheeseboard.

TICKLEMORE

A hard goats' cheese; full-fat, unpasteurized milk; vegetarian rennet.
1.8kg/4lb basket-shaped cheeses; scarce in winter

Ticklemore is very light and delicate, with small holes; the taste is mild, fresh, and sweet, with a mixture of moorland flavours and only the faintest trace of goat.

It is made by heating the milk to 30°C/86°F, adding starter, followed by rennet, and leaving the milk to set for half an hour. The curd is then cut into large chunks and left to stand for twenty minutes before being cut again, stirred, and heated by 2°C/36°F. After being left to rest for another twenty minutes and cut again, it is moulded, not in conventional basket moulds but Woolworth's colanders. Finally, it is left in a warm place for two days, salted, and left at cool room temperature (14°C/57°F) for another two days before being matured for two to three months.

TICKLEMORE SOFT GOAT

A fresh goats' cheese; full-fat, unpasteurized milk; vegetarian rennet.
50g/1¾oz buttons; scarce in winter

This is an exceptionally smooth, delicate goats' cheese, with a mild, sweet, but fresh flowery flavour. Unluckily for those who do not live in the area, it is sold only at his, and Sarie's shop, Ticklemore Cheese, Ticklemore Street, Totnes.

 ## Ticklemore and Apple Mousse

Cooking time: 8–10 minutes, plus 4–5 to crisp the nuts just before serving
Allow at least 3 hours for chilling
For 4

400g/14oz Bramley apples (2 medium), peeled and chopped fairly small
125g/4½oz Muscovado sugar
1 Ticklemore soft goats' cheese (50g/1¾oz)
150ml/¼ pint whipping cream
25g/1oz pecans

Set the apples over very low heat with the sugar and allow them to cook until the sugar has started to melt; stir gently and continue to cook for 7–8 minutes more or until the fruit is soft and submerged in liquid. Blend or sieve it, pressing as much of the pulp through the mesh as possible. Sieve or blend in the cheese. Whip the cream until it stands in peaks; fold it in gently and chill for at least 3 hours.

Shortly before serving, pre-heat the oven to 200°C/400°F/Gas 6, and toast the nuts for 4–5 minutes. Coarsely crush or very finely chop them and sprinkle on top of the mousse.

Sharpham Creamery

DEBBIE MUMFORD, SHARPHAM CREAMERY, SHARPHAM
HOUSE, ASHPRINGTON, TOTNES, DEVON TQ9 7UT.
TEL: 01803 732600

Sharpham House is dramatically situated on the side of a hill above
the Dart, which here, only about 8km/5 miles from Dartmouth, is
meandering and tidal. The house was designed by Sir Robert
Taylor in 1770; in front, on the edge of a steep slope down to the
river, framed by trees and perfectly placed to give scale and focus to
the view, is a large statue by Henry Moore, who was a friend of
Maurice Ash, the former owner. Inside, Oriental rugs on the land-
ings are a reminder that for a time the house was occupied by a
Buddhist community and is still used as a Buddhist educational
centre, with a printing press, library, and programme of lectures
and meditation retreats. Behind the house are gardens, possibly
laid out by Capability Brown, and 200ha/500 acres of farmland,
most of which is on a peninsula made by a bend in the river. The
privacy given by the hill at the back and the river on the other
three sides, the timelessness of the Moore, and perhaps the atmosphere lent by Buddhism, produces an almost tangible sense of
calm.

The estate is now owned by the Sharpham Trust and, besides
the house, consists of four farms, one organic and one biodynamic,
the Sharpham vineyard, and the creamery, which is in the stable-
yard next to the house. The milk comes from a herd of nearly
seventy Jerseys kept on permanent pastures which Debbie and her
partner, Mark Sharman, who makes Sharpham wine, recently converted to organic. When I visited her, she only made the one
cheese, Sharpham, although she had already developed her second,
Elmhirst; since then, she has also taken over Devon (now
Sharpham) Rustic, a rich, moist, semi-soft cheese which used to be

made by Robin Congdon (page 107), with whom she trained for two and a half years.

SHARPHAM

Bronze Medal, British Cheese Awards 1996 and 2001
A soft, white mould rind Jersey cheese; full-fat, thermized milk; vegetarian
rennet. 250g/9oz squares or 1kg/2lb 4oz rounds; 500g/1lb 2oz rounds
occasionally or to order

When ripe, the cheese is gloriously rich and creamy; the taste is grassy and herbal rather than sweet, very individual, and stronger than one might expect, particularly slices from the large size (small cheeses tend to be milder).

Every morning, Debbie collects the milk in a Land Rover fitted with a cooled milk tank. Her first step is to thermize it by heating it to 68°C/154°F: she says that she has tested the treated against the raw milk and the only difference thermizing makes to the cheese is to slow down its development slightly. Sharpham is made by a fairly classic version of the Coulommiers method. After starter is added, the milk is left to ripen for one to one and a half hours, or longer in winter, before the addition of rennet and penicillin for the rind. The curd sets in about an hour; Debbie then cuts it twice, with half an hour between each cutting, and ladles it into the moulds to free-drain. The cheeses are turned four or five hours later and the next morning are taken to a draining room kept at 14°C/57°F; the following day they are brined and for the next three days they are turned daily. They are then moved to a room kept at 10°C/50°F, where they stay for a further twelve days while the rind develops. Thereafter, they are kept chilled until they are ready for eating at seven to ten weeks. If bought unripe, the cheese should be kept in its wrapping, wrapped again loosely in plastic to prevent loss of moisture, and stored at 4°C/39°F, i.e. in the refrigerator, until soft and flowing.

ELMHIRST

A soft Jersey cheese; full-fat, thermized milk and added cream;
vegetarian rennet.
250g/9oz squares and 1kg/2lb 4oz rounds

Elmhirst has a very smooth, silky texture and is soft as opposed to runny, with a taste of butter and cream mingled with grass, wild flowers, and sunshine. So far as I am aware, some eight handmade cheeses with added cream are produced in the UK: Emhirst is one of the most outstanding.

SHARPHAM RUSTIC

Silver Medal, British Cheese Awards 1997 (Chives and Garlic);
Bronze Medal, 2001; Gold Medal (Chives and Garlic) 2002
A hard Jersey cheese, plain or flavoured with herbs; full-fat, thermized
milk; vegetarian rennet. About 2kg/4lb 6oz flattened spheres

I have tried both Robin Congdon and Debbie's versions of this cheese and, despite a possible difference in touch and texture, found both equally exceptional. Like Elmhirst, it tastes of butter, cream, grass, and wild flowers, but, because it is matured and drier, it is sweeter and the flavours more concentrated. To my palate, few more delightful cheeses of the milder, less challenging type are to be found anywhere.

Tala

Hans and Heather White, North Beer Farm, Boyton, Launceston, Cornwall PL15 8NR.
Tel: 01566 785607

On the way to North Beer Farm, in July, I counted over a dozen different types of wild flower on the hedgebanks: pink campion, red clover, yellow toadflax, foxgloves, sheep's-bit scabious, speedwell, mallow. This is not irrelevant to the cause of cheese, since it shows that here at least the herbage is still mixed despite the use of agrichemicals.

Since they embarked on professional cheesemaking ten years ago, Hans and Heather White have confronted many of the problems that cheesemakers are likely to face. Hans was in the Navy and retired at fifty with a pension which needed supplementing: having decided to dairy-farm but disliking goats' milk and feeling unable to cope with cattle, they settled on sheep. They began with twenty British Friesland ewes, a ram, and a cheesemaker in Devon who agreed to take their milk. Before long, the cheesemaker went 'rather seriously' bankrupt, leaving them with an unpaid account and no alternative outlets.

They had both taken cheesemaking courses before starting out, but, as Heather remarked, only a certain amount can be taught in a classroom situation. Having tried freezing and storing the milk, which proved uneconomic, they 'fiddled' with cheesemaking until they produced a cheese which sold. Before long, success prompted them to buy in extra milk: it also soon became obvious that they did not have enough time both to milk their own sheep and fulfil their orders. They therefore gave up the sheep and relied entirely on bought-in milk, which Hans said made him uneasy from the start. His fears were justified: 'We had a lot of trouble, going back over three years, with thousands of

pounds of cheese going off (i.e. "blowing") because of dirty milk.'
However, Hans's next-door neighbour, Terry Perkins, is a farmer
who at that time was raising sheep for lamb: moaning over the
fence to him about his troubles, Hans eventually persuaded him
to branch out into milking, with the result that he now has milk
as fresh as his own had been and Terry supplies the Minsons and
Robin Congdon as well (pages 123 and 107).

The dirty-milk period, however, has left its mark on Hans,
who has kept an entire storeroom of failed cheeses to study:
gazing at row after row of them, all coated with black mould,
some with staring white patches cut out of them, was a strange
experience. Also, when the cheeses first started 'blowing' he
thought that it might be because he hedged, ditched, and did
other farm work as well as making cheese, thus contaminating
the milk with undesirable yeasts and moulds. He therefore withdrew from the actual cheesemaking, leaving it to Heather, and
restricted himself to packing and marketing. Although he now
knows that the milk itself was the problem, this arrangement continued, with Heather making the cheese twice a week (she also
teaches deaf children). At this point, they are thinking of retiring,
which might have meant the loss of a very distinctive cheese: however, it seems probable that it will be taken over by John and Caryl
Minson, who already make several sheep's or partly sheep's-milk
cheeses.

TALA

*A hard sheep's cheese; thermized milk; vegetarian rennet. 450g/1lb and
2.3kg/5lb truckles*

The texture is fine, compact, and velvety; the taste is surprisingly strong and completely unique. As always, it is impossible to

give a true idea of flavour in words, but it is grassy and perhaps the earthiest cheese that I have yet come across. The unusual taste means that you may need to give it a little time: if you are not quite sure about it at first, try it again. It is particularly delicious toasted, when it browns and melts to a toffee-like consistency, with a flavour which if anything is even more intense than when it is uncooked; for best results, drizzle it with a little fruity olive oil.

The particular flavour of Tala is partly due to the fact that it is a washed-curd cheese, like Waterloo and cheeses of the Gouda type. Understandably, in view of their earlier difficulties, Heather takes the precaution of first thermizing the milk, which is heated to 65°C/149°F; rennet is added about an hour after the starter and the curd is left to set for about another hour. It is then cut very small, heated by about 10°C/50°F to give it a firm coating, and washed by gradually replacing the whey with boiled water, which reduces the acidity in the taste of the final cheese. Draining and moulding follow, after which the cheeses are pressed and turned several times, with increasing pressure after each turn. The next day they are moved to a drying room, brined the day after, and finally dried for another twenty-four hours, by which time a firm crust has formed. The maturing time is three to four and a half months, or six weeks for the small size; some are also smoked.

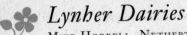

Lynher Dairies

MIKE HORRELL, NETHERTON FARM, UPTON CROSS,
LISKEARD, CORNWALL PL14 5BD. TEL: 01579 362244;
FAX: 01579 362666

Netherton is the largest of a cluster of farms most of which are rented by Mike from the Duchy of Cornwall – who are helpful landlords except that he feels that they would be happier if he farmed organically (which he does not). The farm is open to the public, with a barn which has been converted into a coffee-shop, a farm trail, ornamental poultry, wild boar, and a few pigs. Very properly, the first to greet visitors when they arrive are the pigs, who (deliberately) are kept in the field opposite the car-park.

Serious farming, however, is concentrated on the dairy. Mike, who has been at Netherton since the 1960s, switched from mixed farming about twenty years ago and now has a herd of 500 pedigree Friesian–Holsteins. Cheese was brought to him by the Duchy: aware of the need for a value-added product, he had already been thinking about it when they telephoned to ask if he would take in a couple of cheesemakers who were in need of a home. He said, 'Yes. When?' and they replied, 'Now. Today.' Alan and Jennie Gray from Wales thus arrived with a very old recipe, possibly dating from the thirteenth century, and made the cheese, Yarg (Gray spelt backwards) three days a week for nearly two years. At this point, since the cheese had become popular, Mike asked them to step up production to five days a week: they departed soon afterwards but left the recipe.

Although virtually all the milk comes from his own herd, he pasteurizes, partly to ensure that the cheese has a consistent flavour. Like some others, it nevertheless retains its individuality to a surprising degree: when I asked him why, he answered, 'I don't know', adding that he did not feed the cows for any special effect (at the time of my visit, one of the most eye-catching features of the farmyard was a stack of silage as high as a house).

The dairy makes not only Cornish Yarg, which is wrapped in nettle-leaves, but a new version wrapped in wild garlic leaves, two fresh flavoured cheeses for which the curd is simply drained in cloths, two flavoured semi-hard cheeses based on a traditional West Country recipe, and a plain semi-hard cheese, Stithian's Special.

CORNISH YARG

Gold Medal, British Cheese Awards 2001; Bronze Medal, 2002
A hard cows' cheese coated with nettle leaves; full-fat, pasteurized milk;
vegetarian rennet. 1kg/2lb 4oz and 3kg/6lb 10oz rounds

Cornish Yarg is a moist cheese which tastes fresh and creamy, with a gentle tang and surprisingly wide range of strong yet subtle herbal, grassy, and flowery undertones. The nettle coating, which is dark, greenish grey, is truly artistic, especially when seen on a whole cheese: whether it adds to the flavour is open to question. Mike thinks not; his wife is convinced that it does. I would be inclined to agree with her because of the importance to flavour of the other sorts of rind; however, as the Lynher Dairies soft cheeses show, much of the taste is certainly due to the milk.

Cornish Wild Garlic Yarg is similar except that, far from having a questionable effect on flavour, the coating of wild garlic is extremely potent.

The cheese is made by a method half-way between Caerphilly and Cheddar, although it differs from both in that it is not scalded, which means that it sets less firmly; also it is covered with its distinctive coating of nettle leaves rather than a rind. After pasteurization, the milk is cooled to blood-heat, starter is added, and the milk is left to ripen for about an hour before renneting.

When the curd has set, it is cut very finely with a curd knife (which has vertical blades) and drained. The next stage is cutting it into blocks and piling; this is followed by milling, moulding and pressing overnight. Finally, the cheeses are brined for twenty-four hours, the nettle coating dipped in a sterilizing solution, and applied to the cheese with paintbrushes. The nettles are picked by children and others and frozen, not merely for convenience and to deaden the sting, but because when defrosted they are limp, which makes sticking them neatly over the cheeses much easier.

CORNISH GARLAND

A semi-hard cows' cheese; full-fat, pasteurized milk; vegetarian rennet. 2.3kg/5lb and 3.6kg/8lb wheels

Cornish Garland, which was originally Devon Garland, is a herb-flavoured cheese traditional to the West Country (herbs used to be a popular addition to cheese not only for the sake of flavour and variety but because, in the days before vitamins were identified, people found that they helped to prevent scurvy in the winter). The cheese used to be made by a cheesemaker called Hilary Charnley; when she retired, she sold the recipe to Peverstone Cheese Co. (now defunct), from which it has been taken over by Mike.

The present cheese has a deliciously smoky (rather than herbal) flavour with a pleasant milky overtone, and a distinctive dry, light, slightly flaky texture.

The Devon Garland recipe belongs to the Cheddar group but the curd is cut less finely than for Cheddar, the cheese is only lightly pressed, and the maturing-time is relatively short. After starter and rennet have been added and the curd has set it is cut into 1cm/½-inch cubes rather than pea-sized particles; stirring and 'pitching' (leaving it to rest), draining, and piling in blocks follow.

SOUTH-WEST ENGLAND 121

After the curd has been salted and milled, it is moulded with a layer of the finely chopped herbs in the middle. Finally, the cheeses are pressed overnight and matured for six weeks.

TISKEY MEADOW

A semi-hard cows' cheese; full-fat, pasteurized milk; vegetarian rennet.
2kg/4lb 6oz and 3.6kg/8lb wheels

Tiskey Meadow was the name of a field belonging to the farm at Peverstone. The cheese is made by the same method as Cornish Garland but instead of herbs, it is flavoured with sun-dried tomatoes, oregano, garlic, and basil. I admit that it sounds dubious – but it works. It is moister and mellower than Garland, with a similar almost caramel-like milky flavour which is slightly reminiscent of 'cooked' Alpine cheeses (though it certainly does not resemble them in any other way). I recommend it not only for the cheeseboard but cooking.

 ## Tiskey Meadow Courgettes

Chillies vary greatly in strength: try a tiny piece of the one you are planning to use, and if it is very mild, do not remove all the seeds. The courgettes can be prepared up to twenty-four hours in advance.

Initial cooking time: nearly 1 hour; final baking time: 10–12 minutes
For 4 as a vegetable

450g/1lb ripe tomatoes, peeled, chopped, and the hard cores
    removed
salt and pepper
white sugar
500g/1lb 2oz (4 medium) courgettes, washed and the ends trimmed

5 cloves garlic, peeled and finely chopped

100g/3$^1/_2$oz (2 large) shallots, peeled and finely chopped

1$^1/_2$ tbsp oil

40g/1$^1/_2$oz pine-nuts

1 green chilli, washed, dried, core and seeds (unless needed)
   removed, and finely diced

2 stems basil or enough for 2 tbsp when washed and shredded

100g/3$^1/_2$oz Tiskey Meadow, finely grated

extra virgin olive oil for drizzling

Pre-heat the oven to 190°C/375°F/Gas 5. Put the tomatoes into a small, shallow baking dish (do not spread out in a single layer or they will become too dry); season fairly generously with salt and pepper and sprinkle with a very little sugar. Bake for 40–45 minutes, until the tomatoes are dry but not charred.

Boil the courgettes in lightly salted water for 7–9 minutes, until they are tender when pierced with a blunt knife; drain, refresh in cold water, and leave for a few minutes to cool. Halve them lengthwise and score round the cut side about 5mm/$^1/_4$-inch from the edges to about the same depth, taking care not to penetrate the skin. Scoop out the flesh in the middle with a spoon; turn the shells upsidedown to drain and tip the liquor into the baked tomatoes; chop the flesh into 1cm/$^1/_2$-inch squares.

Fry the garlic and shallots in the oil over medium heat for 2 minutes or until soft, turning constantly; add the courgette flesh and fry for another 1–2 minutes or until the shallots start to be tinged with gold. Add the nuts and stir-fry for a few seconds; add the chilli and stir. Add the tomatoes and cook for 3–5 minutes or until liquified, pressing out lumps of tomato flesh against the bottom of the pan. Stir in the basil. Fill the courgette shells; store in the refrigerator until needed.

To bake, keep the oven at 200°C/400°F/Gas 6, set the courgettes closely together in a baking dish, and cover liberally with the grated cheese. Sprinkle with a few drops of ordinary oil and bake for 10–12 minutes or until the cheese begins to brown. Drizzle with a little virgin olive oil before serving.

CORNISH PEPPER AND CORNISH HERB AND GARLIC

Gold Medal, British Cheese Awards 1996 (Cornish Pepper); Bronze Medal, 2001; Bronze Medal (Herb and Garlic) 2002
A fresh cows' cheese; full-fat, pasteurized milk; vegetarian rennet.
500g/1lb 2oz or smaller and 1kg/2lb 4oz rounds

Both cheeses are rich, creamy, and close-textured; the herbs and garlic in the one are quite strong but, despite pasteurization, you can still taste the natural grassy and flowery flavours of the milk.

Menallack Farm

CARYL AND JOHN MINSON, MENALLACK FARM, TREVERVA, PENRYN, CORNWALL TR10 9BP. TEL: 01326 340333

Besides making cheese, Caryl Minson acts as a wholesaler for cheeses all over Cornwall and part of Devon, which sometimes involves driving 480km/300 miles a day; she also keeps a farmshop selling chutneys and cheeses, bread, pottery, and anything else 'genuine', makes bread for her own and another local shop, and until recently offered bed and breakfast. She is helped in all this by John, who, after a job which took them all over the world, retreated to Cornwall with the aim of living a life of leisure and sailing.

They bought the farm because their son wanted to keep cows: Caryl accordingly experimented with cheese and came up with Menallack, which is based on a recipe for Cheshire from Val Cheke and A. Sheppard's *Butter and Cheesemaking*. This proved so popular that she decided to employ a cheesemaker, which gave her the time to develop her other activities. Meanwhile, the son fell in love with the cheesemaker and carried her off to Kent, leaving Caryl and John with the cows as well as everything else. The cows, except for one or two who were kept for pleasure, were sold: Milk Marque agreed to supply quality-tested milk from a particular farm, and John turned out to be an excellent cheesemaker. Soon after, a couple who made a cheese called Nanterrow, which Caryl sold in her shop, announced that they were giving up; not wishing to lose the cheese, she took it over. When I was working on the first edition of this book, she was making five different cheeses: by now, she has evolved or taken over a list of fifteen, which include several cream-added cheeses, two contrasting goat cheeses, a creamy blue cheese, and a buffalo cheese powerfully flavoured with garlic. Of necessity, she also employs assistants – usually part-time, and nowadays quite a number: often, she told me, there are twelve of them sitting round the lunch-table. (An assistant called Kate, whom I met, was a sculpture student and afterwards graduated with a work featuring the mould growing on a Menallack cheese.)

MENALLACK

Menallack Vintage, Bronze Medal, British Cheese Awards 2002
A hard cows' cheese; full-fat, unpasteurized milk; vegetarian rennet.
10cm/4-inch, 15cm/6-inch, and 17.5cm/7-inch truckles

Menallack has a dryish texture and mild flavour, with a gentle, grassy tang and herbal undertones. It is a good all-purpose cheese suitable for lunches and snacks as well as the cheeseboard; it is excellent toasted.

After slightly warming the milk and adding starter and rennet, Caryl cuts the curd into 1cm/^{1}/$_2$-inch cubes, stirs it for twenty minutes, and scalds (heats) it to 35°C/95°F over another twenty minutes, stirring continuously; she then holds it at 35°C/95°F, still stirring, for a further twenty minutes or until 'the cubes feel like tender, cooked peas ... they should be sufficiently scalded to take on the imprint of your fingers.' Having reached the right point, the curd is left to rest for an hour before being cut into blocks and worked for one and a half to two hours. Draining, milling, and salting follow; finally, the cheeses are packed into moulds, pressed, and matured for a minimum of two months.

NANTERROW

Silver Medal, British Cheese Awards 1996
A fresh sheep's cheese; unpasteurized milk; vegetarian rennet. Made in 1.4kg/3lb disks; sold in 450g/1lb slices

Nanterrow has the delicate, insubstantial, almost trembling texture characteristic of fresh sheep's cheeses; the taste is equally delicate, with the sweetness of the milk balanced by hints of herbs and grass and a very slight tinge of lemon. It comes plain or flavoured with herbs: the herb-flavoured version, which focuses the natural flavours of the cheese without altering its character, is particularly successful.

The milk comes (frozen) from Terry Perkins, near Launceston (page 116). Nanterrow is made by a version of the Coulommiers method: watching John, I was reminded of Charles Westhead at Neal's Yard Creamery (page 190), since both are equally insistent on the need to disturb the curd as little as possible. When set, it is very gently lifted into the moulds, not with a ladle but with a plate: John then covers the mould with gauze and deftly turns it upside-down to drain, like turning a cake to cool on a rack. The herbs for the flavoured cheeses are sprinkled over the curd in layers; the cheeses are then left to drain for twenty-four hours, during which they are turned three times. Finally, they are lightly salted, cut into three, and vacuum-packed.

MRS FINN'S FARMHOUSE CHEESE

A fresh combined cows' and sheep's cheese; full-fat, unpasteurized milk with added cream; vegetarian rennet. 175g/6oz rounds, boxed

Elizabeth Finn founded the Distressed Gentlefolks Aid Association Homelife, a charity which provides care for the old: the cheese was devised by Caryl and John to celebrate its centenary. They have come up with a winner: Mrs Finn's combines the lightness and delicacy of Nanterrow with a slightly stronger, yet overwhelmingly creamy taste in which the sweetness of the milk and cream are offset by a gentle lemon tang. The result is refreshing rather than rich, and I think delicious. I tried it with a rind-smeared cheese, Gubbeen (page 159): the two cheeses set each other off perfectly. All profits will go to DGAA Homelife; available by mail order from the farm.

TREVERVA GREEN is similar to Mrs Finn but coated with green peppercorns.

A third cheese with cream added is HELIGAN (pasteurized), made with mixed sheep's and cows' milk and flavoured with lemon zest.

FINGALS

A fresh goats' cheese; pasteurized milk; vegetarian rennet.
Approximately 120g/4oz rounds

This cheese has a dryish, rather puritanical texture but an interesting flavour in which lemon is more prominent than goat.

VITHEN

A soft goats' cheese; pasteurized milk; vegetarian rennet.
340g/12oz rounds

In contrast to Fingals, this is notable for its rich, creamy, melting texture, but has a very mild taste.

SOFT CHEESE WITH GARLIC AND HERBS

A fresh buffalo cheese; full-fat, pasteurized milk; vegetarian rennet.
115g/4oz, 225g/8oz, 450g/1lb, and 900g/2lb rounds

The buffalo milk, which is even richer than sheep's, gives a nutty, concentrated, but deliciously light, soufflé-like texture; the taste of the cheese is creamy and very garlicky.

CHAPTER 3

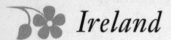 *Ireland*

CROGHAN GOAT FARM

CARRIGBYRNE FARMHOUSE CHEESE CO.

COOLEENEY FARMHOUSE CHEESE

CASHEL BLUE FARMHOUSE CHEESE

INAGH FARMHOUSE CHEESES

ARDRAHAN CHEESE

MILLEENS

DURRUS

WEST CORK NATURAL CHEESE

GUBBEEN

CARRAIG

COOLEA CHEESE

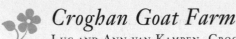

Croghan Goat Farm

Luc and Ann van Kampen, Croghan Farm,
Ballynadrishogue, Blackwater, County Wexford.
Tel: 00353 532 9331; Fax: 00353 532 7331

The first thing to strike us about Ireland was its greenness. We arrived at the end of May, when Britain is green too, but because of the extent and continuity of the grass if not because of the actual colour, the Irish green is much more noticeable and insistent. In the flat basin around Wexford, the land seemed entirely given over to grazing, the grass being interrupted only by equally green trees and the white, blue, and yellow splashes of wild flowers. Cattle were everywhere – but few people and hardly any traffic.

In terms of cheese, one of the major differences between Ireland and Britain was clearly illustrated by our first two visits. Here, the Cheddar and Cheshire tradition does not hold and inspiration tends to come from France, Holland, or Switzerland. Like several other leading cheesemakers, Luc van Kampen is from Holland: one of his cheeses is of the Gouda type, the other French.

To reach him, we drove along a narrow but straight and empty road and turned down a track which reminded me of World's End (page 32). The dairy is small and we would probably have missed it without the tell-tale milk churns outside: if it were bigger, Luc said, they would make more cheese, but at present they are limited by storage space (however, when I spoke to him some months later, he had already begun to extend the storeroom).

He has been interested in cheese for as long as he can remember, having been brought up in a cheesemaking area, Albusset-Waard; after meeting Ann in Dublin and deciding to stay, he started making it himself because at that time (1975) there was very little good cheese of any kind in Ireland. Counting 'everybody', i.e. kids, he and Ann have 100 goats, who supply about half their milk: the rest is bought from two specific farms, one of which is organic, bringing the total on a busy day to about 135 litres/30 gallons. Although their land is organic, the goats, strictly speaking, are not, since the van Kampens cannot afford organic feed; however, they are organic in spirit and do not stagger kidding for winter milk, which means that they make no cheese from November to May. Luc spends the winter equipping the dairy, where he has made his own press and all the wooden shelves, and very occasionally, when he has time, paints. From a large picture hanging in their bathroom, it is clear that he has unusual ability: he has designed their cheese labels and says that one day he would like to take a course in graphic design.

CROGHAN

> *Gold Medal, Best Semi-Soft Cheese, British Cheese Awards 1996;*
> *Silver Medal, 2001*
> *A semi-soft goats' cheese; full-fat, unpasteurized milk; vegetarian rennet.*
> *400–450g/14oz–1lb cakes or 1–1.4kg/2lb 4oz–3lb basket-shaped rounds*

Croghan has an exceptionally fine, velvety texture with a few small holes; the flavour is mild, creamy, and herbal, with a slight tang, not of goat (which is barely detectable) but of herbage and sea breezes (the farm is only 5–6km/3–4 miles inland).

The previous evening's milk is cooled and mixed with the morning's straight after milking; commercial starter is added and the milk is renneted at a temperature of 30°C/86°F, where it is held until the curd has set. It is then cut with a double-pronged curd knife into 1cm/^{1}/$_2$-inch squares, partly drained, and scalded (heated) to 36°C/97°F for about half an hour, by which time it looks like very small white polystyrene balls. These are moulded and pressed for four hours, after which the cheeses are turned out and brined; the maturing time is one month.

MINE-GABHAR

Gold Medal, Best Irish Cheese, Best Soft White-rind Cheese, British Cheese Awards 1996; Bronze Medal, 1997 and 2001; Silver (Roll) 2002
A soft white mould rind goats' cheese; full-fat, unpasteurized milk; vegetarian rennet. 225g/8oz

Mine-Gabhar (pronounced Gower) is notably smooth and velvety but firm-textured; it has quite a strong, very distinctive taste, again not of goat but of blossom and sweet new leaves, with nutty and earthy undertones. The overall impression is rich and luxurious but at the same time sunny and fresh. To suggest using it for cooking seems like libel, but it is wonderful grilled, when the flavour becomes even sweeter and more distinctive: if I had to nominate a Best Cheese for Grilling, this would be my choice.

For this cheese, very little starter and rennet are used and the curd is allowed to set very slowly, which maximizes the natural flavours; in this instance, the starter is home-made. The curd is left for twenty-four hours, drained in a cloth, and moulded for a further twenty-four hours; finally, the cheeses are sprayed with penicillin for the rind and matured for four weeks.

 ## *Carrigbyrne Farmhouse Cheese Co.*

PADDY AND JULIE BERRIDGE, CARRIGBYRNE FARMHOUSE, ADAMSTOWN, COUNTY WEXFORD. TEL: 00353 544 0560

Carrigbyrne is gracious and manorial, with a large, gabled, partly Victorian house and farmyard almost as big but much more orderly than a town square, with a tree in the middle. Round two sides are stables with wooden doors, all painted bright blue; the woodwork on the house is also bright blue. Perhaps because of the blue, and possibly also because of the size and formality of the yard, my instant reaction, before I had seen or spoken to anybody, was that it was French: I felt as if, instead of crossing St George's Channel to Ireland, we were in Brittany. The French impression is not entirely subjective or chance: although Paddy was brought up on the farm, his mother is Belgian, he speaks French like a native, and has a French cheesemaker, Alan Girot.

Before he went into business, two attempts to make Camembert in Ireland, in 1963 and 1972, had already failed; however, a cheese-maker who was involved in the second came to fish in the Berridges' river and taught Paddy, then aged seventeen, to make the cheese in the kitchen. He started out professionally ten years later (on 16 March 1982): everything went 'swimmingly' until the cows came in for the winter. Then, because of the change in the milk, disaster struck: 'The cheese just melted through the racks.' Having by then established that there was a good market for Camembert, he promptly advertised for a cheesemaker: Alan replied and has been with him ever since. After sixteen years, he says that the main lesson he has learnt remains the often-repeated maxim that there are no rules in cheesemaking: judgement has to be exercised afresh every day.

Alongside his commitment to cheese, Paddy loves machines. In the dairy is a French stainless steel washing-up machine, at least 3.6 metres/12 feet long, which washes up and sterilizes all the cheesemaking equipment. When I asked what happened to the whey, he replied, like everyone else, that he used to keep pigs but that they were uneconomic, and without saying more led the way to a barn at the corner of the yard. Inside, an enormous and aston-ishingly elegant sixty-five-year-old engine with a huge, red-painted flywheel generates enough electricity from the whey to service the house and farm and have some left over to sell to the national grid. He later admitted that this probably was not economic either, but I was suitably impressed, feeling, like him, that the machine was sufficient justification in itself.

Not surprisingly, the cheesemaking process is mechanized: only the wrapping is carried out by hand. The milk comes from a closed, i.e. entirely home-raised herd of over 200 Friesians. Besides the Camembert-sized St Killian, a larger version called St Brendan Brie is made; in addition, Paddy is planning to launch a new, washed-rind cheese later this year which he says is something like Swiss Vacherin Mont d'Or.

ST KILLIAN

Gold Medal, British Cheese Awards 1996; Bronze Medal, 2002
A Camembert-type soft cows' cheese; 45% fat, pasteurized milk;
vegetarian rennet. Boxed: 250g/9oz hexagonal rounds; St Brendan Brie,
375g/13oz rounds

The original quality of the milk combined with Paddy and Alan's expertise have produced a first-class result: the cheese has a spectrum of flavours ranging from herbs and grass to mushrooms (mould) and earth. In my tasting notebook, several samples from different shops are marked 'A1 delicious' or 'Wonderful'. Like Somerset Camembert (page 101), yeasts ensure slow ripening, which means that the cheese will almost certainly be at the correct stage when sold.

To encourage the development of yeasts and moulds, the milk is left unchilled for twenty-four hours before use; it is then warmed slightly, a special starter devised by Alan is added, and it is left to ripen for another hour before being 'flash' pasteurized at 72°C/162°F for sixteen seconds. The rennet and penicillin for the

rind are added at the same time: until recently, Paddy and Alan
used the traditional calves' rennet, but they are among the few so
far to have switched to the genetically engineered vegetarian
equivalent, Chymosin. When the curd has set, it is cut into cubes
and left to drain, with turning at intervals, at 25°C/77°F, depending on the time of year, until it has contracted to about half its
original volume. Finally, it is moulded, turned out and brined in
salt which does not contain iodine (iodine inhibits mould), and
ripened for about ten days at 10–12°C/50–54°F before packing.

St Killian is excellent in a pie, fried in egg and breadcrumbs (page
xxix) and served with redcurrant jelly, or simply baked in the oven
and served as a hot dip with biscuits or crudités.

 ## *Cooleeney Farmhouse Cheese*
BREDA, JIM, AND PAT MAHER, COOLEENEY, MOYNE,
THURLES, COUNTY TIPPERARY. TEL: 00353 504 45112

Cooleeney farmhouse is approached via a handsome gateway
crowned with urns and a long drive curving through parkland.
Breda Maher, who is in charge of the cheese, is secretary of the
Irish Cheesemakers Association and had been called away when we
arrived, but I was shown round by her son Pat, who, having
watched her efforts in the early years, when she had to 'push, push,
push' to establish the cheese, has recently taken over as marketing
manager. He told me that she had originally trained in hotel management with the idea of starting a restaurant; however, having
married a farmer, she found herself with cows to manage rather
than a kitchen. This made me wonder whether, as I do, she looks
on cheesemaking as a parallel to cooking: when I spoke to her

later, she said very positively, 'Cheese and cooking go hand in hand. They are both part of the same creative process.' (Sandra Allwood, who also makes soft, mould-ripened cheeses, made a similar comment.)

Her immediate incentive to make cheese was supplied by the milk quota, which interfered with the Mahers' plans for expansion. Almost directly after it was announced, she took a cheesemaking course in Cork, and went into production two years later. She now employs four full-time cheesemakers, who process nearly 2,000 litres/440 gallons of milk a day; all of it comes from a herd of 110 Friesians, the only livestock kept on the farm. Recently, the Mahers launched a second white mould-ripened cheese, Gortnamona, made with goats' milk, which won a Gold award and was judged Best New Cheese at the British Cheese Awards 2002.

COOLEENEY

Gold Medal, British Cheese Awards 1996; Bronze Medal, 1997
A soft, Camembert-type cows' cheese; full-fat, unpasteurized milk;
vegetarian rennet. 200g/7oz rounds (boxed) or about 1.6kg/3lb 8oz wheels

A wonderfully soft, creamy interior contrasts with the crisp, thick rind; the flavour is full and rich, striking the palate at different places and encompassing all the elements of the Irish pastures: sun, rain, wind, grasses and herbs, and flowers – a tribute, if you like, to unpasteurized milk. It loses some of its complexity when heated but is nevertheless delicious fried in breadcrumbs (page xxix) or in a pie. For a pie, enclose the cheese in puff pastry and bake at 210°C/410°F/Gas 6–7 for 15 minutes or until the pastry is risen and golden. With Cooleeney (but not St Killian) sprinkle 1 tsp finely chopped sage over the cheese before wrapping it with the pastry.

As the Mahers do not pasteurize, the cheesemaking process is more straightforward than at Carrigbyrne. The morning and evening milk is warmed, starter and penicillin for the rind are added, and the milk is left to ripen for two hours before renneting. At the time of my visit, calves' rennet was still being used, but because of BSE this has now been replaced by vegetarian rennet. The curd is cut into 2.5cm/1-inch squares, moulded, and left to drain for twenty-four hours, with turning after fifteen minutes and an hour. The cheeses are then brined and matured for two weeks, until the rind has developed, before they are wrapped; thereafter they are kept at 4°C/39°F, either on the farm or by the distributors, for four to six weeks in the case of the smaller size or eight to ten for the larger.

 ## Cooleeney and Fish Salad

Cooking time: 12–20 minutes (for the fish)
For 2 as a main course or 4–6 as a first course

175g/6oz turbot, halibut, or salmon, skinned and boned
salt and pepper
100g/3$^1/_2$oz Cooleeney straight out of the refrigerator
100ml/3$^1/_2$fl oz double cream
1 tsp dill (fresh) or 1$^1/_2$ of sorrel, washed and finely chopped or
    shredded
$^1/_2$ or 1 lettuce, according to the number of servings, washed
    and left to dry
cucumber and other salad ingredients to taste, washed and dried

Pre-heat the oven to 180°C/350°F/Gas 4. Wash the fish in cold water, check for bones, and season it lightly with salt and pepper. Enclose it in a parcel of cooking foil and bake for 12–20 minutes, or until it flakes easily with a fork (salmon cooks slightly more quickly than turbot or halibut). Drain the fish and leave it to cool.

Remove the cheese-rind and chop the cheese into small pieces. Either beat the cream into it by hand, pressing out lumps on the side of the bowl, or process it, but do not over-whip the cream. Stir in the dill or sorrel.

Arrange the lettuce on the serving plates. Flake the fish into bite-sized pieces and place it on top of the lettuce; cover with the cheese dressing. Finely slice the cucumber and arrange it with the other salad ingredients round the edge.

Cashel Blue Farmhouse Cheese
JANE AND LOUIS GRUBB, BEECHMOUNT, FETHARD, COUNTY TIPPERARY. TEL: 00353 523 1151

No one could fail to be impressed by the extreme cleanliness of the dairies everywhere, both in Ireland and Britain: the Grubbs' was so spotless that I swear you would have noticed a single grain of salt on the floor. Louis observed that the hygiene regulations are adhered to here particularly strictly because agricultural products are Ireland's chief export. All his equipment except his cheese mould and a hand-beaten copper vat is stainless steel (which, being non-corrosive, resists moulds as well as rust); some of it is new, including a remarkably elegant spiking machine for pricking the cheeses and the racks in his storeroom, which are fitted with rollers to turn the cheeses automatically. Both were custom-made by a local craftsman, the racks to his own design. However, he takes equal pleasure in other pieces which, far from being new, he picked up in scrapyards and has lovingly restored to pristine condition such as the copper vat, which is at least 100 years old and, although replaced for every-day purposes, is still used from time to time. Similarly, his cheese moulds are waterpipes pierced by local schoolchildren.

When we came to the subject of flavour and pasteurization, he said that as far as he was concerned, the crucial factors were the original quality of the milk and maturity. At that time, he left ten per cent of his cheeses unpasteurized but pasteurized the rest: he was thus able to offer a comparative tasting which, although not decisive because the cheeses were of different ages, illustrated very clearly how the flavour develops. The immature cheeses were hard and sharp whether pasteurized or not, and although the oldest unpasteurized example was soft and subtle, it was not so deep-tasting and interesting as a pasteurized one three weeks older; not surprisingly, he now pasteurizes them all. He emphasized that if the cheeses had been made in the winter, even maturity could not compensate for the inferiority of milk.

CASHEL BLUE

Bronze Medal, British Cheese Awards 1996 and 2001
A blue cows' cheese; full-fat, pasteurized milk; vegetarian and traditional
rennet. 1.5kg/3lb 5oz rounds

The cheese becomes increasingly soft and creamy as it matures; the taste is about as strong as Colston Basset Stilton (page 220) but softer and sweeter, with overtones of sun, rain, and flowers similar to the flavours in Cooleeney (page 135). As well as being outstanding for the table, it is one of the very best blue cheeses made anywhere for cooking, since it melts smoothly and easily and retains its depth of flavour.

The cheese is made three or four times a week by a staff of six; the milk comes from a pedigree herd of 120 Friesians. It is pasteurized, cooled, and starter and *Penicillium roqueforti* for the blue added and cultured at 30–32°C/86–90°F; renneting follows, after which it is left to set for an hour. The curd is then cut and left for another hour before being removed from the vat in scrim (raw Irish linen) cloths, drained, and tipped straight into the moulds. For the next two to three days, it is left to drain, with turning at intervals, until it is sufficiently dry for salting and piercing: the pierced cheeses, before the mould has grown, look like enormous, very thick Bath Oliver biscuits. To develop the blue, they are kept at 10°C/50°F for two weeks, after which the external mould is washed off and the cheeses dried and wrapped to inhibit the growth of further mould. Maturing is carried out at 4°C/39°F: some are sold young, but to reach their full potential, the cheeses need to be kept for four or five months.

 ## Cashel Blue and Fish Salad

This is the same as Cooleeney and Fish Salad but as the cheese is stronger, you need less; also, it suits cod better than salmon. Follow the recipe on page 136, cooking the cod as for salmon and using 40g/1½oz Cashel Blue and 3 tablespoonsful of cream: since these quantities are too small to process, beat the cheese into the cream by hand.

 # *Inagh Farmhouse Cheeses*
SIOBHAN NÍ GAIRBHITH: CHEESEMAKER,
ROISIN BUGLER; INAGH, COUNTY CLARE.
TEL: 00353 656 836633

Here, only about 16km/10 miles from the west coast, the soil is peat or sandy and the Irish green interrupted by dark shrubs and pine trees. The other trees are tall but bent inland by the Atlantic wind; the farm, however, is protected by a slight hill. Originally, the Inagh cheeses were made by Meg and Derrick Gordon at a small farm just down the road. When we visited them, their animals consisted of two Connemara ponies, sixty-eight Saanen goats plus two Toggenburgs, three dogs, seven cats, and an unknown number of hens. The hens included chocolate-coloured speckled Marans, who lay deep brown eggs, and black and white spotted Swiss hens, one of whom laid pale turquoise eggs. Meg's feeling for them was such that she gave them rum punch to drink when they were dying (of old age: no one would ever have thought of eating them). The ponies were a reminder of Derrick's past: he once bred race-horses, but had to give it up when racing became big business because he could no longer afford the stud fees. All the goats had names: I remember sitting in Meg's kitchen eating her delicate-tasting, wonderfully delicious cheeses and watching the goats in a field just outside the window consuming twigs, dock-leaves, and nettles. Meg said that they eat everything except grass; neither she, Siobhan, nor Roisin have ever mentioned consistency of flavour.

For years, Meg made her cheeses entirely alone: once or twice, she had tried hiring assistants, but worried about hygiene: 'People helping don't tuck their hair into their caps properly, or realize how really *very* often they ought to wash their hands.' Four or five years ago, however, she started working with Siobhan and Roisin. Siobhan runs an organic farm a few miles down the road: when Meg and Derrick decided to retire, therefore, it was easy to transfer the goats and cheesemaking (and the ponies) to her farm. She and Roisin now make the cheeses in exactly the same way as Meg: apart from the slight shift in location, the only change is that number of goats is now 200.

ST TOLA HARD CHEESE

Silver Medal, British Cheese Awards 2001
A hard goats' cheese; full-fat, unpasteurized organic milk; vegetarian
rennet. 1.8kg/4lb rounds

Lough Caum has an exceptionally fine, smooth texture; the taste is sweet and nutty, with a gentle tang suggestive of the sea and undertones of peat. It is delicious toasted: serve it with peppery or bitter leaves.

ST TOLA FRESH CROTTIN

Gold Medal and trophy for the Best Organic Cheese, British Cheese Awards
2002
Fresh goats' cheeses, plain or flavoured; full-fat, unpasteurized organic
milk; vegetarian rennet. 85–100g/3–3½oz buttons; seasonal: April–December

The texture is silken smooth and surprisingly compact, much more like matured cheeses than fresh; the taste is of the varied flavours of rich, sweet, organic milk, with the same suggestions of peat and the sea as Lough Caum.

ST TOLA

A soft goats' log; full-fat, unpasteurized organic milk; vegetarian rennet.
1kg/2lb 4oz; seasonal: April–December

St Tola is remarkable for its light, smooth, fine-grained texture: you would hardly recognize it as goat. The taste is creamy and sweet but with any number of sub-flavours, including peat and the sea. It becomes even sweeter when grilled: Meg and Derrick serve it with redcurrant jelly, honey, or pesto.

St Tola and Avocado Salad

For 2

2 tbsp oil
$\frac{1}{2}$ tbsp red wine vinegar
salt and pepper
1 ripe avocado
1 rosy grapefruit, skin and all pith removed
about 85g/3oz St Tola

Beat the oil and vinegar with a little salt and a moderate grinding of pepper. Halve and slice the fruit: arrange it along each side of the serving plates and pour the dressing over the avocado. Place the cheese in the middle.

Ardrahan Cheese

MARY BURNS, ARDRAHAN HOUSE, KANTURK, COUNTY CORK. TEL: 00353 297 8099

I had been particularly curious about Ardrahan because, even allowing for the fact that the rind is washed, it is one of the two or three most unusual and distinctive-tasting cheeses produced in Britain or Ireland. Although we had never met them, Mary and her late husband Eugene invited us (complete with dog) to stay the night. Our visit, delightful and memorable as it was, bore out the theory that cheeses imbibe something of the character of their makers; however, it revealed very little about how Ardrahan acquires its flavour, which one can only conclude is a product of the place, perhaps communicated via the water: a possible clue lies in the name 'Ardrahan', which means 'height of the ferns'. The

(Above) Anglo-Nubian kids. Anglo-Nubians, from Africa, produce the richest goat's milk

(Right) A Toggenburg goat. Toggenburgs originally came from the Alps.

Friesians grazing in parkland on Manor Farm, where Montgomery's Cheddar (page 82) is made.

Leon Downey adding rennet to the milk for Llangloffan (page 169). It will take about thirty minutes for the curd to set.

Testing the curd for Llangloffan to see if it breaks cleanly, which means that it is ready to cut. The next stage is stirring and beating.

Stirring the curd in the oblong vat at Keen's (page 84); while being stirred, it is heated to 40°C/104°F.

Andy Wigmore testing the curd for Waterloo (page 5). The cheese was originally made with milk from the Duke of Wellington's estate.

The curd for Cornish Yarg (page 119) being transferred to moulds after milling.
Once moulded, the cheeses will be pressed and then brined.

Anne and Andy Wigmore's Spenwood in the cheese press.

Cornish Yarg remains in a brine-bath for twenty-four hours before being coated with nettle leaves.

Frozen nettle leaves for coating Cornish Yarg. The effect when finished is very artistic; whether it affects taste is more questionable.

Coolea (page 161), Tyning (now discontinued), and Spenwood (page 7). Coolea is a Gouda-style cheese; Tyning and Spenwood are hard sheep's cheeses.

Blue Vinny (page 79), one of the very few traditional low-fat cheeses to have survived.

Ardrahan (page 143), a washed-rind cheese made by Mary Burns in County Cork.

Robin Congdon with his signature cheese, Ticklemore (page 110). As well as this hard goats' cheese, he makes a soft goats' cheese and three blue cheeses.

country around is lush, with large trees and rich grazing; the house is Georgian, looking over a wide valley, and the farmyard large and immaculate, decorated with pots of red geraniums.

The dairy has a glass screen so that visitors can watch the cheese being made without entering; also, as at Louis Grubb's dairy (page 137), racks turn the cheeses automatically; Eugene also used lengths of pierced piping as moulds, although only for the smaller cheeses. All the milk comes from the Burns own herd, which was lovingly built up by his father from choice imported UK stock and is the oldest registered pedigree herd of Friesians in Ireland.

Very sadly, Eugene died two years ago: one of his sons now runs the farm and the cheesemaking is carried out by Mary.

ARDRAHAN

Bronze Medal, British Cheese Awards 1997; Silver Medal, 2001
A semi-soft washed-rind cows' cheese; full-fat, pasteurized milk;
vegetarian rennet. 300g/10½ oz and 1.5kg/3lb 5oz rounds

The cheese when ripe is creamy all the way through, with a few small holes; it should be soft enough to spread slightly over the knife when cut. The taste, as best I can describe it, is a heady mixture of sea, rain, mushrooms, flowers, oranges, and red wine: the overall effect is powerful but warm and persuasive rather than challenging. Although not an obvious candidate for cooking, it is in fact excellent, retaining its strength and individuality almost unchanged.

The cheesemaking involves both washing the curd, as for Gouda and the soft cheeses made further south, and brine-washing the rind, which has something to do with the flavour but does not in itself account for it. Rennet is added about fifty minutes after the starter and the milk left for another forty-five to fifty minutes to set; the curd is then cut by hand into 2.5cm/1-inch squares, washed, i.e. some of the whey skimmed off and replaced with water, and scalded to blood-heat (37°C/98.6°F). This is followed by moulding and turning at half-hourly intervals for several hours; after unmoulding, the smaller cheeses, which emerge from the lengths of piping in continuous logs, are cut into rounds (the larger ones are made in ordinary moulds). The last stage is brining in sea-salt and washing twice over the next three days. When first made, the new cheeses look like white iced birthday cakes: as they grow older, the rind becomes crinkled and takes on an orange tinge, caused by *Brevibacterium linens*, which proliferates in south-western Ireland. Other cheesemakers encourage it by spraying: Eugene sprayed his cheeses once, after which it has been necessary to add it again.

 Ardrahan Potato Casserole

This is Mary's own favourite recipe for Ardrahan. It is extremely simple: she describes it as 'just an everyday, family sort of dish' – which it can hardly be for anyone else, since the rest of us do not have her access to the cheese; however, I promise that the result is fully worthy even of the quite large amount of cheese needed. The quantity is flexible: you can use less if you wish.

Cooking time: 1 hour
For 4

300g/10½oz Ardrahan
625g/1lb 6oz waxy potatoes, peeled or scrubbed
a little butter for greasing the dish
pepper

Wipe but do not remove the cheese rind and slice the cheese and potatoes. Butter a soufflé or similar ovenware dish and arrange the cheese and potatoes in it in alternate layers, starting with potato and finishing with a thick layer of cheese; season each layer of potatoes very lightly with pepper. Bake at 110°C/225°F/Gas ½ for about an hour.

Milleens

NORMAN AND VERONICA STEELE, EYERIES, BEARA, COUNTY CORK. TEL: 00353 277 4079

Although we had been told that the country is 'very pretty', I was utterly unprepared for the drive over the West Cork mountains and up the Beara peninsula to Eyeries. The mountains do not have the grandeur of the Highlands nor the forbidding quality of the moors and crags of North Wales, but are bright with grass, gorse, and rocks so pale that they catch the sun: little rocky outcrops and boulders scattered all over the slopes shine like white marbles. The first sign of water is the lake at Muckross: once you have ascended the hills beyond, it is never absent from view. The coastline round Beara is so jagged and intricate that land and sea seem inseparably entwined: inlets too land-locked to be penetrated by the tide look like ponds or lakes, with trees, bushes, and flowers growing right down to the water's edge. Here and there, white-washed farmhouses gleam among the boulders on the slopes; in the villages, the houses are painted pastel blue, turquoise, green, yellow, and pink. The area is completely unspoilt: we passed not a single tea-shop, take-away, hotel, or caravan site on the entire route. Despite Veronica's protest at the arrival of supermarkets, little can have changed since Norman first brought her here nearly thirty years ago.

The story of the transformation of the local shop and the origin of Milleens, to which in effect it gave rise, is told by Veronica herself:

There was nothing to eat ... I mean nothing interesting. The old shop in Castletownbere with its saucepans and shovels and Goulding's Manures clock wagging away the time, and smoked hams hanging from hooks in the ceiling, and great truckles of Cheddar on the wooden counter with their mouldy bandages and crumbs of cheese strewn around, scrumptious, tempting, melt-in-the-mouth crumbs which you could nibble as you queued to be served, with your message list. And then she would cut a fine big chunk, golden or white, and what I miss most is the way it crumbled.

So they closed it, gutted it, extended it, and re-opened it. Enter the trolley. Spotless. Sterile. Pre-packed portions perspiring in plastic. Tidy piles. Electronic scales. Keep moving. Don't block the aisles. No idle chatter. Big Brother is watching you. Don't ask for credit. Oh boy.

And then one day we bought a farm and a cow. Her name was Brisket and she had only one horn. She lost the other one gadding down a hill, tail-waving, full of the joys of spring. Her brakes must have failed. We had to put Stockholm tar on the hole right through the hot summer. And all the milk she had. At least three gallons a day. Wonder of wonders and what to do with it all. For two years I made Cheddars. They were never as good as the ones in Castletownbere had been but they were better than the sweaty vac-packed bits. Very little control at first but each failed batch spurred me on ... I was hooked.

One day Norman said, 'Why don't you try making a soft cheese for a change?' So I did.

Now while all this was going on we had a mighty vegetable garden full of fresh spinach and courgettes and French beans and little peas and all sorts of things you couldn't buy in a shop for love or money. And we would sell the superfluity to a friend who was a chef in a restaurant and took great pains with her ingredients. Annie would badger fishermen for the pick of their catch and come here on a Monday morning to root through our treasurehouse of a garden for the freshest and best. Now I was no mean cook myself and would have ready each Monday for her batches of yoghurt, quiches, game pies (made with hare and cream – beautiful), pork pies, skate pies, all adorned with pastry leaves and rosettes and as light and delicious as you can imagine, and my speciality, gâteau St Honoré – profiteroles oozing with cream and chocolate and freshly roasted almonds.

So there was the soft cheese beginning to run. We wrapped up the last of it and away it went with the vegetables and the pies and all the other good things to Sneem and the Blue Bull restaurant where it made its debut. As luck would have it Declan Ryan of the Arbutus Lodge Hotel in Cork was having dinner there that very night. Attracted no doubt by Annie's growing reputation, Declan had ventured forth to sample the delights of Sneem, and the greatest delight of them all was our humble cheese. The first, the one and only, Irish Farmhouse Cheese. At last, the real thing after so long.

Since then, vast quantities of learning have been ingested and applied, from the many journals of dairy science through *Scientific American* and even pamphlets from New Zealand on bacteriophage. All grist to the mill. The making of Milleens is not a slap-happy matter but a carefully controlled scientific process. Thermometers have replaced elbows. Note is taken of pH and acidity. Milk quality is carefully monitored.

> Starters are recognized as a most important influence on
> flavour and quality and are as well looked after as the crown
> jewels, and to better effect.

Having established Milleens, Veronica became aware not only of
the commercial potential of cheese in Ireland but also the advantage
of conditions in Cork, where the growth of moulds is fostered by
humidity of 100 per cent; she remarked that moulds rather than
bacteria were the determinant factor for cheeses made in this part
of the world. Partly by dint of a personality which Giana Ferguson
(page 157) describes as 'visionary', she encouraged others to make
cheese, notably Giana and Jeffa Gill (page 150), and consolidated
their position by founding the Irish Cheesemakers' Association.
The Steeles themselves have progressed from their first one-
horned cow to a herd of twenty-four which includes 'mad, bad'
black Kerry cattle, whose milk, according to Veronica, has fat
globules almost as small as goats': with two assistants and additional milk from neighbouring farms, she now makes 72kg/158lb
of cheese a day. Norman, who used to be a lecturer in philosophy,
has given up his job to manage the farm; they no longer keep pigs,
to their great regret, but still have hens and a large flock of ducks.

MILLEENS

Gold Medal and Supreme Champion, British Cheese Awards 1997
A semi soft washed rind cows' cheese; full fat, pasteurized milk; vegetarian
rennet. 225g/8oz and 1.4kg/3lb rounds

The texture is rich and creamy, not as runny as Camembert but soft
enough to flow over the knife when cut. It tastes of mushrooms,
earth, grass and the flowers which grow here in astonishing profu-
sion. The rind is a deep marigold yellow, caused by the growth of
B. linens mould.

Veronica Steele's Puff-Balls

Entirely by chance, I met Veronica's daughter Jenny soon after returning to London: she says that of all the dishes her mother cooked when she was a child, this is the one she remembers most vividly. In fact, it is simply tiny choux buns fried very crisp and stuffed with Milleens while still hot. It is essential to eat them as soon as they are ready, before the cheese has had time to liquefy. They literally melt in the mouth. The dough, which should be chilled before frying, can be made the previous day.

Makes 24–30

85g/3oz butter, chopped small
salt
125g/4½ oz plain white flour
3 large free-range eggs, broken and beaten in separate cups
about 225ml/8fl oz sunflower oil for deep-frying
a deep-fat thermometer *or* a few squares of bread to test the oil
about 100g/3½oz Milleens straight out of the refrigerator, cut into
    1.25cm/½-inch squares just before use

Put the butter, 225ml/8fl oz water and a moderate pinch of salt into a small saucepan. Set it over low heat until the butter has melted; then raise the heat and bring it to a brisk boil. Remove the pan from the heat, tip in all the flour at once, and beat until the mixture is smooth and comes away from the sides of the pan. Return the pan to very low heat and continue beating for 1–2 minutes, until the dough is stiff and cohesive and no tiny pockets of unmixed flour remain. Leave it to cool for a moment or two. Add the first egg and beat until it is completely amalgamated; the mixture will again become stiff. Repeat with the second and third eggs; after the third, the dough will be as soft as paste. Chill until needed.

Line a plate with absorbent paper to drain surplus fat from the puff-balls after they have been fried. Heat the oil to 175°C/350°F or until squares of bread brown in 40 seconds. Adjust the heat to maintain the temperature and slide heaped teaspoonsful of the dough into the oil: take care to avoid splashing and do not add more at a time than will fit into the pan without touching. Fry to a deep golden brown (if fried only to pale brown, the centres of the balls will be spongy instead of hollow). Roll the puff-balls on the absorbent paper, make a slit in the side of each and stuff with the cheese. Serve directly, while you fry the next batch.

Durrus

JEFFA GILL, COOMKEEN, DURRUS, COUNTY CORK.
TEL: 00353 276 1100

On the way to Durrus from Goleen, the roadside verges were covered with violets, lady's-smock, stitchwort, clover, dandelions, buttercups, large, yellow-centred daisies, and wild garlic; on marshy land were yellow flags, on patches of moorland, gorse. Jeffa's farm is in the armpit of the Sheep's Head and Mizen peninsulas, up a long moorland track which makes it seem very remote; the house when you arrive, however, is immaculate and welcoming – though we were not welcomed by Jeffa's Connemara pony, who had given birth that morning and was guarding her foal against all comers.

When Jeffa bought the farm, twenty-four years ago, she hoped to run it organically and sell a mixed range of produce, but was forced to revise her ideas by lack of demand: inspired by Veronica Steele (page 145), she experimented with cheese, starting, like almost everyone else, in the kitchen. With the support of local shops and restaurants, the business gained momentum slowly but steadily. Unable to manage both cows and the cheese, she sold the cows and now buys milk from a nearby farm: although not organic, the wide variety of flora means it is probably the equivalent in terms of taste.

DURRUS

Bronze Medal, British Cheese Awards 1995, 1997, and 2002
A semi-soft cows' cheese; low-fat, unpasteurized milk (morning only);
vegetarian rennet. 375g/13oz or 1.5kg/3lb 5oz rounds

The cheese varies considerably according to age and season. At a few weeks old, it bends slightly over the knife when cut; at three months, it flows slightly. The taste is rich, mellow and above all buttery, with a distinct hint of russet apples in the autumn; when young, the cheese is mild, but the more mature version can be quite strong. It seems to improve every year: whereas when I first tried it I liked it, now it seems to me outstanding.

Like Bill Hogan's (below), Jeffa's method is based on Swiss principles: like him, she uses a copper rather than stainless steel vat and a 'harp' with vertical blades to cut the curd. When made, the cheeses are sprayed with a preparation which encourages the growth of *Brevibacterium linens*. They are matured on the farm for three to five weeks but they remain in good condition for up to five months.

West Cork Natural Cheese

BILL HOGAN AND SEAN FERRY, ARDMANAGH, SCHULL,
COUNTY CORK. TEL: 00353 282 8593

In his own way, Bill is as visionary a personality as Veronica Steele
(page 145); he is also a practised and adroit interviewee and I
swiftly abandoned any thought of asking why he became a cheesemaker, although he gave full details of how. He was trained in
Costa Rica by the late Josef Dubach, a well-known Swiss cheesemaker who, under the auspices of the Swiss Development
Corporation, made it his mission to teach sound, hygienic principles of cheesemaking in developing countries where it could
substantially raise standards of living (as the production of
Gruyère, Emmental, and other cheeses had in the Swiss valleys).
Subsequently, Bill translated Dubach's book, *Traditional
Cheesemaking*, and instead of payment spent a summer at Dubach's
farm in Switzerland. He set up his dairy in West Cork partly
because, with its cheeses, fish, and several good restaurants, it is the
accepted gourmet centre of Ireland, but also because of its varied
herbage and exceptional grazing. There was never any question of
producing his own milk since, according to Dubach, the milk for
first-class cheese should be taken only in high summer, when the
grass is at its best and the stage of lactation most favourable. Thus
Bill makes all his cheese in four months of the year, which means
that in order to be economic he needs creamery-sized quantities
over this period. He buys from seven farms in the area: as with
Durrus, the milk is not organic but the quality of the grazing
means that it tastes as if it were.

His house and dairy are just across the bay from Schull: at the
time we went, the house was being converted and little more than
a shell, as was his dairy for making butter, but the cheese dairy and
maturing room were unaffected and more than enough to absorb

on one visit. Before looking over them, however, we went for a walk round his reed bed, or, in less polite language, organic cesspool. It was laid out more than three years ago and treats both the household waste and the whey. It was striking not only for its magnificent bulrushes but also the slightly unnerving size and succulence of all the other plants growing around: were it not for this, it would look like an ordinary, if somewhat overgrown ornamental pond.

We then went into the cheese dairy, or rather, as I wrote in my notes by mistake, studio, which is really what it is. In the centre is a huge, round, gleaming copper vat – copper because, according to Bill, the very slight reaction of the copper with the acid of the curd gives the cheese a deeper, livelier taste than stainless steel, which he says has a deadening effect. At the far end is an elegant Victorian boiler, dating from about 1880, which he uses for scalding the curd (all his cheeses are hard and scalded to a high temperature). As the entire cheesemaking process except separating some of the milk is carried out by hand, a Swiss harp for cutting the curd and a forty-year-old Swiss separator are the only other items in the room. Both are worthy of being there solely for their aesthetic value, but they are not its most remarkable feature, since, unlike any other dairy I have seen, it is painted from floor to ceiling in bright turquoise. This is not (or not only) for decorative reasons but because the colour repels flies.

The maturing room is in a large, outwardly shabby barn with one small window half blacked out by gauze. Inside, having shut the door immediately lest a tiny, new season's fly might slip past us, we could see nothing: the smell of cheese and the almost disinfectant fragrance of wood were sufficiently powerful to convince me for ever after that wood must surely contribute to taste, but in no way prepared us for the amazing display of cheeses revealed when Bill switched on a single, dim light. From end to end of the barn, great, dark sculptural wheels of cheese, some as large as 31kg/68lb, and one or two (Mizen) of 45kg/100lb or more, were laid out at an angle on tilted wooden racks. Instead of labels, each was embossed with its name on top in black. As they are all matured from one summer to the next, the whole of the last season's production was on view – worth perhaps £35,000. Any cheese bought will therefore be almost a year old; some are matured for two.

GABRIEL

> *Bronze Medal, British Cheese Awards 1996; Silver Medal, 2002*
> *A hard cows' cheese; 85% fat, unpasteurized milk; vegetarian rennet.*
> *6.8kg/15lb and 27kg/60lb wheels*

In texture, this is hard and grainy, rather like Parmesan; the taste is deep and powerful, with the tang of the sea at one level, earthy undertones at another, and a warm peppery, almost spirituous aftertaste. Like other cheeses of this class, it melts in strings; because of its dryness, it is better not heated alone, but is marvellous for fondue or sauces made with wine.

Bill cultures his own starters, skims fifteen per cent of the milk, and uses relatively little rennet to produce a soft curd from which a large proportion of the moisture can be expelled (for soft cheeses, a firm curd is needed). Also to expel moisture, the curd is cut progressively smaller the harder the cheese: for Gabriel, it is cut to the size of rice grains, i.e. slightly smaller than for Cheddar, and for Mizen, the hardest, which he no longer makes, it was 'as fine as dust'. The curd is then stirred for a considerable time and scalded, respectively, to 46°C/115°F, 53°C/127°F, and 57°C/135°F. By the time the cheeses are matured, their yield per gallon of milk is less than nine per cent and weight for weight they contain three times as much protein as steak.

DESMOND

A hard cows' cheese; 85% fat, unpasteurized milk; vegetarian rennet.
6.8kg/15lb and 27kg/60lb wheels

This is the least hard of Bill's three cheeses: though dry and grained, the texture is slightly fudgy. All three taste of the elements, i.e. sun, rain, earth, and the sea, as much as herbage. Although like the classic definition of a good soup, the flavours are mingled and balanced, Desmond is more on the side of grass and herbs than the others. When heated, the taste intensifies: it is delicious toasted, excellent for fondue, and also very good for sprinkling, although it is not as salty as pecorino and Parmesan.

At a tasting in London, Bill (who was once a chef) made a fondue which was universally acclaimed: this is the recipe as he later sent it to me.

 A Theory of Cheese Fondue

A true cheese fondue must be made with thermophilic cheese. Gruyère, Emmental, Appenzell, Gabriel and Desmond are all suitable. A fondue may be cooked with a single kind or any combination of these, depending on the flavour and effect that is desired. The word fondue simply means sauce.

Many white wines blend perfectly with thermophilic cheeses. I suggest light, crisp wines like Swiss Fendant or Alsatian and Luxembourgeoise Riesling or Pinot Blanc, the latter two embellishing the taste with special tone and glow. Personally, I avoid sharp or steely wines because they can overpower the dish.

Formula

Cut at least 2kg/4lb 6oz of thermophilic cheese into half thumb-sized chunks, removing the hard outer rind. Heat a cup and a half of white wine [350ml/12fl oz] nearly to the boil, preferably in a ceramic pot which may be pre-scented and rubbed with a dot of garlic. Add half the cheese and stir slowly at first with a flat wooden spoon.

Keep the heat fairly high for eight to ten minutes, until the cheese suddenly begins to melt. As the cheese dissolves, stir very briskly and lower the heat. Later, more wine may be added if the fondue becomes too thick. Or more cheese added if it gets too thin. The flame should be adjusted accordingly. A second batch may be prepared forthwith, if the pot is not scorched.

A small quantity of soft cheese may be added near the finish to achieve an extra layer of aroma. I often create a party fondue using Milleens, Gubbeen and Durrus as special taste ticklers. Try adding a few cubes of your favourite soft cheese. At this point a few drops of Kirsch or other spirit may be thrown in the pot, just as the fondue is being served ...

The Meal

Traditionally fondue is eaten with small lumps of bread skewered on long forks or sticks. Each guest or family member gets an individual fork which is tipped with bread then dipped into the pot, twirled to gather the sauce, then eaten as quickly as possible to avoid drips.

Cheese fondue is perhaps the only European dish still eaten out of a communal pot. For this reason and the wonderful wine fumes which rise from it, fondue parties can be amiable and intimate occasions.

Instead of bread, I sometimes serve fondue over lightly

sautéd or steamed vegetables like leeks, cauliflower, or tomatoes. An exciting modern choice is to offer raw or lightly cooked asparagus and broccoli spears for dipping in the hot fondue. Usually, I accompany a cheese fondue with a tart green salad and give simple ice-cream or sorbet with fruit for dessert.

To drink with the meal, I enjoy Pinot Gris for perfect resolution and clarity. But this is a matter of mood and fancy. Experiment yourself with fine white wines and thermophilic cheeses. Devise your own stratagems ...

Gubbeen

Tom and Giana Ferguson, Gubbeen House, Schull, County Cork. Tel: 00353 282 8231

Gubbeen House is on a blunt peninsula just to the west of Schull, surrounded by trees so that one's chief impression is of luxuriant foliage rather than proximity to the sea. The Fergusons have farmed here for five generations but Giana, who is partly Hungarian, was brought up on a Spanish mountain-top where her father, a writer and believer in what she terms 'Kitchen-culture', encouraged the family to gather in the kitchen every evening to drink wine, watch their gypsy cook preparing their meal, eat, and talk. Since they kept goats, the cook would make curd cheese; Giana was also able to watch cheese being made at her uncle's house in the south of France, near Nice. After she married Tom and had constant access to milk, making cheese thus seemed obvious and natural; she did not start seriously, however, until Veronica Steele (page 145) had convinced her of its possibilities and she had taken a course in hygiene and microbiology at University College, Cork.

Now, having made cheese for eighteen years, she says that she finds it 'obsessional' but as creatively satisfying and personal as writing or painting. However, she considers eighteen years not nearly long enough: a lifetime, she declares, might be too short to come to know and develop a cheese to its full potential. It took her five or six years simply to become used to the characteristics and seasonal variations of her milk – and she now wishes that she did not feel obliged to make cheese during the winter, when the cows live on silage and the milk is correspondingly inferior. She also sometimes regrets the need for consistent quality because of the barriers to excellence that it imposes: as an example, she cited the fact that she uses a commercial starter because a home-cultured one is less reliable, although in certain conditions it gives much better results.

The milk for Gubbeen is from a mixed herd of Jersey, Friesian, Simmenthal, and the local (but now very rare) black Kerry cattle. The two most distinctive points about the cheesemaking are that the whey is diluted to slow down bacterial activity (as opposed to washing the curd, which implies draining off some of the whey) and that particular trouble is taken over maturing or 'curing' the cheeses. It goes without saying that humidity and temperature are carefully controlled, but the cheeses are also turned and washed frequently to discourage the growth of all but *Brevibacterium linens*, which is promoted by daily applications of 'goo'. This system is time-consuming and labour-intensive: partly because of it, Giana employs a staff of ten, which, given her output, nevertheless seems generous. When I commented on it, she smiled happily and said, in the melodious voice which is the first thing you notice about her, 'Well, yes, we *do* over-employ, but then, you see, the people round here need the work.'

GUBBEEN

Silver Medal, British Cheese Awards 1995 and 1997; Gold Medal, 2002
A semi-soft washed-rind cows' cheese; full-fat, unpasteurized milk;
vegetarian rennet. 1.4kg/3lb discs

The texture is slightly firmer and more elastic than that of the other semi-soft Cork cheeses, with small holes; the rind is temptingly crisp and crinkled, greyish but overlaid with a pink blush. In taste, the cheese is probably an accurate reflection of the West Cork flora, with flowery tones overlaid by grass and savoury herbs. Bill Hogan (page 152) once described Durrus as tasting like 'violins' – in which case Gubbeen resembles violas. A smoked version is also produced.

Carraig

LIEKE AND AART VERSLOOT, BALLINGEARY, COUNTY CORK.
TEL: 00353 264 7126

The farm is up a narrow track off the road from Bantry to Macroom in the Shehy Mountains. After driving along the track round a frighteningly tight hairpin bend, you bear left up a hill until you come to a gate, with goats on the other side. Some of them look, not exactly thin but unusually bony, with slightly bedraggled coats, as though they led a hard life: however, when I talked to Lieke, I found that the reason for their appearance was simply age. The Versloots' feeling for them overrides commercial considerations and instead of culling them when they are too old to milk, they keep them until they die naturally. In fact, their lives are probably ideal, since the farm is in a sheltered situation and the hillsides are wooded, with a wide variety of tasty shoots and twigs.

CARRAIG

A Gouda-style goats' cheese; full fat, unpasteurized milk; traditional rennet (imported from Holland). 400g/14oz, 800g–1kg/1lb 12oz–2lb 4oz rounds

Carraig has a velvet-smooth texture with small holes; at six to eight weeks it is moist and elastic but becomes harder as it ages. The taste is a blend of sweet, flowery flavours, including gorse, with hints of herbs and nuts; the cheese has a gentle tang when young which becomes stronger with maturity. Virtually the only indication of goat is that the flavours are fuller and more intense than the usual Gouda-style cows' equivalent. To my mind, it is one of the most interesting hard goats' cheeses made. Unfortunately, it is only sold locally, notably in Bantry market on Fridays, but mail orders are welcomed (Lieke will send it anywhere: it has even been to Japan).

Lieke makes the cheese entirely by hand to a recipe which she says is much the same as the Willems' (below) but adapted to goats' milk. As the goats' curd is more delicate than cows', she does not heat it to such a high temperature nor stir it for so long. After moulding and pressing, the cheeses are brined and matured for a minimum of six weeks, with daily turning for the first two or three; Lieke also brushes and washes them at intervals to prevent mould from developing on the surface. Although she herself prefers the cheese at six to eight weeks, it can be kept for up to a year.

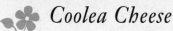

Coolea Cheese

HELEN AND DICK WILLEMS, COOLEA, MACROOM, COUNTY
CORK. TEL: 00353 264 5204

From Schull to Coolea, in the hills west of Macroom, is a slow
journey: there was hardly any traffic, but I shall never again
comment on the straight roads of Ireland. Of all the farms that
I have visited, including the Versloots' just across the hills, the
Willems' seems the most isolated, although in fact it is only
about 5km/3 miles from the main road to Killarney. It is in a
spectacular situation facing a wide valley, with a skyline of hills.
The Willems come from Linburg, in Holland, where Helen ran
a pub and discotheque until she came to feel the need for silence
and space. Her intention in coming to Ireland was to paint: for
fifteen years, her time and attention were monopolized by the
cheese, but her son Dick, after training in Belgium, has now
effectually taken it over, leaving her with the leisure to pursue
her ambition.

COOLEA

Gold Medal and Best Modern British Cheese, British Cheese Awards 1997
A Gouda-type cows' cheese; full-fat, pasteurized milk; traditional rennet.
1kg/2lb 4oz, 2kg/4lb 6oz, 4kg/8lb 13oz, and 10kg/22lb rounds

Louis Grubb of Cashel Blue (page 137) remarked that the reason
for the popularity of Gouda-type cheeses in Ireland is that they
are sweet and fairly mild, so that one can eat them continuously
without getting tired of them: this certainly applies to six-
month-old Coolea, which tastes subtly but positively of grass
and flowers. When matured for longer, the flavour becomes
deeper and richer, with a strong note of peat which gives it a

sweet/salt tang that can compete with a blue or mature Cheddar on the cheeseboard.

Some of the cheeses are flavoured with cumin seeds.

Consistent with the fact that the cheese is Gouda-type, the milk comes from a herd of Dutch MRI cows. Starter is added half an hour before the rennet, which is calf, imported from Holland. When the curd has set, it is cut to the size of peas and washed twice to remove some of the lactose, which speeds up acidity and makes for a sweeter-tasting cheese; it is then scalded twice over about two hours, with continuous stirring (by machine). This is followed by moulding, pressing for six hours, and brining for up to four days. To keep the surface free of mould and promote ripening from the outside inwards, the cheeses are sprayed with a coating which dries into a hard skin. The maturing time is a minimum of six months, but for the large cheeses can be up to two years.

CHAPTER 4

 *Wales*

PENBRYN

LLANBOIDY CHEESEMAKERS

LLANGLOFFAN FARMHOUSE CHEESE

TEIFI

GORWYDD CAERPHILLY

LITTLE ACORN PRODUCTS

CAWS CENARTH

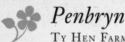

Penbryn

TY HEN FARM, PENBRYN, SARNAU, DYFED SA44 6RD.
TEL: 01239 810347

Ty Hen is just behind Penbryn beach, which is a National Trust property and presumably for this reason totally unspoilt: a small road twists down one of the narrow wooded valleys which are typical of this part of Wales to a car-park and sandy beach where there are no huts, no motor boats, and, even on a fine Saturday in August, very few people. The farm, perched on the hill above, is in rolling country similar to that around Glynhynod (page 172): one is also reminded of Glynhynod by the fact that the cheese is Gouda-style. It used to be made by Andrea Degan, who is Dutch and before she started making cheese had been a psychiatric nurse. By a curious coincidence, Alison is also a trained nurse, and works four days a week for the NHS (although in administration rather than on the wards). This means that she can cheesemake only on one working-day a week, so that packing and marketing have to be done at weekends. Before she and Trevor moved to the farm, neither of them had ever made cheese before: however, Andrea made them a video (a very useful way of teaching cheesemaking) and her assistant, Sarah, who had worked with her for some time, stayed to help them during their first year.

PENBRYN ORIGINAL

Silver Medal, British Cheese Awards 2002
A Gouda-type cows' cheese; full-fat, unpasteurized milk; vegetarian rennet.
1kg/2lb 4oz and 2.7kg/6lb rounds

At two months, it tastes very distinctly of butter, grass, a wide variety of herbs, and the sea; by eight or ten, it has developed a powerful, characteristic tang and, like Teifi, leaves a strong peppery, almost spicy aftertaste. It is excellent toasted and for cooking (one of Andrea's favourite ways of eating it was in a toasted sandwich buttered on the outside). Since Andrea left, the herd has doubled from twenty-five to fifty; the cows are Friesians with a dash of MRI, which means that the milk has a relatively high solids content.

The recipe for the cheese is a modified rather than strictly traditional form of the Gouda method. A home-cultured starter is added at the same time as the rennet; when the curd has set, it is cut for ten minutes, left to rest for ten minutes, and washed and scalded once, to 37°C/98°F. This is followed by draining, moulding, and pressing for an hour, after which the edges of the cheeses are trimmed (although rounded when finished, they are pressed in truckle moulds). They are turned and pressed for a further two and a half hours, trimmed again, and brined; the maturing time is two to ten months.

Llanboidy Cheesemakers

SUE JONES, CILOWEN UCHAF, LOGIN, WHITLAND, DYFED SA34 0TJ. TEL: 01994 448303

Rather as Charles Martell has devoted his life to Gloucester cattle (page 56), Sue is the saviour of Red Polls, a cross between the rare-breed Norfolks and Suffolks and, like other older breeds and MRIs, dual purpose. She started out as a teacher rather than farmer but kept goats and made goats' cheese in her spare time; then one day her husband, a TV journalist, gave her four Red Polls as a result of working on a feature. This unusual present led to their moving to Cilowen, where they kept a few other cows besides the

Red Polls and sold beef and the milk direct. A few years later they divorced, and she agreed to stay at the farm so that she could keep the cows. It was a brave decision, since it left her to run the farm without help between, as she put it, a bank manager and two children. Having already made cheese, she was aware of its worth as a value-added product but also of the fact that she could not both make it and manage the cows single-handedly: she therefore called on her sister, at that time a 'scientific cook', who duly became her cheesemaker – and is still with her. She now has thirty-three Red Polls in milk, plus four Friesians; a man is employed for the milking and a second cheesemaker alternates with her sister. As well as sitting on several National Farmers' Union committees, she is President-elect of the Red Poll Association. Recently, she developed a semi-soft, or almost semi-soft organic cheese called Cilowen, made with milk from two local farms.

LLANBOIDY

Silver Medal, British Cheese Awards 1997; Gold Medal, 2001
A hard cows' cheese; full-fat, unpasteurized milk; vegetarian rennet.
4.5kg/10lb wheels

Perhaps partly because of the homogeneous nature of the milk, the texture is exceptionally smooth, almost silky, in contrast to the more robust flavour. The taste varies according to maturity and season but is herbal and buttery with an almost spicy tang which appears to be characteristic of the area, since it is similar to that of nearby Teifi and Penbryn. When young, the cheese is mild, but as it matures the tang becomes increasingly powerful.

The Red Poll milk is higher in protein and has smaller fat globules than Friesian, rather like Ayrshire, and is thus especially suitable for cheese. After starter and rennet have been added, it is top-stirred;

when the curd has set and been cut, it is blocked and piled, as for Cheddar. Draining, milling, and salting follow; it is then packed into muslin-lined moulds and pressed for thirty-six hours. The maturing time is from two to ten months.

CILOWEN

Gold Award and the Dougal Campbell trophy for the best Welsh cheese, British Cheese Awards 2002
The cheese is on the borderline between hard and semi-soft; full-fat, organic milk; vegetarian rennet.

As the Dougal Campbell trophy and Gold Medal suggest, this is an outstanding cheese. It has a smooth, melting, almost semi-soft texture and an exceptionally sweet, caramel-like flavour with herbal hints and quite a strong taste of wild flowers: the taste, according to Sue, is partly due to the red clover on the swards where the cows graze. The recipe was developed by taking elements from a number of different cheeses, including Caerphilly, Lancashire and Wensleydale, although the result is nothing like any of them (though it is perhaps nearer to Caerphilly than the rest).

 ## *Llangloffan Farmhouse Cheese*
LEON DOWNEY, LLANGLOFFAN FARMHOUSE, CASTLE MORRIS, HAVERFORDWEST, PEMBROKESHIRE.
TEL: 01348 891241

Leon Downey ties with Lyn Jenner (page 32) as the cheesemaker with the most unlikely background; also, in line with the TV chefs, he has turned cheese into theatre and his farm into the perfect set –

though, as the results of the British Cheese Awards show, without sacrificing quality in the slightest degree: indeed, it would seem that the opposite is true. The farm, which is about 3km/2 miles from the sea, is spruce and welcoming but in no way prettified: the various alterations he has made, which include converting some of the buildings into a shop, teashop, and house for his daughter and son-in-law, who helps him with the cheese, are scarcely noticeable from the outside. The dairy is in a former barn and one of the most attractive I have seen, with a warm-coloured stone floor, smooth for easy cleaning rather than flagged, and the original rafters, which to conform to hygiene standards have to be scrubbed regularly – but Leon does not mind: given the importance of the look of the dairy both to himself and to his demonstrations, the extra work is well worthwhile.

Before he made cheese, he spent fifteen years as the co-principal viola player with the Hallé Orchestra, where he performed with Barbirolli and Menuhin: he left because he was afraid of becoming stale, perhaps even ending up hating music. He chose to make cheese instead, he says, because it is just as creative and 'a natural progression' for a musician. However, cheesemaking *per se* lacks the performance element of music: he has remedied this by inviting the public to watch him – and people come, sometimes 150–200 in a morning. One may wonder how he can make first-class cheese and entertain at the same time, but he can. I stayed at a hotel further up the coast where a girl on a walking holiday had sprained her ankle: unable to walk, she went to see the cheese-making at Llangloffan instead and came back declaring that she had never seen anything so interesting in her life and wanted to train as a cheesemaker herself.

For some years, the cheese was made with milk from Leon's own herd, but as he has only 7ha/18 acres, he had to keep it down to fourteen. The land, fertilized by cow-dung and seaweed, is organic; formerly, however, the cheese was not because the cows were fed with non-organic barley. Now he buys his milk from local farms, some but not all of which is organic (in response to customers' preferences rather than availability: not all of them, he says, favour organic produce).

LLANGLOFFAN ORGANIC

Llangloffan Gold Medal and Dougal Campbell Memorial Trophy for the Best Welsh Cheese, British Cheese Awards 1996; Llangloffan Organic Bronze Medal, 2002
A hard cows' cheese; full-fat, unpasteurized milk; vegetarian rennet.
1.4kg/3lb, 4.5kg/10lb, and 13.5kg/30lb

The texture is light and slightly crumbly; the taste is fresh, buttery, and mild or deep according to age, with a mixture of grassy and herbal flavours. Of all cheeses, it is one of the most adaptable, with enough character to serve alongside potent partners on the cheeseboard but not too strong to be eaten every day. It is also surprisingly effective as a flavouring in cooking, when it adds vivacity and interest without the obvious tang of Cheddar. Some of the cheeses are flavoured with garlic and chives.

The starter is home-cultured and the milk left to ripen for an hour and a half before the addition of rennet; when the curd has set, after about another half-hour, it is cut with multiple-bladed curd knives. For the next hour it is stirred and scalded (heated) slightly according to acidity; it is then drained and milled. The salt, plus chives and garlic for the flavoured versions, is added during milling. Finally, the cheese is packed into cloth-lined moulds and pressed again until the following day. At the time of my visit, the maturing-time on the farm was ten weeks, although stockists such as Neal's Yard Dairy may mature the cheeses on for another one and a half to three and a half months; Leon said that he is aiming to mature them himself for up to nine.

 Llangloffan and Spinach Pies

Total cooking time: just over 20 minutes; baking time: 13–15 minutes
Makes 12–14

200g/7oz spinach, picked over and washed
salt
$^1/_2$ tbsp oil
15g/$^1/_2$oz butter
3 cloves garlic, peeled and finely chopped
$^1/_2$ mild green chilli, washed, core and seeds removed, and finely diced
1 large free-range egg, beaten
4 tbsp single cream
1 tsp Dijon mustard
2 tbsp dry white wine
pepper
150g/5$^1/_4$oz Llangloffan, finely grated
1$^1/_2$ quantities short pastry (page xxv)

Pack the spinach into a saucepan with $^1/_2$ teaspoonful of salt (but no water). Cover and set over medium heat for 4 minutes; stir and cook (still covered) for another 1–2 minutes, until the spinach is submerged in juices and tender. Drain in a sieve, pressing out as much liquor as possible with the back of a spoon, and chop.

Warm the oil and butter over medium heat and fry the garlic until it begins to show signs of changing colour (it should not be allowed to colour further because it will continue to cook in the hot oil). Add the chilli, turn it briskly, and remove the pan from the heat. Stir in the spinach.

Beat together the egg, cream, mustard, wine, a pinch of salt, and a fairly generous grinding of pepper. Stir in the cheese and spinach. Roll out the pastry thinly and line a patty tin or tins; fill just to the top of the cases with the spinach mixture. Do not add more because it will overflow during cooking. Set the oven to 200°C/400°F/Gas 6. Cut out tops for the cases, moisten the edges on the undersides to ensure that they stick, and cover the pies, pinching or stamping the edges firmly together. Make air-holes in the middle and bake for 13–15 minutes, until the pies are well browned. Serve them hot.

LLANGLOFFAN COLOURED CHESHIRE

*Gold Medal and Dougal Campbell Memorial Trophy, British Cheese
Awards 1997*
*A semi-hard cows' cheese; full-fat, unpasteurized milk; vegetarian rennet.
4.5kg/10lb or 13.5kg/30lb*

This cheese was originally made as a joke. Leon had never made Cheshire before, but his grandmother had, and he decided to try, partly to show that Cheshire cheese can be made outside Cheshire. He then entered it for the British Cheese Awards, where (as at all similar events) the cheeses are judged blind, so that no one knew who had made it until afterwards. It won not for its Cheshire-like qualities but simply because it was so delicious. The texture is quite wonderfully light, flaky, and melting, while the taste hits the palate at so many levels that you could call it mild and powerful simultaneously. The overall impression is rich and piquant, but the piquancy is not the salty/sweet tang of Appleby's (page 206) but a slightly peppery, mellow tang with (as one might expect) affinities to Llangloffan.

Teifi

JOHN AND PATRICE SAVAGE-ONSTWEDDER, GLYNHYNOD
FARM, FFOSTRASOL, LLANDYSUL, DYFED SA44 5JY.
TEL: 01239 851528

Even though they are now as hooked as everyone else, John and
Patrice set out to make cheese simply in order to live where they
do. This area is not mountainous, but broken by sudden, convex,
irresistibly pretty river valleys densely wooded with oak trees.
Their farm is high up on the side of a wide valley (Glynhynod
means 'remarkable valley') with a view across rolling, fertile
country sloping down to the sea, only 10–11km/6–7 miles to the
west.

John met Patrice in Holland, where he taught at the Small
Earth, a leading organic farming and alternative living centre. As a
result of translating a book into Dutch, *The Complete Book of Self-
Sufficiency*, he and Patrice were invited to stay with the author in
Pembrokeshire. This prompted their decision to move to Wales:
before moving, however, Patrice spent a year in Brabant as an
apprentice to a Dutch cheesemaker, Mrs Vermeer, who made the
first post-war organic farmhouse Gouda in Holland.

As the farm is very small, they only keep six organically reared
Jerseys, whose milk is used for butter and buttermilk; the milk for
the cheese comes from a herd of about forty-five Friesians on the
other side of the valley. Patrice makes the Teifi to an allegedly
500-year-old recipe, using the traditional wooden vat; as from
about two years ago, she now also makes Caerphilly. This was
originally made for them by a cheesemaker called Cyril Woolley,
who celebrated his fiftieth anniversary of cheesemaking while he
was working with them; he has since retired but taught Patrice his
method (and, as his experience was only with British territorial
cheeses, she taught him in return to make Gouda).

TEIFI

Silver Medal, British Cheese Awards 1997; Bronze Medal, 1997 (Herbs);
Bronze Medal, 1997 (Garlic); Gold Medal, 2001; Bronze Medal (Herbs),
2002
A Gouda-style cows' cheese; full-fat, unpasteurized milk; vegetarian rennet.
450g/1lb, 900g/2lb, and 3.5kg/7lb 11oz truckles or
7.2–11.3kg/16–25lb wheels

Teifi has a very wide range of flavours which includes grass, flowers, earth, and a selection of herbs. When it first hits the tongue, it seems sweet and mild, but the flavours develop as you eat it and it ends by being surprisingly strong, with an almost spicy tang which, like that of Llanboidy (page 166), resembles cheese made nowhere else. Patrice may have begun to make cheese for practical reasons but she is a natural: both her cheeses are exceptional. Sometimes she flavours them, e.g. with garlic, garlic and herbs, cumin, or peppercorns with sweet red pepper: I have not tried all the flavours, but rather to my surprise found that I liked the peppercorns with red pepper as much as the original, since the sweet pepper brings out the spiciness of the cheese and the peppercorns its herbal tones. John also matures some of the smaller sizes into Celtic Promise (page 175). The cheese loses none of its power when heated and is excellent toasted or as a flavouring; as it melts in strings, it is also suitable for pizza.

For both Teifi and Caerphilly, Patrice uses a homemade starter, added when the milk (morning and evening) is at 20°C/68°F. For Teifi, she adds rennet when it has been left to ripen for twenty minutes and warmed to 29°C/84°F. When the curd has set, she cuts it to the size of peas and washes and scalds it twice, to 32°C/90°F and 36°C/97°F, draining off a third of the whey the first time and half of the remainder the second. It is then drained, scooped into moulds, and pressed for two and a half hours, which leaves it with enough moisture for the acidity to rise overnight. In the morning, it is unmoulded and brined for eight hours to three days according to size; it is matured for up to a year.

 Gougère

This is traditionally made with Gruyère but works wonderfully with the powerful flavour of Teifi. Serve with Burgundy. The dough can be made up to twenty-four hours in advance.

Cooking time: 35–40 minutes
Makes 8 portions

125g/4$^1/_2$oz plain white flour
1 tsp dry mustard
$^1/_2$ tsp salt
generous grinding of pepper
55g/2oz butter
3 large free-range eggs, broken into separate bowls
20g/$^3/_4$oz Parmesan, finely grated
110g/nearly 4oz plain Teifi, finely grated

Sift together the first four ingredients. Chop up the butter and melt it over low heat in 220ml/just under 8fl oz water; raise the heat, and as soon as it is boiling vigorously, tip in the seasoned flour all at once. Remove the pan from the heat and beat with a table-spoon to a firm, smooth dough with no remaining pockets of flour: this will take 2–3 minutes. Return the pan to low heat and continue to beat for another 2 minutes, until it is shiny and leaves the sides of the pan in a smooth mass. Beat in the eggs one at a time; do not add another until the previous one is completely absorbed and the mixture is homogeneous. When all three eggs have been amal-gamated, the mixture will be a stiff paste but not quite stiff enough to hold its shape. Stir in the Parmesan or pecorino and 80g/nearly 3oz of the Teifi, leaving the rest to sprinkle over the top. The dough can now be stored until needed.

To bake, set the oven to 190°C/375°F/Gas 5. Thoroughly butter a small baking sheet (unless it is thoroughly greased, the gougère will stick) and place tablespoonsful of the dough in a circle, each spoonful just touching the next. Sprinkle the tops thickly with the rest of the cheese and bake for 35 minutes without opening the oven door. The gougère will rise and turn golden, but if it is only pale gold, continue to bake it for another 5 minutes, until it is well browned and very crisp. The outside should be as crisp as a well-baked croissant but the inside slightly hollow and as soft as a soufflé. Serve hot or warm. Any portions left over are delicious heated up the next day: the hollow middles can be stuffed with soft cheese or butter.

CELTIC PROMISE AND SAVAL

Saval: Gold Medal and trophy for the Best Semi-soft Cheese,
British Cheese Awards 2001; Celtic Promise, 2002
A washed-rind cows' cheese; full-fat, unpasteurized milk; vegetarian
rennet. Celtic Promise 600g/1lb 5oz; Saval, 2kg/4lb 6½oz

The basic cheese is Gouda-style, with herbal and rich, spicy undertones; the rind-washed version is cool-tasting and brings out the herbal rather than spicy side of its character. The two cheeses are similar but Saval larger.

CAERPHILLY AND REMARKABLE VALLEY

Bronze Medal, British Cheese Awards 1997 (Remarkable Valley)
A semi-hard or hard cheese, according to age; full-fat, unpasteurized milk;
vegetarian rennet. Caerphilly, 2.7–3.7kg/6–8lb; Remarkable Valley,
8kg/17½ lb

Like other Caerphillies, the cheese varies enormously at different ages. When very young, it is creamy; by about five months, it is mild and sweet, tasting of grass, flowers, and the soft Welsh water. At six months, it has begun to develop a tang; by eight, the tang is deep and lasting, although not strong. The same cheese made in a larger size becomes Remarkable Valley after maturing for over eight months.

The milk is heated to 31°C/88°F after the starter is added and renneted after thirty minutes. When set, the curd is heated to 35°C/95°F and cut over an hour; it is then drained and cut very small by hand rather than milled, which means that it retains a higher proportion of moisture. This is followed by moulding, pressing for twenty-four hours, and brining for up to twenty-four hours depending on size. At ten days, some of the smaller size are smoked; the rest are matured for up to fifteen months.

Gorwydd Caerphilly

TODD TRETHOWEN, GORWYDD FARM, LLANDEWI BREFI,
TREGARON, CEREDIGION SY25 6NY.
TEL: 01570 493516

The Trethowens senior downshifted from Sussex eleven years ago, when Todd started at London University: his father, who had been a headmaster, decided to retire early, although he has now taken a job at Lampeter University. Nowhere makes down-shifting look so tempting as Gorwydd. The house looks over the Teifi valley, facing west so that it catches the afternoon sun; in the front, the light is caught by the soft pinks and orange of the flowers in the borders. The farm is a very old foundation: to one side of the present house is the original farmhouse, and on the other an enormous barn which will probably become Todd's cheese store. The walls of the buildings are 0.9 metres/3 feet thick, which creates the ideal conditions for cheese, since the temperature is kept cool and constant and humidity is over 90 per cent. In the smaller maturing room behind the dairy which he now uses, he says that even in very hot weather the temperature never rises by more than two degrees.

Todd's commitment to cheese originated at Neal's Yard Dairy, where he worked during vacations; when he went to Wales to stay with his parents, he helped Dougal Campbell, whose farm was only about 8km/5 miles away. After graduating, he took up a full-time job at the Dairy before training, first with Charlie Westhead (page 190), then with Chris Duckett (page 91), whose recipes for both the cheese and starter he now uses. At present, he makes cheese four days a week and delivers it on the other days; as the Trethowens do not keep animals, his milk comes via First Milk from four neighbouring farms. Every stage of the cheese-making is carried out entirely by hand; a bulk milk-tank serves as a vat and his moulds, of the traditional cake tin-like shape, are made by the local blacksmith (where else in the UK could you still find a local blacksmith?). The maturing time on the farm is two months, but Neal's Yard matures the cheeses on for an extra month.

GORWYDD CAERPHILLY

Bronze Medal, British Cheese Awards 1996
A semi-hard cows' cheese; full-fat, unpasteurized milk; vegetarian rennet.
1.1kg/2lb 7oz, 1.8 kg/4lb, and 3.6kg/8lb truckles

The Trethowens gave us a two-month-old cheese which I tried directly and again after a week, having kept it from necessity rather too warm but in an atmosphere of high humidity. At first, the texture was open and slightly crumbly and the taste full, complex, and with just a hint of sharpness. A week later, it had already become much sweeter and creamier: the sharpness had completely disappeared. It was delicious both ways, but the riper version more so: in fact, at this stage it was so rewarding that as I write we have just ordered another (the Trethowens will send them to order, not by post but by twenty-four-hour dispatch). True to Welsh tradition, it is wonderful toasted, melting to a rich cream and becoming even sweeter.

 Gorwydd Lemon Tart

To give contrast to the filling, these should be made with part-wholemeal or almond pastry: the almond pastry is delicious but friable and tends to be sticky to roll. You can make either small tartlets or one large tart.

Cooking time: 12–15 minutes for tartlets or 20–25 for a large tart
Makes about 16 or enough to fill a 22cm/8½-inch tart tin

short pastry (page xxv) made with equal quantities of wholemeal and
    white flour *or* 100g/3½oz white flour, 50g/1¾oz wholemeal flour,
    and 50g/1¾oz ground almonds
75g/2¾oz Gorwydd Caerphilly, finely grated
4 large free-range egg-yolks, beaten

zest of $^1/_2$ large organic lemon

2 tbsp lemon juice

1 tbsp brandy

115g/4oz caster sugar

100ml/3$^1/_2$fl oz thick double cream

Roll out the pastry thinly: if using almonds, knead it slightly before use and dust with plenty of flour. Lightly butter and line the tart or patty-tins.

Mix together the cheese and egg-yolks; wash the lemon and grate in the zest. Stir in all the other ingredients. Bake in a pre-heated oven at 190°C/ 375°F/Gas 5, 12 minutes for tartlets, 20 minutes for the larger tart, or until the filling is firm and just beginning to bubble. Serve hot or warm with more thick cream.

Little Acorn Products

DON AND KAREN ROSS, MESEN FACH FARMHOUSE,
BETHANIA, LLANON, CEREDIGION SY23 5NL.
TEL: 01974 821348

Don and Karen moved from Manchester in search of the good life. It is now nearly twenty years since Don worked for a vending-machine company, Karen in a fashion boutique. Their transition was carefully planned: Don had already worked on a farm, both studied cheesemaking in Devon before they left, and they travelled all over Britain looking for the right place prior to choosing Mesen Fach. They nearly settled in Orkney, where they would have milked cows, but at the last moment had to abandon their plans because the milk quota was introduced just at this time, which put the initial outlay beyond their means. At Mesen Fach (the name means 'Acorn') they have 6ha/16 acres suitable for sheep on which they still keep a pedigree Friesland flock, although they now buy in their milk because they found that they did not have time both to milk and make cheese. Even with a staff of four, their wide range of speciality cheeses means that they work almost round the clock.

They developed their first cheese, Acorn, slowly and patiently, trying out different variations on a standard recipe and test-marketing the results until they were satisfied that it was distinctive enough to be interesting but not too strong to be popular (to start with, it was stronger than most of their customers liked). After two or three years, they took over the recipe for a Caerphilly-style cheese marinated in mead which had been made on Skirrid, a mountain near Abergavenny. Eighteen months later, they introduced two more sheep's cheeses (both now discontinued), one smoked and the other flavoured with horseradish. They became increasingly fascinated by flavourings and began a series of experiments with spices, fruit, wine, and spirits and liqueurs as well as the more traditional herbs; however, the cost of the flavourings on top of sheep's milk (which is much more expensive than cows') encouraged them to produce a cows' cheese which they use as the basis of most of their flavoured products. These now include a total of ten flavoured Cheddar-style cheeses and the three described here.

ACORN

A semi-hard sheep's cheese; unpasteurized milk; vegetarian rennet.
2.3kg/5lb truckles

This is a distinctive, very unusual cheese with a soft, crumbly texture reminiscent of Wensleydale; the taste, however, is very different, since it has the herbal tang which seems to be characteristic of this area. Sub-flavours include grass, nuts, and a hint of the sea, which is only about 11km/7 miles from the farm. The cheese is particularly good with hazlenuts or apple cheese (page xxx), and excellent toasted, when it becomes mild, rich, and sweet.

SKIRRID

A semi-hard sheep's cheese; unpasteurized milk; vegetarian rennet.
2.5kg/5½ lb truckles

Although made by a different method, the taste and texture are similar to Acorn but less pronounced: partly because the cheese has been marinated, the texture is softer and moister, and the mead imparts an overtone of honey which modifies the tang and accentuates its nutty character.

LADY LLANOVER

A saffron-flavoured semi-hard sheep's cheese; unpasteurized milk;
vegetarian rennet. 2.3kg/5lb truckles

This is softer, smoother, and less crumbly than the other two, with sweet, flowery notes which mask the natural flavours; to my taste, less successful than Skirrid, but I gather that plenty of customers take the opposite view. It is named after the well-known Welsh cookery writer.

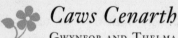

Caws Cenarth

GWYNFOR AND THELMA ADAMS, FFERM GLYNEITHINOG,
ABERCYCH, NEAR NEWCASTLE EMLYN, DYFED SA37 0LH.
TEL: 01239 710432

Thelma Adams's television appearances and the numerous articles about her in newspapers and magazines mean that she is probably already well known to many readers. While the Ducketts have made Caerphilly in Somerset for generations, she is the only remaining maker born to it in Wales. She learnt by watching her mother, and after marrying Gwynfor made it for her family for years before deciding to turn it into a business, largely, as with others, in response to the milk quota. Even now, however, despite her success (she has won dozens of awards), the Adamses run their farm primarily to produce liquid milk. They have just over 100 Friesian–Holsteins and make cheese three times a week, using morning milk only, which means that the cheeses are relatively low in fat. Thelma has not had them analysed but reckons that, allowing for the shorter maturing time and higher retention of moisture, the fat content of her Caerphilly is about ten per cent lower than that of mature Cheddar. They have never used pesticide or herbicide on their land (which perhaps accounts for the varied flowery flavours in their cheese): after a two-year conversion period, they qualified for fully organic status last year.

Besides the plain Caerphilly for which they are chiefly known, the Adamses produce smoked and garlic-and-herb versions, and also a second, Cheddar-style cheese, Caws Mamgu. They are helped by their son and daughter, but make the cheese without additional staff and entirely by hand. Like Leon Downey (page 167), they are happy to have an audience: on cheesemaking mornings, visitors can watch from a viewing gallery where there is also a small museum and shop.

CAWS CENARTH FARMHOUSE

Silver Medal, British Cheese Awards 2002
A semi-hard cows' cheese; morning-only, organic, unpasteurized milk;
vegetarian rennet. 225g/8oz, 450g/1lb, 900g/2lb, and 4–4.5kg/9–10lb
rounds

Despite its lower-fat content, the cheese is notable for its deliciously rich, creamy feel: though not as soft as the Ducketts' after maturing, it is almost semi-soft rather than semi-hard, very smooth-textured, and slightly elastic. The taste is mild and sweet: the very gentlest herbal background is overlaid with delicate grassy and flowery flavours which very much bring to mind the countryside where it is made.

The milk is used while it is still warm from the cow: starter is added without further heating and the milk allowed to ripen for 1–1¾ hours. After renneting, it is left to set for another hour. For Caerphilly, the curd is cut with knives, stirred and scalded to 34.5°C/94°F over nearly a further hour, and left to settle before draining. It is then 'textured' by cutting into progressively smaller pieces until the right acidity is reached; salting, milling, and moulding follow, with turning after an hour. Finally, the cheeses are pressed overnight and brined; the maturing time is three to four weeks.

CAWS MAMGU

A hard cows' cheese; morning-only, organic, unpasteurized milk.
Sizes as above

This is similarly sweet, mild, and gentle-tasting, with a slightly fudgy feel. Rather than a Cheddar-like tang, it develops a soft herbal, peppery edge in the mouth which leaves a gentle spicy aftertaste on the tongue.

CHAPTER 5

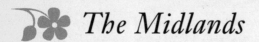 *The Midlands*

MALVERN CHEESEWRIGHTS

ANSTEYS OF WORCESTER

NEAL'S YARD CREAMERY

WOMERTON FARM

RAVEN'S OAK DAIRY

H. S. BOURNE

APPLEBY'S CHESHIRE

BERKSWELL

HIGHFIELDS FARM DAIRY

COLSTON BASSETT AND DISTRICT DAIRY

STAFFORDSHIRE ORGANIC

LINCOLNSHIRE POACHER

Malvern Cheesewrights
NICHOLAS HODGETTS, POND FARM CHURCH LANE,
WHITTINGTON, WORCS WR5 2RD. TEL: 01905 350744

I met Nicholas just a year after he had moved to Pond Farm, when
he felt that he had still hardly settled in. From a cheesemaking
point of view, the farm is ideal, since it is only 3km/2 miles from
the M5 and has accommodation for animals and an enormous
dairy with a correspondingly large drying room and storeroom
and an office as big as a sitting room. He remarked that when he
arrived, he had wondered if he would ever be able to fill so much
space – but of course he has. Altogether, he now makes ten cheeses,
including Malvern, which he launched some fifteen years ago,
when he was still milking his own sheep, Hereford Red and
Hereford Red with Chives, Hereford Hop, coated with toasted
hops, Worcester Gold, so named because the milk is Channel
Island, i.e. rich and golden, plus several flavoured cheeses, English
Oak Smoked, a smoked Cheddar-style cheese which won a Bronze
Medal at the British Cheese Awards 2002, and (his newest), a goats'
cheese, Whiteladies Goat, which won a Gold Medal at the 2001
Awards. When I visited him, he was making a buffalo cheese with
a caramel-like, almost burnt-orange flavour which was quite unlike
any other cheese I have tasted, and delicious. He has now stopped
making it: I wish he would revive it, along with a lovely, soft-
tasting organic cheese, Whittington, made to an old recipe that he
found in a museum.

MALVERN

Bronze Medal, British Cheese Awards 1996 and 2002; Silver Medal, 1997
A hard sheep's cheese; unpasteurized milk; vegetarian rennet. 200g/7oz and
1.5kg/3lb 5oz truckles or 2.3kg/5lb wheels

Although a hard cheese, Malvern has a soft, moist, notably smooth texture and delicate, creamy taste overlaid with the sweetness of the milk and wild flowers. Its gentle flavours make it more suitable for the cheeseboard than cooking, but left-over pieces can be used in the same way as pecorino for grating over vegetable dishes.

To make Malvern, Nicholas uses an adaptation of a white Wensleydale recipe (Wensleydale was originally a sheep's cheese). Starter is added when the milk is at 20°C/68°F; it is heated to 31°C/88°F before the addition of a little rennet, left to set for half an hour, and cut into 1.25cm/$^1/_2$-inch cubes. This is followed by scalding to 38°C/100°F over an hour, during which it is stirred continuously. The stirring is mechanical, but as the curd is very delicate, the rest of the process is carried out by hand. The curd is tipped on to a draining table and gently blocked and piled before being broken into walnut-sized pieces; it is then salted in three sessions, moulded, and piled into blocks of three to drain. Finally, it is re-moulded in cloths and pressed with increasing pressure for twenty-four hours. The maturing time is five months, with turning four times during the first week and once a week thereafter; the cheeses are also regularly rubbed to keep them free of mould.

HEREFORD HOP

Gold Medal and Best Speciality Cheese, British Cheese Awards 1995; Gold Medal, 1997; Bronze Medal, 2002
A semi-hard cows' cheese; full-fat, unpasteurized milk; vegetarian rennet.
1.8kg/4lb wheels

The cheese derives its name from its thick coating of dried hops. It has a moist, slightly fudgy texture and a sweet taste of grass and flowers strongly impregnated with the flavour of the hops.

WORCESTER GOLD

A hard Jersey cheese; full-fat, unpasteurized milk; vegetarian rennet.
400g/14oz and 1.5kg/3lb 5oz truckles or 2.5kg/5lb 8oz wheels

Worcester Gold has a rich, creamy texture and a very mild taste which develops flowery and herbal flavours on the tongue.

 Ansteys of Worcester
ALYSON AND COLIN ANSTEY, BROOMHALL FARM,
BROOMHALL, WORCESTER WR5 2NT.
TEL: 01905 820232

When Colin's grandfather bought Broomhall Farm in 1923, it was presumably well out into the country: it is now almost in Worcester, on the A38 to Tewkesbury. However, largely thanks to Alyson's initiative and energy, the Ansteys have gained considerably from their urban situation. Before they married, Colin produced only liquid milk, but Alyson, a trained cheesemaker, insisted that they needed a challenge, and helped him to develop their first cheese, Old Worcester White – called 'White' because they had originally hoped to make a blue cheese: however, the blue refused to grow. A second cheese was launched just after the birth of their second child (each of their three cheeses, they say, coincided with the birth of a child). This new cheese was Worcester Sauce, made by request because Lea & Perrins' factory is just down the road 'within smelling distance' when the wind is in the right direction. To start with they did not regard the cheese as a serious proposition, but it turned out to be exceptionally popular. By the time they had evolved the third cheese, Double Worcester, so many people were coming to buy cheese from the farm that they decided to start a shop, where they now sell not only about forty per cent of their own output but also a discriminating range of other British cheeses, accompaniments such as olives, and stiff, nubbly, not-too-sweet Worcestershire honey. As at Neal's Yard Dairy and Iain Meliss in Scotland, all the cheeses they sell are British and, because they are cheesemakers and know how to look after them, invariably in perfect condition. Around Christmas, they may have homemade mince pies, but otherwise all their stock is connected with cheese except the honey, which is produced (though not by them) on the farm.

OLD WORCESTER WHITE

Bronze Medal, British Cheese Awards 2002
A hard cow's cheese; full-fat, unpasteurized milk; vegetarian rennet.
450g/1lb and 3.5kg/7lb 11oz truckles

The cheese has a hard-pressed, dryish but cohesive texture and creamy, nutty taste with a distinctive tang: as it matures, the taste deepens and the tang develops. At five months it is a pleasant all-purpose cheese; when more mature, it becomes surprisingly powerful.

All the cheeses are based on the Old Worcester White recipe. After adding starter and rennet and waiting for the curd to set, which takes about fifty minutes, the curd is cut into 1.25cm/$^1/_2$-inch squares, scalded slightly, and blocked and piled. Draining, milling and salting follow; the cheeses are then pressed for twenty-four hours and dipped in hot water to encourage a crust to form. They are pressed for a further twenty-four hours, coated with lard to inhibit the growth of mould, and matured for a minimum of five months.

DOUBLE WORCESTER

Silver Medal, British Cheese Awards 2001; Bronze Medal, 2002
An annattoed cow's cheese; full-fat, unpasteurized milk; vegetarian rennet.
450g/1lb and 3.5kg/7lb 11oz truckles

Double Worcester has a slightly crumbly texture and a deep, rich taste slightly mellowed by the annatto but with a sharp punchy tang: when well matured it is strong enough to serve on a cheese-board in place of a blue cheese.

Double Worcester is called 'Double' because everything in the Old Worcester White recipe is doubled: the curd is cut smaller and scalded to a higher temperature, cut into blocks twice, and milled twice. The minimum maturing time is six months.

Neal's Yard Creamery

CHARLES WESTHEAD, CAPERTHY, ARTHURSTONE LANE,
DORSTONE, NEAR HAY-ON-WYE, HEREFORDSHIRE
HR3 6AX. TEL AND FAX: 01981 500359

Charles came to cheesemaking by instinct rather than design: one day when he was on the dole and wondering what to do next, he happened to pass Neal's Yard Dairy in London, went in, and in effect never emerged again. He served his apprenticeship, first behind the counter and then driving round the country collecting cheeses. His first dairy was on top of Ragstone Ridge in Kent, only a few minutes from the M25: you drove down an unremarkable wooded road, turned right – and there, without warning, was the Weald of Kent spread out before you. However, the dairy, perched on the hillside, was very small and it was no surprise to hear that he had moved. More surprising was where to: even after writing this book, I would have thought that it would be virtually impossible to find a view to equal the one he has left – but he has succeeded, and now makes cheese on top of Dorstone Hill on the edge of the Black Mountains, overlooking the Golden Valley. Here, as before, he makes goats' curds (the equivalent of cows' curd cheese) and three goat cheeses, Perroche, Ragstone (called after the Ridge in Kent) and Dorstone, plus cows' crème and fromage frais and two cows' cheeses, Wealden Round and Finn (he chose the name Finn, which means 'White Ancient One' in Irish, because the cheese is the only one he makes which is matured). The cows' milk, which he collects himself, comes from the September Organic Dairy at Almeley, about six miles away: Charles collects it himself directly after milking (for a new, white-rinded cheese which he is still developing, he is able to use it while it is still warm from the udder). The goats' milk (non-organic) is from a herd at Lime Kilns Farm, north of Gloucester.

NEAL'S YARD CREAMERY GOATS' CURD

Fresh curds; full-fat, unpasteurized milk; vegetarian rennet. Sold by weight

The curd has a light, creamy consistency and mild, sweet taste crossed with just enough tartness to give it character. Like cows' curd cheese and fromage frais, it makes an excellent base for a wide range of dishes, including fools, ices, and cheesecake.

The delicate texture which is the hallmark of Charles's cheeses is the result of his touch, or rather the lack of it: perhaps more than anyone, he takes enormous care to treat both the goats' and cows' curds gently and handle them as little as possible. All the cheeses are made by the same basic method. The milk is heated to 30°C/86°F, starter and rennet are added more or less simultaneously, and the curd is left overnight. In the morning, except for Wealden, the curd is cut into 3cm/1¼-inch squares with a steel ruler. For plain goats' curds, it is drained briefly and hung in a cloth until the next morning, when it is ready for use; for the other cheeses, it is transferred into moulds with a shovel rather than a ladle because a shovel has an open front and thus disturbs it less. I offered to help with moulding the Perroches and (in the nicest possible way) was rebuked for disturbing it by dragging the shovel over the surface. The moulds are topped up at intervals as the curd settles, left overnight, and brined.

Goats' Curd and Strawberry Fool with Maraschino

One way of serving goats' curd with strawberries is simply as an alternative to cream: to take the edge off its sharpness, beat it with 15g/½oz caster sugar per 250g/9oz curd or to taste (it should not, however, be sweet). Since the strawberries can be puréed the previous day, the fool is an excellent way of preventing berries picked in advance from going mouldy. To disguise its ever-so-pretty pale pink colour, pour a little extra purée over it before serving. A similar mixture makes a very rich, delicious ice.

For 6–8

125g/4¹/₂oz caster sugar
400g/14oz strawberries, hulled, washed, and left to dry
1 tablespoonful maraschino
400g/14oz goats' curd

Add 55g/2oz of the sugar to the strawberries, leave them to soften for 15–20 minutes, and pass them through a sieve, pressing as much pulp through the mesh as possible. Stir in the maraschino. Beat the curd with the rest of the sugar and gradually stir in as much of the strawberry purée as is necessary to give them a stiff, creamy texture. You will have about a quarter of the purée left over: pile the fool into the serving bowls and pour a little over each.

Strawberry Curd Ice

For 6

400g/14oz strawberries, hulled, washed, and dried, plus extra for
    serving
190g/generous 6¹/₂oz caster sugar
juice of ¹/₂ lime
200g/7oz goats' curd

Cover the berries with some of the sugar and leave them to soften for 15–20 minutes. Pass them through a sieve with the rest of the sugar, and add the lime juice. Beat the purée into the curd until smooth. Freeze for 2¹/₂–3 hours or until the ice has half-set; beat thoroughly and freeze for another 1–2 hours or until firm. Serve decorated with whole or half strawberries.

PERROCHE

Gold Medal, British Cheese Awards 1995; Silver Medal, 1996; Bronze
Medal (Plain) and Gold Medal (Herbs), 1997; Silver Medal (Herbs), 2002
A fresh goats' cheese; full-fat, unpasteurized milk; vegetarian rennet.
150g/5¼oz rounds

Perroche has a wonderfully light, melting texture and a sweet, mild taste shot with hints of honey, herbs, and lemon. Some of the cheeses are flavoured with herbs (rosemary, tarragon, or dill).

The curd for Perroche and Ragstone is prepared in the same way as the goats' curd. The Perroches are piled in towers to drain so that the cheese is pressed lightly; after draining, they are brined and the flavoured cheeses rolled in herbs.

 Hot Chocolate Creams

The operative word here is rich rather than delicate; however, the background of goats' cheese gives the chocolate a surprisingly refreshing quality. The texture is actually almost cake-like. The creams be prepared up to twenty-four hours in advance (store them in the refrigerator).

Cooking time: 25–30 minutes
For 6–7

100g/3½oz Valrhona cooking chocolate
200ml/7fl oz (⅓ pint) extra thick double cream, plus extra for serving
2 large free-range egg yolks, beaten
100g/3½oz Perroche or Innes Button (½ a Perroche or
    2 Innes Buttons)
75g/2¾oz caster sugar
1 tbsp brandy

The chocolate comes in buttons or a solid block: cut the block into small pieces if you can or grate it coarsely. Set it with the cream over very low heat and stir gently until it is about two-thirds melted. Remove from the heat and continue stirring until the mixture is completely smooth.

Beat together the yolks, cheese, and sugar until smooth (the mixture will soften as you proceed). Stir in the brandy, then the chocolate. Heat the oven to 180°C/350°F/Gas 4; spoon the creams into ramekins and bake for 25–30 minutes, until they just begin to bubble. Serve hot covered with more cream.

RAGSTONE

Bronze Medal, British Cheese Awards 1996; Gold Medal, 2001
A white mould rind goats' cheese log; full-fat, unpasteurized milk;
vegetarian rennet.
200g/7oz logs

Again, the texture is outstandingly light and smooth; the taste includes a flash of lemon and a strong infusion of honey. In fact, it is probably fair to say that Ragstone and Dorstone (below) are the sweetest as well as among the subtlest goats' cheeses in Britain. In one way, it seems a pity to use it for cooking, but it is particularly outstanding grilled.

Ragstone is moulded in tall pipes which are set on end, the cheese inside being pressed by its own weight. The maturing time is two to three weeks. The cheese is at its lightest if eaten promptly but can be kept for at least another two weeks.

DORSTONE

A goats' cheese rolled in ash with a slip-coat rind; full-fat, unpasteurized
milk; vegetarian rennet. 200g/7oz truncated cylinder

In my notes, instead of describing Dorstone as tasting of honey, I
have called it 'nectarian'. Though still deliciously sweet, it is milder
and fresher-flavoured than Ragstone, with a tremblingly light, delicate texture. The rind, which is often seen on French goats'
cheeses, gives a bluish rather than white bloom and contributes
considerably to flavour. At the time of writing the cheese has not
yet been launched, but a few are already on sale at Neal's Yard
Dairy.

WEALDEN ROUND

Silver Medal, British Cheese Awards 1996 and 2002
A flavoured, fresh cows' cheese; full-fat, unpasteurized organic milk;
vegetarian rennet. 200g/7oz rounds

Of all Charles's cheeses, Wealden is the most remarkable for its
texture, which is as light, moist, and delicate as a baked egg custard.
The mild taste is strengthened by a choice of flavourings (tarragon, chives, parsley and garlic, or spring onion).

For Wealden, the curd is not cut but left as a solid block floating in
the whey and placed in the moulds in layers, between which the
flavourings are sprinkled. The fresh herbs are snipped very finely
and evenly by Charles's wife.

FINN

Bronze Medal, British Cheese Awards 2001 and 2002
An unpressed, white mould rind cows' cheese; full-fat, unpasteurized
organic milk with 10% cream added; vegetarian rennet. 200g/7oz rounds

Finn is soft but firm and compact rather than runny; the taste is sweet and nutty, with a mild but distinctive, slightly salty tang.

For Finn, which is a cream cheese, ten per cent of cream and penicillin mould for the rind are added to the milk with the starter and the cheeses are matured for a fortnight while the rind develops.

 ## Finn and Watercress Soup

This is very quick to prepare and cook, and can be made the previous day.

Cooking-time: 15–17 minutes
For 4–5

1 large or 2 small onions (150g/5¼oz), peeled and finely chopped
1 tbsp oil
25g/1oz butter
2 cloves garlic, peeled and finely chopped
150g/5¼oz watercress, washed, and roughly chopped (keep the stems)
850ml/1½ pints vegetable or strong, fresh chicken stock (page xxvii)
salt and pepper
3 tbsp extra thick double cream
100g/3½oz Finn, chopped very small, including the rind

Fry the onion in the oil and butter over low heat for about 2 minutes; add the garlic and continue to fry for another 5 minutes or until the onion is soft but not brown. Add the cress and stir until it is thoroughly coated with oil. Add the stock, 1 teaspoonful of salt, and a moderate grinding of pepper and bring it to a simmer; simmer, covered, for 4–5 minutes. Liquidize the soup, allow it to cool, and chill until needed. When you are ready to serve, reheat it over fairly high heat; when just simmering, stir in the cream and cheese. Remove from the heat and stir until the rind of the cheese has melted: return to the heat very briefly if necessary. Serve at once.

 ## *Womerton Farm*

RUTH LAWRENCE, WOMERTON FARM, ALL STRETTON, NEAR CHURCH STRETTON, SHROPSHIRE SY6 6LJ.
TEL: 01694 751260

You could spend a lifetime searching for somewhere with a situation like this: Ruth, however, did not have to look, since she inherited the farm from her parents and was brought up here. It is nearly 300 metres/1,000 feet up on the Long Mynd, an isolated outcrop of hills just south of Shrewsbury, with a view over Shropshire to the east and sheep-cropped slopes dropping into steep, bracken-covered valleys to the north and west. It was and still is primarily a sheep farm, but Ruth's father raised a few beef cattle, and Ruth keeps goats. The goats are crossed Anglo-Nubian, which means that the milk is very rich milk: its quality is evident from her soft cheese, St Francis, but was also immediately obvious to us when she gave us tea. The tea itself was perfectly ordinary but so transformed by the creamy milk, only a few hours old and full of sweet flavours, that it was a revelation. Until recently, she was milking a herd of ninety: now, however, in order to leave more time to make the cheese, she has sold all but ten and buys in the rest of the milk, much of which still comes from her own former goats.

WOMERTON

A hard goats' cheese; full-fat, unpasteurized milk; vegetarian rennet.
1.4kg/3lb and 4.5kg/10lb truckles

The texture is slightly fudge-like; the taste is mild, with a mixture of earthy and herbal flavours. A smoked version is also available. Womerton is based on a Cheddar-type recipe and I think does not do Ruth's goats' milk justice, as St Francis certainly does: when I put this to her, she replied that she is not particularly satisfied with it herself, and is already planning to replace it with a new hard cheese.

ST FRANCIS

A soft white mould rind goats' cheese; full-fat, unpasteurized milk;
vegetarian rennet. Various sizes, ranging from 55g/2oz buttons to
675g/1lb 8oz logs

The texture of the cheese is like very thick cream but much lighter; the taste is a blend of clear, delicate, refreshing flowery flavours. If there is any trace of goat, it is in a slight undercurrent of lemon. It is delicious instead of cream with fruit and can be used as a filling for pies and tarts.

Only the richer evening milk is used: it is used directly after milking and cooled to 20°C/68°F. Starter, rennet, and penicillin for the rind are added simultaneously and the curd is left to incubate overnight. The next day, it is drained in baskets for an hour and a half, moulded, and left, still at 20°C/68°F, until the following day, or for a shorter period for the small sizes; finally, it is brined and left to ripen for a fortnight while the rind develops.

Raven's Oak Dairy

MIKE AND SANDRA ALLWOOD, RAVEN'S OAK DAIRY,
BURLAND FARM, WREXHAM ROAD, BURLAND, NANTWICH,
CHESHIRE CW5 8ND. TEL: 01270 524624/524210;
FAX: 01270 524724

As soon as I started talking to Sandra Allwood, I realized that here was a kindred soul. When I asked her why she and Mike had started to make cheese, she replied that she had spent fifteen years running a Bed and Breakfast, which she had enjoyed partly because she loves cooking and offered not only breakfasts but dinners. And – this is the point: 'I regard cheesemaking as an extension of cooking.' It is precisely for this reason that the methods for making the cheeses given here are placed after the descriptions of them, like the recipes in a cookery book.

Sandra is American and was brought up in Florida; Mike's family are the descendants of a Wesleyan preacher who settled at Burland Farm in 1768. The Allwoods have farmed there in unbroken succession ever since. To begin with, Mike rebelled against his destiny and went to Cambridge to read economics with the idea of making a career in banking: he met Sandra while studying for his Masters at Reading. However, by the time he had finished at university his father was sixty-five and announced his intention of retiring. This meant that either Mike managed the farm or it was sold. There was no real choice. Sandra smiled: 'Fortunately, we both took to it.'

Cheesemaking had been in her mind for years but the immediate spur to begin was the effectual present of a ready-made dairy. Mike had set up a company for making frozen yoghurt for which a dairy had been equipped: when the company disbanded, it became vacant. At the time, feeling that her brain was rusting, Sandra was working on a Ph. D. at Keele, but she laid aside her books and has not looked at them since. She started experimenting with cheese immediately, at first with unpasteurized milk from their own herd. Soon afterwards, the equipment used for making a Scottish Camembert-style cheese, Bonchester (which I remember and loved) went up for sale, and they bought it: 'That made everything much easier!' Success came rapidly: in their very first year, Sandra entered three cheeses for the British Cheese Awards, won a medal for all of them and carried off the award for the best new British cheese with her mould-ripened goats' cheese, Whitehaven. It was only the eighth batch that she had ever made.

As her analogy with cooking suggests, she works mainly by touch. 'When I get my hands into the cheese, I can feel it. It's slightly different every day. Texture is the result of touch.' The Allwoods now make a plain fresh and a white mould-ripened cheese from all the four kinds of milk available: cows', from their herd of 168 Friesians and twelve Shorthorns, plus sheep's, goats', and buffalo; chiefly for cooking purposes, they also produce two logs, goats' and cows' (to order only). As the non-cows' milk is bought, they feel obliged to pasteurize it and, sadly, pasteurize the cows' as well. However, rather than the more usual 'flash' pasteurization, which involves heating the milk to 72°C for fifteen seconds, they heat it only to 63°C and hold it there for half an hour, which Sandra believes is far less detrimental to flavour. Both the fresh and mould-ripened cheeses are made by the same method except that the ripened ones are dipped into a penicillin solution after they are made. (Most producers of mould-ripened cheeses inoculate the milk with the mould when they add the starter bacteria, but Sandra says that they have never found this necessary.)

BURLAND GREEN

Bronze Medal, British Cheese Awards 2000
A soft, white mould-ripened cows' cheese; full-fat, pasteurized organic milk;
vegetarian rennet.
1kg/2lb 3¹/₂oz, 375g/13oz, and 150g/5¹/₄ oz rounds

Of the four cheeses of this type, Burland Green and Whitehaven seemed to me the most successful. I have tried Burland Green on many occasions and always been delighted by its luscious texture and, given that it is pasteurized, remarkably full flavour. Sandra attributes this not only to the method of pasteurization but the Burland microflora: in addition, the organic milk almost certainly plays a part. The taste is sweet and flowery, with a gentle but distinctive peppery tang and after-taste which gives it character. A bonus is the admirably crisp, well developed rind which contrasts wonderfully with the creamy interior.

WHITEHAVEN

Gold medal and Best New Cheese award, British Cheese Awards 1999;
Silver medal, 2000; Bronze Medal, 2001
A soft, white mould-ripened goats' cheese; full-fat, pasteurized milk;
vegetarian rennet.
1kg/2lb 3¹/₂oz, 375g/13oz, and 150g/5¹/₄ oz rounds

This is deliciously creamy and clean-tasting, with just enough flavour of goat to be identifiable. Again, it is characterized by a slight pepperiness and exceptionally crisp, thick rind.

RAVEN'S OAK

Bronze Medal, British Cheese Awards 2000; Silver Medal, 2002
A fresh cows' cheese; full-fat, pasteurized milk; vegetarian rennet.
1kg/2lb 3½oz, 357g/13oz, and 150g/5¼oz rounds

This has a pleasingly firm, nutty texture and distinctive, fresh taste; in fact, no cheese that I have tried for some time has such an unmistakable flavour of grass.

SPURSTOW

Bronze medal, British Cheese Awards 1999 and 2000; Gold medal and
award for the Best Fresh Cheese, 2001
A fresh buffalo cheese; full-fat, pasteurized milk; vegetarian rennet.
1kg/2lb 3½oz, 375g/13oz, and 150g/5¼oz rounds

The rich, homogeneous nature of buffalo milk, which makes it so suitable for mozzarella, is also ideal for a simple, fresh cheese like this. The flavour is predominantly creamy and the texture silken and mousse-like. I think it is delicious.

The milk is heated to a higher temperature than usual (37°C) before the starter is added and left to ripen for an hour. After renneting, it is left to set for an hour and a half. The curd is then cut into fingers, allowed to rest for another half hour, and tipped into the moulds. These are turned three times at hourly intervals before being left overnight at 26°C-30°C depending on the external temperature (Sandra discovered the importance of maintaining the storeroom temperature the hard way, i.e. with failed cheeses). In the morning, all the cheeses are brined: the ones to be sold fresh are packed immediately and those to be ripened dipped in penicillin and kept at 10°C for two to three weeks.

H. S. Bourne

JOHN AND JULIET-ANNE BOURNE, THE BANK, MALPAS,
CHESHIRE SY14 7AL. TEL: 01948 770214;
FAX: 01948 770288

'Someone once said to me that you couldn't sell Cheshire south of Birmingham,' said John as he stood at his stall in Borough Market, London SE1 wrapping endless packages of cheese for a continuous succession of customers. 'Well, as you see, I can – but it's got to have flavour.' Along with others from the midlands and north, including the Allwoods (page 199), the Bournes travel down to London every Friday, leaving at dawn, and return after the market closes on Saturday. It is extremely hard work, but the size and prestige of the market make it an important part of John's mission to reinstate Cheshire to what he considers to be its rightful status. Before the first world war, he said gloomily, Cheshire held over fifty per cent of the UK market. Now, he feels, it is not taken seriously as a cheese at all, for which he blames the bland, plastic-wrapped mass-produced versions sold in the super-markets.

His, in contrast, is genuinely farmhouse-made and almost cer-tainly the nearest to Cheshire of past centuries as one will find. His family have made it for 200 years and he does his best to ensure that nothing is changed. In a nutshell, this means that every stage of the cheesemaking process is carried out by hand, including cut-ting and subsequently breaking the curd. The fact that all his pasture is permanent, with an unusually wide variety of grasses and herbs, also contributes to the traditional character of the cheese; in addition, although he does not farm organically, he uses very little nitrogen, preferring to rely on clover. Despite all this, as he emphasizes, it is impossible to imitate his ancestors' cheeses accurately because of the nature of modern milk: his herd, which consists of 120 Friesians, yields milk which is far richer than in his grandfather's or even his father's day.

As well as cheese from the milk of his own herd, which he makes red (annattoed) and white, and pasteurized or unpasteurized, he produces organic cheese with milk from a neighbouring farm and, so far as I know, is the only cheesemaker currently making blue Cheshire. The last person to make it was Mrs Hutchinson Smith of Hinton Bank Farm, Whitchurch, who sold the recipe some years ago to a dairy: however, none forthcame, and until I discovered John's, I thought that it had disappeared for ever.

MRS BOURNE'S TRADITIONAL CHEDDAR (UNCOLOURED)

Bronze Medal, British Cheese Awards 2001
A semi-hard cows'cheese; full-fat, unpasteurized milk; vegetarian rennet.
10kg/22lb cylinders and smaller sizes on request

Before describing any of John's cheeses, I should emphasize that they vary considerably according to season, maturity, which might be anything between two and fifteen months, and whether or not they are pasteurized. In general, he sells the unpasteurized ones younger, partly because he knows that they will have plenty of flavour, whereas the taste of the pasteurized ones needs time to develop. The particular sample I tried on this occasion was two and a half months old, with a light, crumbly texture, just as Cheshire is supposed to have, very moist, and with a sufficiently strong tang to stand up to Westcombe or even Keens' Cheddar (pages 89 and 86).

BOURNE'S 'BOROUGH SPECIAL' (UNCOLOURED)

A hard cows' cheese; full-fat, pasteurized milk; vegetarian rennet.
10kg/22lb cylinders and smaller sizes on request

John tends to take his oldest cheeses to Borough, chiefly because some of his customers there ask for them specially. This cheese was fifteen months old, still light, like the younger one, with a nutty taste and texture and a gentle, salty-sweet tang.

JOHN BOURNE'S ORGANIC CHESHIRE (COLOURED)

Silver Medal, British Cheese Awards 2001
A hard cows' cheese; full-fat, pasteurized organic milk; vegetarian rennet.
10kg/22lb cylinders and smaller sizes on request

The texture was again light and crumbly, but the taste relatively soft and mellow, which was at least partly due to the annatto used for the colouring.

JOHN BOURNE'S BLUE CHESHIRE (COLOURED)

Silver Medal, British Cheese Awards 2001
A semi-soft cows' cheese; full-fat, pasteurized organic milk; vegetarian
rennet. 10kg/22lb cylinders

Apart from probably being unique, this cheese is interesting because it is made with natural mould rather than mould which has been inoculated into the milk. Perhaps because of the annatto, the blue actually looks green, although John assures me that it tastes different from the more usual streaks of 'green fade' which sometimes invade normal Cheshire in places where air can enter (just as Cheddar sometimes develops blue veins, usually near the rind). The taste of the natural mould is quite different from the usual kind: instead of being pungent and peppery, it is surprisingly gentle and herbal, with a hint of aniseed.

Appleby's Cheshire

EDWARD APPLEBY, HAWKSTONE ABBEY FARM, WESTON-
UNDER-REDCASTLE, SHREWSBURY, SHROPSHIRE SY4 5LN.
TEL: 01948 840221/01948 840387

The salty/sweet tang associated with Cheshire, and which certainly characterizes the Appleby's, is said to be due to the salt under the soil not only in Cheshire, but also parts of Lancashire, Staffordshire, and Shropshire: Hawkstone, at the edge of the Dee and Mersey basin, lies at the southern end of the area. The country is lush, with thick hedges, spreading trees, and rich grazing.

The first building to catch the eye as you approach the farm is a long black and white Tudor barn, which faces the back of the house and the cheese-room. The house, which was also originally Tudor but rebuilt on a larger, grander scale, seems unremarkable until seen from the front, when it is revealed as a particularly fine, tall, four-square, eighteenth-century Shropshire manor house. It faces a lawn bounded by shrubs and banks of foxgloves, lupins, larkspur, and delphiniums; at one end is an orchard and vegetable garden fruitful (in June) with ripe strawberries and nascent apples, gooseberries, and raspberries. Here we met Mr Appleby, or so we deduced. When I said, 'How do you do? Are you Mr Appleby?', he replied with dry humour, 'You may presume so. I am just the gardener.' These days (by now he is ninety-four), his main interest is the garden; Mrs Appleby, however, who comes from a farming family and has made cheese all her life, is still as preoccupied with it as ever, although the actual work is now carried out by a cheese-maker and three assistants.

Although not on the scale of Quicke's (page 102), the Applebys are one of the largest cheese-farms in the country, keeping a closed herd of 300 Friesians or part-Friesians and handling an average of 4,000 litres/800 gallons of milk a day. The milk vat is as large as a small swimming-pool; of necessity, the curd is stirred and broken after scalding by machinery. The most impressive piece of machinery connected with the cheese, however, is not in the dairy but a slowly revolving carousel which replaces a con-ventional milking parlour. It is one of only two so far installed in this country and the only one for cows (the other is for sheep). To reduce the amount of power needed and the noise, which might upset the cows, it floats on a bed of water; the cows took about a year to get used to it but now queue up to board it willingly. Each chews a feed of concentrates calculated by computer to meet her individual needs as she goes round; the milking appara-tus falls off when she is dry, her yield is automatically registered, and the milk piped directly to the dairy.

The whey is separated, pasteurized, and used for particularly excellent whey-butter; the Applebys also make ordinary butter, small quantities of smoked Cheshire, and Double Gloucester instead of Cheshire once a week.

APPLEBY'S CHESHIRE

Gold Medal (coloured), Silver Medal (white), British Cheese Awards 1997
A hard cows' cheese; full-fat, unpasteurized milk; vegetarian and
traditional rennet. 1.25kg/2lb 12oz, 2.3kg/5lb, 9kg/20lb, and a few
28kg/62lb Traditionals

The white and coloured cheeses are exactly the same except that
the white ones are made without annatto. The texture is short,
light, and crumbly; when young, the taste is mild and mellow,
giving only a promise of the lively flavours of the mature version.
After six months or (in the case of the larger sizes) more, they
become rich, piquant, deep-tasting, and surprisingly powerful,
with a sharp sweetness offset by an almost smoky tang; occasionally, they may have a few veins of green under the rind which are
an assurance of age and enhance flavour. The cheese is not only
superb on the cheeseboard, but also excellent for cooking (before
the days of creamery-made Cheddar, Cheshire was the standard
cheese recommended for flavouring).

The cheese is made with morning and evening milk; a home-cultured
starter with annatto for the coloured cheeses is added and the milk is
left to ripen for two hours before renneting. When it has set, which
takes the usual forty minutes, the curd is stirred and scalded very
slightly, and stirring continued until the correct acidity is reached; it
is then cut into blocks and turned and broken rather than blocked
and piled, as for Cheddar. Salting, milling, and moulding follow,
after which the cheeses are pressed overnight; finally, they are turned
and pressed again, briefly for the small sizes or for another day in the
case of the 28kg/62lb size. The maturing times are a minimum of six
weeks for the smallest size and from two to ten months for the
largest, with twice-weekly turning and wiping throughout.

Over tea with homemade lemon cake, Mrs Appleby recalled that her father ate the cheese with raspberry jam – which is unexpectedly good, perhaps because the two flavours have a similar richness. A deep, rich six- to ten-month-old cheese also goes well with gooseberry jam.

 ## Cheshire Rarebit with Whisky

There is nothing traditional about whisky with Cheshire; however, the taste of whisky has an affinity with the matured cheese which makes this the most interesting and successful rarebit mixture that I have tried.

For 2

slice from a large loaf
butter
2 level tsp plain white flour
salt
Cayenne pepper
$^3/_4$ tsp Dijon mustard
2 tbsp whisky
150g/5$^1/_4$oz mature Applebys' Cheshire, finely grated

If you like, trim the crust from the bread; butter it, cut it in half, and bake it (page xxviii). Mix together the flour, a pinch of salt, and a generous pinch of Cayenne. Put 15g/$^1/_2$oz butter into a small saucepan over low heat until it melts; remove the pan from the heat and stir in the seasoned flour. Return it to the heat and add the mustard, whisky, and 2 tablespoonsful of water. Cook for 1–2 minutes, stirring continuously, until the mixture is very thick but not too stiff to mix with the cheese. Stir in the cheese off the heat: it should just melt but no more. If necessary, return it to the heat for a second or two, but be careful only to warm it gently. Pile the cheese mixture over the pieces of toast, making sure that it covers them completely: any exposed edges will burn. Place the rarebit under a hot grill until it turns pale brown and serve at once.

APPLEBYS' DOUBLE GLOUCESTER

A hard cows' cheese; full-fat, unpasteurized milk; vegetarian and traditional rennet.
1.8kg/4lb, 6.8kg/15lb, and 13.5kg/30lb wheels

The Double Gloucester has a similar salty/sweet tang to the Cheshire but the texture is crumblier and the taste milder, mellower, and smokier. It leaves quite a strong, smoky aftertaste.

 Applebys' Jerusalem Artichoke Soup

You can make this with either Cheshire or Double Gloucester: Cheshire is livelier and tangier, Double Gloucester deeper and richer.

Cooking time: just under 1 hour
For 4

1 tbsp oil
15g/½oz butter
125g/4½oz (1 small) onion, peeled and diced
2 cloves garlic, peeled and diced
1 small leek, finely sliced, washed, and dried
250g/9oz carrots, peeled and finely sliced
salt and pepper
150ml/¼ pint dry white wine
250g/9oz floury potato, peeled and sliced

450g/1lb Jerusalem artichokes, peeled and sliced
1 litre/1³/₄ pints vegetable or fresh chicken stock (page xxvii)
2 tbsp double cream
a little milk for thinning if needed
at least 125g/4¹/₂oz Applebys' Cheshire or Double Gloucester, finely
    grated

Warm the oil and butter in a large saucepan or wok and fry the
onion over low heat for 4–5 minutes; add the garlic and fry for
another 4–5 minutes or until the onion is soft but not brown. Add
the leek and carrots, season with 1 teaspoonful of salt and a moderate grinding of pepper, and turn for about 2 minutes. Pour in the
wine; raise the heat, and boil it away. Add the potato, artichokes,
and stock, bring to the boil, and simmer for 25–30 minutes or
until the carrot is soft. Liquidize the soup until it is very smooth;
return it to the pan and heat it very gently until simmering. Stir in
the cream. If it is very thick, add a little milk. Remove from the
heat and add half the cheese: sprinkle the rest over each serving.

Berkswell

STEPHEN AND TESSA FLETCHER, RAM HALL DAIRY SHEEP,
RAM HALL, BERKSWELL, COVENTRY, WEST MIDLANDS
CV7 7BD. TEL: 01676 532203

Ram Hall is of ancient origin: the Fletchers are not sure how long
a farm has been on the site, but the present farmhouse is sixteenth
century and as little altered as you could hope to find. You go in
through a deeply weathered, iron-studded wooden side-door to
the former kitchen, where a huge, curving brick flue leads from
where the bread-oven used to be up through the rafters. An

original staircase, complete with banisters, is in the main part of the house, as is the room (still labelled) which was used for maturing cheeses. In Cheshire this was usually an attic, but in the Warwickshire area the maturing room was often on the first floor, with another storey above, as was the case here. The cheesemaking room was directly underneath and below that a cellar which may also have been used for maturing. It was almost certainly used for cheese at some point, since it is connected to a nearby pond so that the atmosphere could be kept moist by flooding.

Originally, the Fletchers milked cows, selling the milk direct; in the late 1980s they decided to keep sheep as well, although at first without any thought of making cheese. Milk sales started well but fell off; then a goats'-cheesemaker who supplied the local farm shop gave up and the shop asked them for sheep's cheese instead. Although Stephen did not know how to make cheese, he seems to have a talent for collecting willing helpers: first, he found Sally, a trained cheesemaker, who produced a cheese based on a Caerphilly recipe; then his mother took a short cheesemaking course. Soon afterwards, they were joined by Tessa, who is now Stephen's wife. When Sally left, Tessa took over, and now makes Berkswell with a full-time and several part-time assistants. In summer, when there is plenty of milk, Stephen's mother also sometimes makes soft cheese (which is sold only locally).

For some time, the Fletchers continued to keep both cows and sheep: however, the cows were sold in 1995. At the time of my visit, they had 250 Frieslands, who took three hours twice a day to milk; by now, there are 400–500. The cheese is made two or three times a week to a recipe which no longer bears any significant resemblance to Caerphilly, but involves cutting and working the curd and then scalding it and allowing it to free-drain. The cheeses are finished with cheese-paint to ensure that they have firm but thin rinds; the maturing time is four to eight months.

BERKSWELL

Gold Medal, British Cheese Awards 1994, 1995 and 2001;
Bronze Medal, 1997 and 2002
A hard sheep's cheese; unpasteurized milk; vegetarian rennet.
3–4kg/6lb 10oz–8lb 13oz baskets

At eight months, Berkswell is close-textured, silky and yet slightly crystalline, and as hard as a mature pecorino; however, instead of being salty and smoky, it is full, rich, and sweet, with exceptional power and layers of taste which unfold on the tongue by degrees. The flavours are unmistakably of the rich grass and herbage of Middle England: eating it seems almost like eating distilled meadow. It is wonderful on the cheeseboard and for sprinkling. In particular, its sweetness brings out the flavour of sweet vegetables.

Spaghetti with Berkswell, Basil, and Courgettes

Cooking time: under 30 minutes
For 2

400g/14oz medium to small courgettes, washed and trimmed
fine salt
250g/9oz fresh or dried spaghetti
1 small clove garlic, peeled and roughly chopped
about 24 basil leaves, washed and dried
2$\frac{1}{2}$ tbsp oil
pepper
2 large cloves garlic, washed and finely chopped
25g/1oz pine-nuts
70g/2$\frac{1}{2}$oz 8-month-old Berkswell, finely grated

Cut the courgettes into slices about 8mm/$\frac{1}{3}$-inch thick, sprinkle with salt, and leave them to sweat for 20 minutes. Rinse and blot them dry.

Set a large pan of water to boil for the spaghetti. Start cooking dried pasta if you are using it: when the water is boiling vigorously, add a little salt (about 1 teaspoonful per litre/1¾ pint) and the pasta, bring back to the boil, and stir. Cook for the shortest time given on the packet.

Crush the small clove of garlic in a mortar. Roughly chop, add, and crush the basil; moisten the paste with about a ½ tablespoonful of oil.

If you are using fresh pasta, start cooking it, which takes about 5 minutes, and warm the rest of the oil over medium to high heat in a large frying pan. With dried spaghetti, heat the oil 5 minutes before you think the pasta will be ready. Add the courgettes to the oil, season lightly with pepper, and fry until they begin to change colour. Add the garlic and fry, turning constantly, until the garlic and courgettes are a light gold. Add the nuts, stir-fry for a few seconds, and remove from the heat. Stir in the garlic and basil paste.

Drain the pasta as soon as it is *al dente*. Toss with half the cheese. Serve with the basil, courgettes, and the rest of the cheese on top.

MARLOW AND KELSEY LANE

Bronze Medal (Kelsey Lane), British Cheese Awards 2002
Soft white mould-ripened sheep's cheeses; full-fat, unpasteurized milk;
vegetarian rennet.
Marlow, 200g/7oz and 500g/1lb 2oz squares; Kelsey Lane,
350–450g/13oz–1lb rounds

Both cheeses are examples of the rich diversity of flavours given by unpasteurized milk. Marlow is predominantly sweet, tasting of flowers and grass, with soft earthy undertones. The sweetness, however, is balanced by a perhaps unexpectedly positive cheesey flavour. If not exactly a strong cheese, it is certainly not mild. To do its depth of flavour justice, I suggest serving it alone, or with just one other non-competing hard cheese such as Gabriel (page 154). Kelsey Lane is similar.

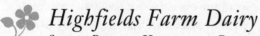

Highfields Farm Dairy
STELLA BENNET, HIGHFIELDS, CLIFTON LANE, STATFOLD, TAMWORTH, STAFFS B79 0AQ. TEL: 01827 830197

Innes became famous in 1994 when it won the Supreme Championship at the first British Cheese Awards. It was started by Hugh Lillingston, heir to Thorpe Park, as part of his strategy to make enough money for the upkeep of the house: having launched Innes cheeses, he went on to found a partner venture in the form of a bakery. Some of the bread, like the cheese, was made in Staffordshire, but he also had a large bakery under London Bridge Station, where, looking faintly incongruous with his white baker's coat covering a velvet jacket and handmade shoes, he told me that his original ambition was to be a musician (he was sacked from Eton because of the time he spent playing with rock groups). The importance to him of music led him to experiment with it on his goats, whom he found gave ten per cent more milk if they were entertained by Mozart on rainy afternoons. (The effect of music on animals has in fact become quite well known: similar experiments have shown that music encourages hens to lay more eggs.)

He originally chose goats because he rented Highfields from his father 'on the usual terms – no favours' and did not have enough land for cows or sheep. He went to Angoulême to study cheese-making but never made the cheese himself commercially because, apart from his other commitments, he feels that he is too impatient. To make good cheese, he says, you need a passive, quiet temperament so that you can fill in the intervals while the curd sets or the acidity rises with thought. Instead, he found a local cheese-maker, Stella Bennet, who has made it ever since. When Hugh withdrew, she bought the business herself, and now carries it on independently.

The particular quality of the cheese is due partly to her almost obsessive concern for hygiene, to the fact that the milk is used lit-erally within twenty minutes of leaving the udder, and her extraordinarily light touch. The goats are part-organically reared, since the Highfields land is organic, but they are given non-organic concentrates. The freshness of the milk is assured by the fact that either the cheese is made twice a day or the afternoon's milking is sold in liquid form.

INNES CURD CHEESE

Bronze Medal, British Cheese Awards 2002
A soft goats' curd cheese; full-fat, unpasteurized milk; vegetarian rennet.
175g/6oz pots or 1.8kg/4lb tubs

As with all the Innes cheeses, the texture is so light and delicate that it floats down the throat like air. The taste is similarly delicate, with the sweetness of the absolutely fresh milk and virtually no hint of goat. The version I tried was flavoured with garlic and chives but, as with the Button, the sweetness of the cheese means that the plain version would go excellently with fruit.

INNES BUTTON

Gold Medal and Supreme Champion, British Cheese Awards 1994; Bronze Medal, 1996; Gold Medal, Trophy for the Best Fresh Cheese, and Supreme Champion, 2002; Silver Medal (with pink peppercorns), 2002
A fresh goats' cheese; full-fat, unpasteurized milk; vegetarian rennet.
40g/1½oz buttons or 170g/6oz rounds

This is the lightest and most soufflé-like cheese that I have ever tried. To enjoy it at its lightest, buy and eat it as soon as possible after it has been made. Like the curd cheese (above), the flavour is very mild, with the sweetness of fresh milk: some of the cheeses are rolled in flavourings, including ginger, caraway seeds, and pink peppercorns.

 ## Grilled Innes Button with Cherries in Brandy

This can also be made with peaches. The fruit benefits from being soaked in the brandy overnight.

Grilling time: 4–5 minutes
For 2

75g/2¾oz red or black cherries, washed, dried, halved, and stoned *or*
  1 large peach, sliced
1 tbsp brandy
1 tbsp demerara sugar (for cherries) *or* caster sugar (for peach)
4 tbsp double cream
2 Innes Buttons

If possible, soak the fruit in the brandy and sugar overnight; beat together the cream and cheese. Place the fruit, cut-side up, in two individual ramekins or similar ovenproof dishes, pour the juices over them, and cover with the cheese mixture. Place under a hot grill for 4–5 minutes, or until lightly browned. Serve at once.

INNES LOG

A goats' cheese with an ash coating covered with a white mould rind; full-fat, unpasteurized milk; vegetarian rennet. 175g/6oz log

Like the other Innes cheeses, the log has an exceptionally fine, light texture. It tastes mild and sweet, with flavours of nuts and mushrooms and virtually no trace of goat. It is delicious toasted, when the nutty flavour is intensified and it melts to a creamy consistency.

BOSWORTH AND CLIFTON LEAF

White mould rind, Camembert-style goats' cheeses; full-fat, unpasteurized milk; vegetarian rennet. Bosworth, 150g/5¼ oz rounds; Clifton Leaf, 70g/2½ oz rounds

The cheeses flow slightly; the taste is mild and sweet, with overtones of mushrooms and nuts, as before. The leaf, which is sweet chestnut, emphasizes the sweet, nutty flavour.

Colston Bassett and District Dairy

RICHARD ROWLETT, COLSTON BASSETT AND DISTRICT DAIRY, HARBY LANE, COLSTON BASSETT, NOTTINGHAMSHIRE NG12 3FN. TEL: 01949 81322

The country around Colston Bassett is very open, predominantly flat, but punctuated at intervals with small hills or wolds. You pass woods, but I did not notice a single ploughed field: the entire area seems to be grazing, which perhaps is as one would expect in a region famous for cheese for two and a half centuries. As with other cheeses, the distinctive taste of Stilton is associated with a particular type of soil: the most northerly Stilton dairy is at Hartington, near Matlock in Derbyshire, and those furthest south at Melton Mowbray, Leicestershire.

No farmhouse Stilton has been made since before the war; Colston Bassett, however, is the smallest of the creameries. Colston Bassett itself is a village in the proper sense of the word, with an old-fashioned post office-cum-shop and large church, designed to accommodate all the families on the surrounding farms. The creamery is professional and workmanlike, with a small shop, which was empty on the day of my visit but, as I was assured, becomes extremely busy in the autumn, when people are stocking up on Stilton for Christmas.

I went just before Ernest Wagstaff retired after being the manager for thirty-five years (the creamery has only had one other manager since it was founded in 1920). Two relatively recent changes introduced during his time were pasteurization and the use of the genetically engineered rennet, Chymosin. Remarkably, he held out against pasteurization until the listeria scare in the early 1990s with only memory to serve as a comparison, I cannot judge its effect on the cheese. At that stage, Chymosin was used only for Shropshire Blue, which Ernest felt that it positively improved, and a few Stiltons produced for vegetarians. When I tried two Stiltons of nearly the same age, one made with Chymosin and the other with traditional rennet, I marginally preferred the Chymosin version, which I thought had a creamier taste; however, the difference could have been due to other factors, such as the weather. According to Ernest, Stilton is especially sensitive to weather, or more particularly, humidity: 'Anybody can make Stilton cheese in September when it is dry outside.'

COLSTON BASSETT STILTON

Gold Medal, British Cheese Awards 1996 and 2001; Silver Medal, 1997 and 2002

A blue cows' cheese; full-fat, pasteurized milk; vegetarian and traditional rennet. 2.3kg/5lb cylinders and 7.2kg/16lb

The texture is creamy but not so moist as to be semi-soft, the blue deep and powerful, and (despite pasteurization) the cheese itself distinctive, with a strong herbal, almost spicy flavour: the herbal flavour lingers on the tongue as an aromatic aftertaste. As well as being a splendid cheese for the table, it keeps its flavour perfectly when heated and is exceptionally adaptable for cooking. It also freezes perfectly.

The milk comes from five farms in the district and is left to stand for twenty-four hours before pasteurization. Starter and *Penicillium roqueforti* are added when it has cooled to 30°C/86°F; after renneting, the curd is left to set for seventy minutes before being cut and left to settle for a further three hours. Whey is then drawn from the top of the vat and the curd ladled into cooling trays by hand – by hand because Ernest, like others, is emphatic about the importance of disturbing it as little as possible. It remains in the trays until the next morning; milling, salting, and moulding in tall moulds lined with 'bits' (cloths) at the bottom follow. For the next five days, it is turned and the 'bits' are renewed daily, after which the sides of the cheeses are smoothed by hand and left to dry further, with turning every day, for another three weeks: at this stage, the smoothed cheeses are deep butter-yellow, with a skin which looks like a thick coat of paint, and still contain sixteen per cent more moisture (which is needed by the *Penicillium*) than after they have matured. Piercing to supply the mould with extra air, which is repeated once and if necessary twice, is carried out at five to seven weeks, depending on acidity level; thereafter, the cheeses become covered with a film of calcium, which is drawn out as the pH rises and causes them to become progressively softer and creamier. Subsequently, they develop a crusty, almost rocky-looking brownish-gold rind. The maturing time is twelve weeks from when they are made: before being sent out, every cheese is ironed, i.e. a small piece is removed from the middle, to test for quality. Shropshire Blue is made in exactly the same way but with vegetarian rennet only and annatto, which gives it a deep marigold colour and mellower, slightly earthy flavour.

 ## Stilton Mashed Potato

You might not think of serving mashed potato as a first course, but the following is quite interesting enough to stand on its own. It can be prepared ahead of time.

Cooking times: 1 hour for the potato; 20 minutes to brown
For 3–4

450g/1lb baking potato or potatoes, e.g. Estima, Cara, King Edward
1 tbsp red wine vinegar
2 generous tbsp low-fat fromage frais
1½ tsp Dijon mustard
salt and pepper
140–150g/5–5¼oz Colston Bassett Stilton, crumbled or finely grated
watercress or chicory to garnish

Pre-heat the oven to 200°C/400°F/Gas 6. Wash the potatoes if they are muddy, prick them as a precaution against bursting, and bake for 1 hour, until they are soft all the way through. (Baking, although it takes longer, gives a lighter, drier result than boiling.) Halve and scoop out the flesh while the potato is still warm. Add the vinegar, fromage frais, mustard, about $^1/_3$ teaspoonful of salt, and a generous grinding of pepper, and mash the potato thoroughly; finally, mash in 100g/3$^1/_2$oz of the Stilton.

If the dish is prepared ahead of time, allow it to cool before chilling it; when needed, reset the oven to 200°C/400°F/Gas 6. Transfer the potatoes to individual ramekins or similar ovenware dishes and sprinkle the rest of the Stilton on top. Bake for 20 minutes or until brown. Serve surrounded with watercress or chicory.

Staffordshire Organic

BETTY, MICHAEL AND DAVID DEAVILLE, NEW HOUSE
FARM, ACTON, NEWCASTLE-UNDER-LYME, STAFFS,
ST5 4EE. TEL: 01782 680366

Acton is about 5km/3 miles to the west of the M6; directly opposite on the other side of the motorway are Newcastle-under-Lyme and Stoke-on-Trent. The motorway is effectually a green-belt boundary: Acton is small and rural, although prosperous and obviously a dormitory village, and New House Farm is surrounded by hills and woods. So far as I was concerned, the farm marked another boundary: Ulceby Grange in Lincolnshire (page 225) is in fact further north, but New House was the last I visited in England where a Cheddar-style cheese is made: after this, open-textured cheeses such as Cheshire, Lancashire, and Wensleydale prevail until one reaches Scotland.

When Betty married Michael, he did not farm organically but kept a dairy herd; he sold it soon afterwards, preferring to concentrate on meat, but kept a few 'house cows' for their own use. Some years later, when they became interested in converting to organic, Betty began to experiment with cheese as an added-value product, using milk from the house cows; never having made it before, she taught herself from books and did not attempt commercial production for some time. In 1984, however, they bought more cows, bringing the total to a dozen, and she went into business in a small way. The next year, they doubled the number of cows; in the third year, they started buying in milk and thereafter, like many others, gave up the herd in favour of the cheese. After a time David, who had been studying music, finished his course and joined them: he turned out to be a first-class cheesemaker and has now entirely taken over from his mother, leaving her to grow the herbs for the cheese and run their farm shop where, besides the hard cheese, they sell their own curd and cottage cheeses, delicious eggs (which are not registered as organic), meat, including occasional Gloucester Old Spot pork, and a range of organic wines.

The cheese is made once or twice a week with milk from an organic herd only a few miles down the road; the entire process is carried out by hand, which accounts for its fine, delicate texture but is extremely hard work. David said that if he made it every day, he would need an assistant.

When I visited him, he had just been offered a supply of organic sheep's milk and was planning a weekend with James Aldridge to decide what sort of cheese to make with it: as a result, he is now producing one of the only three hard organic sheep's cheeses made in Britain and Ireland (the others are Sussex Pecorino and some of the Duddleswells: page 22). However, he is currently developing another, St Thomas, which should be on the market by summer 2003.

STAFFORDSHIRE ORGANIC

Bronze Medal, British Cheese Awards 1997
An organic cows' cheese; full-fat, unpasteurized milk; vegetarian rennet.
1.4kg/3lb, 9kg/20lb and 18kg/40lb truckles

The cheese is distinguished by its fine-grained, velvet-like texture: at three months, when it is still fairly moist, it is mild and sweet, tasting of butter and a wide range of herbage, with a soft, fairly discreet tang; at six months the tang is more developed. At either age, it is an outstanding all-purpose table cheese, just as good for a quick lunch as on the cheeseboard.

As well as plain, it is made flavoured with wild garlic, chives, or apple-mint grown by Betty, or mixed dried organic herbs. Usually, I find that I prefer the plain version of a really good cheese such as this, but the flavourings are so beautifully balanced and suit the cheese so well that I can heartily recommend them all: particularly good are the mixed herbs and apple-mint (apple-mint is softer and sweeter than the usual spearmint). A smoked version, which is similarly smoked just enough to bring out the natural flavours of the cheese, is also available.

After adding starter and rennet, David cuts the curd to the size of peas and stirs and scalds it over thirty minutes to 40°C/104°F, or a few degrees lower in winter, when the cows are living on dried fodder and the curd is correspondingly drier. Stirring continues for another fifteen minutes before pitching (leaving to rest) and draining; blocking and piling follow. For this, David cuts the curd first into 25cm/10-inch squares, then into 5cm/2-inch strips which he piles eight or ten times: this takes about two hours. Salt is added during the final piling: he uses relatively little because his aim is only to bring out the natural flavours in the cheese rather than produce a salty tang. The curd is then put through a fine mill, moulded, and pressed at increasing pressure overnight, after which it is capped in muslin and pressed overnight again. On the third day the cheeses are wrapped entirely in muslin and left at 12–14°C/54–57°F for two weeks; finally they are moved to a cooler store and matured for a further three to six months.

WHITMORE

A hard sheep's cheese; unpasteurized organic milk; vegetarian rennet.
About 1.8kg/4lb truckles

The cheese has a fudgy, slightly gritty texture and combines a soft, smoky tang with a flavour of grass and flowers: the strength of the tang depends on its age. It is delicious on the cheeseboard, but also excellent for sprinkling, in the same way as pecorino.

Lincolnshire Poacher

Simon and Jeanette Jones, Ulceby Grange, Alford, Lincolnshire LN13 0HE. Tel: 01507 462407

Lincolnshire Poacher is remarkable for several reasons: besides winning the Supreme Championship at the 1996 British Cheese Awards, it is the only cheese made in Lincolnshire, part of which is fen and most of which, like the counties further south, is arable – and in fact, milk production at Ulceby is partnered by a large arable acreage. The farm, however, is at the southern tip of the Lincolnshire Wolds, where the country is undulating rather than flat and the soil lies over chalk, yielding milk with an enviable range of flavours; less satisfactory for dairying purposes is the low rainfall, which means that the grass tends to dry out in the summer.

Simon counters this by reversing the usual pattern and making cheese throughout the winter instead of the summer: from June to September, when relatively little milk is produced, he sells it directly. As was pointed out by his father, who used to sell all the milk in liquid form, a reduced yield in summer is economically advantageous because milk prices are then at their highest.

Another interesting feature of the cheese is that Simon was taught to make it by the late Dougal Campbell. To start with, Simon spent a week at Dougal's farm in Wales; later, Dougal came to make cheese with him at Ulceby. In between, he continued to act as Simon's mentor: 'He was always at the end of the telephone. It was really Dougal who inspired us and got us going.' As well as commitment to cheese, Simon share Dougal's belief in organic farming and set about converting Ulceby by degrees. In terms of the land, this is now complete, although the cheese is not yet fully organic.

Everything except the initial cutting of the curd is carried out by hand: Simon works with a full-time cheesemaker, Richard Tagg, an assistant who comes three days a week, and Jeanette, who makes cheese on Mondays. The cheese is made four days a week: Wednesday is given over to preparing the cheeses for sale. The Joneses not only go to local farmers' markets but on the last weekend of the month Simon, his sister, and Jeanette take the cheese to London, where each of them sells at a different market on Saturday and Sunday (e.g. Simon goes to Pimlico and Islington and Jeanette to Notting Hill and Palmer's Green).

LINCOLNSHIRE POACHER

*Gold Medal and Supreme Champion, British Cheese Awards 1996; Gold
Medal, 1997 and 2001; Bronze Medal, 2002
A Cheddar-style cows' cheese; full-fat, unpasteurized milk; vegetarian and
traditional rennet. 2.3kg/5lb 'Babies' and 18kg/40lb truckles*

A full-sized, eleven-month-old Poacher (the small ones mature
more quickly) and a two-year-old Vintage Poacher are almost different cheeses. In the younger, the taste of milk and herbage is still
very much to the fore, balanced but not overwhelmed by a sweet,
clean tang; the older has a much more pronounced tang, but the
milky flavour is overlaid. I took away a year-old 'Baby', unironed
and chosen by me solely for its mould pattern. If the cheese which
won the Championship was like this one – well, it deserved its
success. It was not only a beautiful cheese, but had that indescrib-
able soft, earthy overtone which sometimes characterizes matured
cheeses and, I think, makes them exceptional. It made us happy for
several weeks: I still mourn its passing.

The evening and morning milk, which is used while still warm
from the udder, are mixed, starter is added, and the milk is left to
ripen for an hour before renneting. When the curd has set, it is cut
to the size of baked beans over fifteen minutes: this is followed by
scalding to 40°C/104°F and stirring for one and a half to two
hours, 'until the curd is springy and squeaks between the teeth'.
After pitching (leaving it to rest) and draining, the curd is blocked
and piled three times at half-hourly intervals; it is then simultaneously milled and salted. The salt is rubbed in three times, which is
the hardest part of the whole process and demands a team of three.
This is followed by moulding, pressing for over forty-eight hours,
and finally coating the cheeses with a plastic cheese coating, which
protects them until they have grown their own firm rind. The
maturing time is eleven to twelve months for ordinary Poachers,
and up to two years for the Vintage cheeses.

CHAPTER 6

The North of England

KIRKHAMS LANCASHIRE

J. J. SANDHAM LTD

CARRON LODGE

RIBBLESDALE CHEESEMAKERS

WENSLEYDALE DAIRY PRODUCTS LTD

FORTMAYNE FARM DAIRY

SHEPHERD'S PURSE

SWALEDALE CHEESE CO.

COTHERSTONE

NORTHUMBERLAND SHEEP DAIRY

NORTH DODDINGTON FARM

Kirkhams Lancashire

JOHN AND RUTH KIRKHAM, BEESLEY FARM, GOOSNARGH,
PRESTON, LANCASHIRE. TEL: 01772 865335

There are some who maintain that plants need to be loved, even talked to, if they are to flourish: Ruth Kirkham loves her cheeses, along with her cows and the plants in the meadows where they graze. John sells the bullocks for beef but she has never been persuaded to eat any of them. Occasionally, to enhance the taste of the cheese, she goes out to plant extra meadowsweet; she also encourages dandelions and clover (rather than daisies, which she does not think add to flavour).

The country round Goosnargh is green and lush, not picturesque but surprisingly unspoilt, given that it is only about 6km/4 miles out of Preston and less than 3km/2 miles from the motorway. Beesley Farm is by no means as large as the fame of the cheese might lead one to expect: unlike the Applebys (page 199) or the large Cheddar-makers in the south, the Kirkhams have a modest herd of thirty-eight Friesians, who supply all their milk and, apart from the calves, are the only livestock they now keep. In today's economic climate, only the cheese enables them to survive. They employ no help: John looks after the cows and Ruth makes the cheese in a tiny but immaculately clean dairy. Every day, seven days a week, Christmas Day included, she processes an average of 450 litres/100 gallons of milk, yielding 52kg/114lb of cheese, which works out at two large cheeses and two small.

The storeroom smells of cheese and meadowsweet. As is often the case with Kirkham's Lancashire, all the mature cheeses were sold at the time of my visit, but I bought an 11kg/24lb, ten-week-old one to give to a relative in Shropshire as a wedding present. Having nowhere to mature it myself, I took it straight to his house, which has a large cellar. He stored it in a basket, and manfully turned it twice a week until, nearly three months later, it was cut and served at the wedding reception. Even amateur maturing had not spoilt it: it was superb.

KIRKHAM'S LANCASHIRE

Gold Medal and Supreme Champion, British Cheese Awards 1995; Gold Medal, 1996 and 1997
A semi-hard cows' cheese; full-fat, unpasteurized milk; traditional and vegetarian rennet. 1.4kg/3lb, 1.8kg/4lb, 2.7kg/6lb, 11kg/24lb, and 20.3kg/45lb truckles

Traditional Lancashire, known for its pale colour, crumbly texture, and excellent toasting properties, is made partly or entirely with curds that have been prepared one or more days previously: partly because of the crumbly result, this method of production has never been adopted by creameries, so that mass-produced Lancashire bears virtually no relation to the farmhouse original. The texture of Ruth Kirkham's is melting and delicate as well as crumbly; the taste is mild, flowery, and above all buttery, with no hint of sharpness or acidity. It is wonderful toasted or added to the pastry cream underneath the apples on a tart, or, as Ruth suggests, slipped under the lid of an apple pie.

She makes her Lancashire in exactly the same way as her mother and grandmother before her, using curd made on the previous two days. The first part of the morning's work is to prepare that day's curd. The morning and evening milk are mixed, heated to 29.5°C/85°F, and a very little cultured starter and rennet added. When the curd has set, after about an hour, it is cut into cubes and left to stand for another hour; the whey is then drained off and the curd scooped into a drainer lined with a cloth, where it is crumbled by hand three times, with half an hour between each session. This completes its preparation: it is then covered and set aside until the next day, when some of it is added to the previous day's curd.

The rest of the cheesemaking process is straightforward. The mixed two- and three-day-old curds are milled and salted, with sea-salt when available (the Kirkhams have difficulty in buying large amounts). At this stage, the curd is a mass of little white bobbles which already taste deliciously of cheese. Moulding and pressing follow; halfway through the pressing, the cheeses are covered in muslin with a drawstring top. Two or three days later, when the rinds are dry enough, they are sealed by rubbing them with melted butter. The maturing time is usually four to six months, although Neal's Yard Dairy sometimes keep them for up to eight.

 ## J. J. Sandham Ltd

CHRIS SANDHAM, ROSTOCK DAIRY, GARSTANG ROAD, BARTON, PRESTON, LANCS PR3 5AA. TEL: 01995 640247

Rostock Dairy is about 6km/4 miles from Beesley Farm (page 229) and Park Head at Inglewhite (page 234). As you realize as soon as you leave the main roads, this is the main dairying area of the north-west: both Beesley and Park Head are impossible to find without foolproof directions because the entire landscape is chequered with dairy farms (even with directions, I went to several before finding the right ones).

Several generations ago, the Sandham family were farmers, and almost certainly made cheese; however, the present dairy was founded by Chris's grandparents in 1930, using milk produced on farms nearby. As the Milk Marketing Board had not yet been formed, the milk was brought by private contract which, because the quantities were inflexible, led on occasion to over-production: Chris described how surplus cheeses were piled two deep at the sides of the staircase in the house and, when the staircase was fully stacked, in the sitting room; finally, if sales did not catch up with supply before they became too mature to keep, they were buried in the field at the back.

Chris continues the family tradition, using milk from farms within a 1.6-km/1-mile radius. As he does not produce the milk himself, he pasteurizes; apart from this and the use of vegetarian rennet, he uses the same recipe as his grandparents. It is not unlike Ruth Kirkham's but differs in three important respects: the curd is only two- rather than three-day, the cheeses are matured in wax, and the maturing times are four to five weeks for the mild or about fourteen for the 'Tasty' version.

SANDHAM'S LANCASHIRE

Creamy Traditional Lancashire, Silver Medal, British Cheese Awards 2001; Gold Medal, 2002; 'Tasty', Bronze Medal, 2002; 'Crumbly', Silver Medal, 2002
A semi-hard cow's cheese; wax rind; full-fat, pasteurized milk; vegetarian rennet.
450g/1lb, 1kg/2lb 4oz, 6.3kg/14lb, 9.9–10.4kg/22–23lb, and 18kg/40lb truckles

The mild version is very moist, with a fairly smooth, soft, creamy texture, to the point that it is almost semi-soft: the taste is warm and mellow but with a slight peppery tang which develops in the mouth and leaves a gentle aftertaste. 'Tasty' is drier and crumblier, with a more noticeable tang, although it is still warm and mellow rather than sharp. It melts smoothly and is delicious toasted, when its sweetness intensifies but the tang disappears: add a little crushed rather than ground pepper.

For the curd, the milk is 'flash' pasteurized (72°C/162°F for fifteen seconds), a traditional starter made and cultured at the dairy added, and the milk allowed to stand for 'as long as is needed', which is usually about fifteen minutes; rennet is stirred in for another fifteen minutes, and the curd is left to set for about fifty minutes. When sufficiently formed, the curd is cut to the size of baked beans, stirred and rested briefly, and drained; Chris and his assistants then divide it into two and break it by hand in six sessions at twenty-minute intervals. The half for use the next day is set aside and kept at 21°C/70°F: this dries it slightly and protects it from off-flavours. The half for immediate use is mixed with the previous day's curd, milled and salted, milled again, and moulded, after which it is pressed at increasing pressure for twenty-four hours (sudden strong pressure would cause uneven moisture distribution). Next day, the cheeses are turned out, bound in muslin, and briefly pressed again; finally they are dried in a drying room and waxed. All are turned daily during the maturing period, including the 'Tasties', which are kept for fourteen weeks.

As well as his regular Lancashire, Chris makes an organic version from Jersey milk and 'Crumbly', a quickly produced variation which is enormously popular: I had the impression that he did not expect me to like it, but I found it pleasantly mild and refreshing. The Jersey cheese, which he introduced last autumn, is made by the same method as his other Lancashires; for Crumbly, he uses a relatively enormous amount of starter, adds rennet and cuts the curd as before, and breaks it twice. It is then left at 21°C/70°F overnight; thereafter, it is milled and salted, pressed, and finally bound and waxed for consumption within twelve days.

Carron Lodge
ADRIAN RHODES, PARK HEAD FARM, CARRON LODGE,
INGLEWHITE, LANCS TEL: 01995 640352

As he himself admitted, Adrian could talk about cheese for days
on end; however, the two points he emphasized in a relatively
short space of time were that his first priority is the quality of the
milk and his second pleasing his customers, which he puts far
above selling to prestigious shops or even winning at shows
(although he has so many award certificates, kept in a large box,
that finding the ones for the British Cheese Awards proved to be
impossible).

Milk quality is taken care of by his herd of 250 elegant, high-
yielding Friesian–Holsteins, built up and cherished by his father
over the years. Pleasing his customers has led him into wholesaling
as well as making cheese: in consequence, his storerooms are a
wonderland of cheeses of every kind, ranging from his own
double-curd Lancashires to Ribblesdale (page 238), imported
smoked Brie, Wensleydale with blackberries, and a striped composition of different sorts of cheeses: 'very useful when people
can't make up their minds which to choose'. Altogether, he makes
fourteen kinds, including several variations of Lancashire,
Wensleydale, Sage Derby, Caerphilly, and a Cheshire which won
the Championship at the Cheshire Show despite not being made
within the prescribed area.

He is not sure how far cheese goes back in his family but his
great-grandmother, grandmother, and mother all made it; nor is he
the only only member of the family to keep up the tradition, since
the Singletons, also well-known makers of Lancashire, are rela-
tions. Initially, he tried to avoid cheese by going to university, and
subsequently tried to strike out in a new direction by taking
courses in ice-cream and soft cheesemaking; however, instinct

prevailed. He started his present business eleven years ago and was spectacularly successful right from the start. A helpful factor was that his father managed the farm and cows, leaving him free to concentrate on the cheese, until he retired three years ago and sold the farm to Adrian – for a fair price: muttering that he does not believe in inheritance, Adrian stressed that he did not take it on special terms but bought it just like anyone else.

The Lancashire is made according to the family recipe, which he preferred not to divulge; however, as he observed, its quality is due to many factors, including the cows, the rich, mixed soil on which the farm is situated, and in particular the fact that the cheese is not hurried. The total cheesemaking process is spread over five to six days: 'We take longer than anyone else. It is a low-acid cheese with a steady build-up which can't be rushed – that's what gives it its rich, creamy texture.'

CARRON LODGE LANCASHIRE

Gold Medal, British Cheese Awards 1994
A semi-hard cows' cheese (natural rind); full-fat, unpasteurized milk;
vegetarian rennet. 450g/1lb, 900g/2lb, and 10kg/22lb truckles; also
20kg/44lb 'Traditionals'

The cheese has a soft, light, nutty texture; the taste, like Sandham's, develops in the mouth. To start with, it seems innocuously mellow and mild, but as you eat it becomes full, fruity, and complex, with earthy undertones and quite a pronounced peppery tang. The overall effect is not exactly strong but vigorous and robust. It is totally different from Kirkham's but just as delicious in a more muscular way: it is a pity that it is not more widely available in the south.

MRS RHODES' FARMHOUSE TOASTER

A hard cows' cheese; full-fat, pasteurized milk; vegetarian rennet.
20kg/44lb 'Traditionals'

You could say that this is the opposite of Chris Sandham's
'Crumbly' (page 232). 'Toaster' originated with cheese which was
over-mature and had developed a strong, sharp tang: to start with,
it was sold at a discount, but, perhaps because a little went a long
way, soon became popular in its own right. Adrian has revived an
old recipe: raw, the cheese has an earthy rather than acidic tang;
heated, it becomes much sweeter but retains a strong distinctive
flavour.

Ribblesdale Cheesemakers

Chris and Iain Hill, Ashes Farm, Horton-in-
Ribblesdale, Settle, North Yorkshire. Tel: 01729
860231

Ashes Farm is high up in the Dales, an oasis of trees and (in
August) flowers on the bare moors, with a skyline of hills rising
from the Ribble valley in both directions. It is small and in parts
very old: the back of the farmhouse, where a hard buttermilk
cheese called Old Whangby was once made, dates from about
1660. The rooms are still used for cheese by the Hills, but because
of lack of space and the situation of the farm in the Dales National
Park, which means that further building is prohibited, the actual
making is now carried out further down the Ribble, at Longridge,
near Preston (in fact, it is quite near the Kirkhams: page 229).
However, every single cheese is sent to the farmhouse for inspec-
tion, waxing, and maturing before sale.

Iain is an engineer, and has also worked in retailing, which he found intensely dispiriting but is useful to him now. Cheesemaking was a hobby, which he would almost certainly never have developed further had it not been for one of his sons, force of need, and Chris. The son announced that he wanted to go into farming and make cheese: as part of setting him up, Iain invested in a herd of 300 goats. The son then changed his plans, leaving the goats and the disposal of the milk to Iain (who, until then, had been planning to retire). Iain first tried to sell the milk in liquid form, but because of competition succeeded only in the winter, when many of the rival herds were dry. Next, he tried yoghurt, but found himself delivering absurdly small orders enormous distances. The situation became so serious that 'we were down to only one car' (which if you live in a place like this has more meaning than to the rest of us). By then, however, he had married Chris, who is a cheesemaker: as they were warned that, again because of competition, very mild goats' cheese would be difficult to sell, she invented the recipe for Ribblesdale Original, which is relatively strong but with a smoky tang rather than the flavour of goat. This was followed by Ribblesdale Superior, plus smoked versions of both. To start with, Iain's other son, Adrian, smoked them himself over a mixture of oak and beech; although Adrian is no longer involved, the same mixture is still used. Iain's contributions are Ribblesdale Original Dairy Cheese, based on a Wensleydale recipe, and a buffalo cheese.

Part of the reason for the distinctive character of the goats' cheeses is the starter, which, like the rest of the recipe, is Chris's own; special care is also taken over applying the wax rinds with which they are coated. A crucial point about waxing is the moisture content of the cheese: traditionally, this was judged by placing the cheese on absorbent paper to see how much liquid was released. The goats' milk comes from St Helen's Farm in Yorkshire, the cows' from the Longridge area, and the buffalo milk from Warwickshire.

RIBBLESDALE ORIGINAL GOAT CHEESE

Bronze Medal, British Cheese Awards 1996
A hard goats' cheese; yellow wax rind; full-fat, pasteurized milk; vegetarian
rennet. 1.8kg/4lb wheels

Ribblesdale Original has a hard, dryish, slightly grained texture;
the taste is of smoke and peat, with a tang which makes it almost
the goat equivalent of matured pecorino. The taste of goat is
scarcely noticeable as such but adds to the strength of flavour.
Altogether it is interesting, punchy, and different – very much an
original. The smoked version is also very successful, chiefly
because the taste, which is delicate and slightly charcoal-like,
echoes the natural smokiness of the cheese.

RIBBLESDALE SUPERIOR GOAT CHEESE

A hard but moist goats' cheese; yellow wax rind; full-fat, pasteurized milk;
vegetarian rennet. 1kg/2lb 4oz half-wheels or 2kg/4lb 6oz wheels

The Superior Goat has a notably smooth, soft, creamy texture; it is
much milder than the Original, with (given pasteurization) a surprisingly wide range of herbal flavours. It is delicious with fruit or
nut breads, e.g. apricot or hazelnut. The smokiness of the smoked
version is more in evidence than with the Original because the
cheese itself is milder.

RIBBLESDALE ORIGINAL DAIRY CHEESE

A semi-hard cows' cheese; yellow wax rind; full-fat, pasteurized milk;
vegetarian rennet. 2kg/4lb 6oz wheels

The cows' cheese has a very delicate, crumbly texture with a mild,
sweet, creamy taste. Like white Wensleydale, its sweetness makes
it suitable for cheesecake, apple tart, and similar dishes.

Ribblesdale Lemon Cheesecake

This is as light and luscious as mousse: for the best texture, how-ever, you need a curd cheese sufficiently drained to hold its shape.

Cooking time: 7–8 minutes; allow at least 2 hours for setting and chilling
For 6–10

55g/2oz butter, chopped
100g/3¹/₂oz low-sugar digestive biscuits, finely crushed
25g/1oz hazelnuts, crushed
¹/₂ tsp ground ginger
150g/5¹/₄oz caster sugar
nutmeg
225g/8oz curd cheese
1 lemon, preferably organic (you need the zest)
125g/4¹/₂oz Ribblesdale Original Dairy cheese, finely grated
200ml/7fl oz (¹/₃ pint) whipping cream
1 tbsp brandy
9g/¹/₃oz gelatine

Pre-heat the oven to 200°C/400°F/Gas 6. Melt the butter over low heat and mix it with the biscuits, nuts, ginger, 25g/1oz (1 table-spoonful) of the sugar, and a little freshly grated nutmeg. Spread the mixture over the base of a 22cm/8¹/₂-inch tart dish, pack it down firmly, and smooth the surface with the back of a spoon. Crisp the base in the oven for 7–8 minutes, when you should be able to smell the spices. Allow it to cool completely.

Beat the curd cheese and the rest of the sugar until smooth. Wash the lemon and finely grate about half the zest into the cheese mixture; then add 2 tablespoonsful of the juice. Stir in the Ribblesdale.

Put 3 tablespoonsful of the cream and the brandy into a small saucepan and heat almost to boiling. Sprinkle in the gelatine, remove from the heat, and stir until it has dissolved completely. Allow it to cool a little before stirring it very thoroughly into the cheese mixture.

Whip the rest of the cream until it is very stiff and fold it gently into the cheese and gelatine. Spread the mixture evenly over the base and chill for at least 2 hours.

RIBBLESDALE BUFFALO CHEESE

A hard buffalo cheese; white wax rind; full-fat, pasteurized milk; vegetarian rennet.
1.8kg/4lb wheels

I tried two samples of the cheese, at four and eleven months old. The older one was rich and nutty, with a robust, grassy tang; the younger, which I preferred, has a wonderfully light, silky feel and is mild and creamy. It was excellent with fruit bread but would also go well with oatcakes.

Wensleydale Dairy Products Ltd
WENSLEYDALE CREAMERY, GAYLE LANE, HAWES, NORTH YORKSHIRE DL8 3RN. TEL: 01969 667664

The story of the Creamery is given in more detail in its own brochure than is possible here. In brief, however, it was effectually founded by a corn and cheese merchant called Edward Chapman, who delivered flour and corn to the local farms in return for cheese. Some of the cheese was so badly made that in 1897 he started to take milk instead and made the cheese himself, first in his flour mill, then in a converted woollen mill in Hawes. The creamery came to play a central role in the area, since the farmers at that end of the Dale were assured of an outlet for their milk and housewives, who might not be able to afford meat, could be confident of the quality of the cheese.

The creamery flourished until the Depression of the 1930s, when it ran into debt: it was almost bought by the Milk Marketing Board but was rescued by a farmer called Kit Calvert, who managed it successfully for over thirty years; he also bought up a number of dairies further east, including the original Fountains Dairy. As the time approached for him to retire, the Milk Marketing Board made a second offer and purchased both the dairies; Fountains regained its independence by means of a management takeover in 1987 and Hawes followed suit five years later. It is now not only successful in economic terms but has turned itself into a quite astonishingly popular tourist attraction. Visitors are catered for with a shop, coffee-shop, restaurant, and museum; a video illustrates the cheesemaking process, which can also be watched from a corridor with windows facing into the dairy. On a Saturday in August, the video-room was constantly packed and the windows overlooking the cheesemaking room lined with an audience two or three deep. As at Leon Downey's in Wales (page 167), everyone was enthralled. The staff at the Creamery have themselves been surprised at the response: originally, they say, they decided to open to the public simply in order to boost confidence in the product. 'People are so worried now about food: we thought that the best way to convince them that the cheese is exactly what it is supposed to be was to let them see it being made for themselves.'

Besides blue and white Wensleydale, the creamery produces flavoured versions of the white (waxed rinds: chives and onion, blueberry, cranberry, apricot, ginger, and fruit and nut), smoked, white cows' and sheep's combined, and small amounts of Red Leicester.

WHITE WENSLEYDALE (TRADITIONAL AND MATURE)

Bronze Medal (Mature), British Cheese Awards 1997
(Traditional), 2001 and 2002
A semi-hard cows' cheese; full-fat, pasteurized milk; vegetarian rennet.
Traditional: waxed rind, 250g/9oz truckles; cloth-bound, 400g/14oz,
500g/1lb 2oz, 900g/2lb, 2kg/4lb 6oz, 4kg/8lb 13oz, 4.5kg/10lb, and
6kg/13lb truckles; Mature: cloth-bound, 2.5kg/5lb 8oz and 4.5kg/10lb
truckles

The Traditional is moist and open-textured, with a very mild, fresh taste; the Mature is light and crumbly, with the sweet flavour which is characteristic of the area.

The milk comes from forty-three farms, all within 16km/10 miles of Hawes, and is flash pasteurized (72°C/162°F for fifteen seconds). When it has cooled, a cultured starter made at the Creamery is added and it is left to ripen for one and a half hours; after renneting, the curd takes forty to forty-five minutes to set, to a 'semi-soft junket'; it is then cut to the size of baked beans. This is followed by scalding slightly, stirring until the acidity has reached the desired level, and 'pitching', i.e. leaving the curd to settle. Next, the curds are drained, blocked, and moved to the sides of the vat to release further whey. The next step is 'cutting and ripping', which is crucial to the texture of the cheese and consists of slicing the curd into small squares with knives. The squares are forked over, salted and milled, moulded, and lightly pressed for twenty-four to seventy-two hours depending on size. Directly after unmoulding, all the cheeses except the smallest size of Traditional are wrapped in muslin, which is stuck to them with flour paste; finally, they are dried and turned daily for four or five days in a drying room. Traditional are matured for four to six weeks, Mature for twelve.

Wensleydale and Whisky Walnut Cake

The Yorkshire custom of eating Wensleydale (blue or white) with fruit cake has been followed up by Hawes with fruit and nut flavoured Wensleydale: I have turned this the other way round by using the cheese in a fruit and nut cake.

Like the cheese, the cake has a light, slightly crumbly texture; for maximum lightness, bake it in a 23cm/9-inch tin. You can also use the mixture for small cakes.

Cooking time: 35–40 minutes for a large or 20–25 for small cakes

150g/5¼oz butter, softened
200g/7oz caster sugar
2 large free-range eggs
zest of 1 lemon
1 tbsp whisky
150g/5¼oz Traditional or Mature Wensleydale, finely grated
150g/5¼oz walnuts, roughly chopped or crushed
100g/3½oz raisins
100g/3½oz sultanas
200g/7oz plain white flour
2 tsp bicarbonate of soda

Cream together the butter and sugar and beat in the eggs; continue to beat until the mixture is homogeneous. Stir in first the lemon zest and whisky, then the cheese, nuts, and fruit. Sift together the flour and bicarbonate of soda, add the sifted ingredients to the mixture, and stir thoroughly.

Pre-heat the oven to 150°C/300°F/Gas 2, butter the cake tin (use cake-papers for small cakes), and bake until the cake turns a deep brown and a knife inserted into the centre comes out clean. The cake is particularly enjoyable while still warm.

BLUE WENSLEYDALE

Silver Medal, British Cheese Awards 1996 and 1997; Bronze Medal, 2002
A blue cows' cheese; full-fat, pasteurized milk; vegetarian rennet.
2kg/4lb 6oz, 4kg/8lb 13oz and 8kg/17lb 10oz truckles

The Blue Wensleydale has a firm, slightly crumbly texture, a soft, sweet, aromatic flavour, and a moderately strong, deep rather than salty blue taste.

The cheese is made by a method about halfway between those used for the white version and Stilton. *Penicillium roqueforti* for the blue is added a little while after the starter; like Stilton, the curds and whey are left undrained for some hours but, unlike Stilton, the cheeses are lightly pressed. Piercing is carried out at about five weeks; the maturing time is four months or more.

WENSLEYDALE EWES' AND COWS' (WHITE)

A semi-hard combined sheep's and cows' cheese; full-fat, pasteurized milk; vegetarian rennet.
500g/1lb 2oz, 2.5kg/5lb 8oz, and 5kg/11lb truckles

The texture is short, open, and slightly crumbly; the taste is mild and flowery, with a soft, lemon-like tang and definite undertone of the moors: a delicious cheese.

Fortmayne Farm Dairy

Suzanne Stirke, Fortmayne Cottage, Newton-le-Willows, Bedale, North Yorkshire DL8 1SL.
Tel: 01677 450660

Almost the first thing Suzanne said to me was 'I'd rather be described as a business woman than a cheesemaker. I'm here to make money, I'm not here to make cheese.' That she might choose cheesemaking as her way of making 'just a little' money is natural enough, since she is a farmer's daughter and a farmer's wife; however, she did not start just because the milk was there (which it was not in the usual sense) but because she had already become fascinated by the history and social significance of cheese. This has led her to become a popular speaker, giving lectures locally and appearing from time to time on TV.

She decided to follow up her academic interest by actually making cheese when she realized that Wensleydale was originally made with sheep's milk, which on the face of it suited her because her husband and brother raise sheep. The sheep had never been milked, and the flock did not include the higher-yielding breeds (e.g. Frieslands), but were divided into two groups, one for early lambing from whom the lambs were taken before the mothers were dry. She tried milking some of these, which with the untrained ewes was extremely hard, slow work, and after persisting for two years still found that milking took so long that there was no time left to make the cheese. She therefore abandoned the idea of using the sheep and instead developed her cheeses with bought cows' milk. Determined not to let cheesemaking dominate her whole life, she now makes cheese twice a week; to start with, she made it on her farm, but now works in a separate dairy. At present, she makes only the one cheese, a white Wensleydale which she has named King Richard III because Richard III was brought up at

Middleham Castle, only a few miles away. The name is confusing in that the cheese is white whereas in Richard III's day it would have been blue: however, she is remedying this with a Blue King Richard III, which at the time of writing is still under development but will be on sale very soon.

KING RICHARD III WENSLEYDALE

A semi-hard cows' cheese; full-fat, unpasteurized milk; vegetarian rennet. 500g/1lb 2oz and 2.3–2.7kg/5–6lb truckles

Like the double-curd Lancashires, this is a cheese truly described by the term 'semi-hard': it is moist, crumbly, and nutty yet creamy in texture, almost like a moist, rich but light cake. The taste is a blend of gentle flavours which includes a distinct hint of the local limestone soil. It steals on you rather than rushes at you: even those with a preference for strong cheeses acknowledge its quiet, low-key appeal.

Suzanne adds rennet an hour after the starter, leaves the milk for another hour to set, and chops the curd coarsely; she then stirs it for fifteen minutes, leaves it to settle for about forty-five, and runs off the whey. Next, she blocks and piles it to assist draining and leaves it to rest again for about half an hour. This is followed by milling, salting, and breaking up the curd by hand before moulding (without cloths). After moulding the cheese for the first time, she washes up the cheesemaking equipment before turning and remoulding them (still without cloths). The next day, she turns and moulds them in cloths; on the third day she turns them again, and on the fourth brines them briefly and wraps them in muslin, using an edible, starch-based glue which inhibits the growth of mould. The usual maturing time is three weeks, but some of the cheeses are made for storing longer: to ensure that they stay moist, Suzanne does not block and pile the curd for these but mills it directly after draining. Similarly, she encourages the development of a harder, 'bloomy' rind by extending brining from a brief dip to two days.

Shepherd's Purse

JUDY BELL, LEACHFIELD GRANGE, NEWSHAM, THIRSK, NORTH YORKSHIRE YO7 4DL. TEL: 01845 587220; FAX: 01845 587717

In the fourteen years since Judy went into business, Shepherd's Purse has gone from strength to strength. Aside from the cheeses themselves, there are obvious reasons for its success, one of which is Judy's vigorous and imaginative approach to marketing. The need for it was obvious to her from the beginning, since when she started out, in 1989 (the year of the Festival of Food and Farming in Hyde Park), prejudice against sheep's products was still very marked. When she took her cheeses to shows, 'everything went swimmingly *until* people noticed the pictures of sheep with the cheese – then all at once they would stop and look horrified. They equated it with goat and were convinced that it would be horrible. They thought that they only liked cows' cheese.' The change that has taken place over the last six or seven years she describes as 'incredible', but easier sales have produced other problems, notably how to ensure that her cheeses are properly treated in supermarkets. The policy she has adopted gives pleasure all round. She invites the staff, in parties of not more than fifteen, to come to the dairy and watch the cheese being made, gives them a tasting of all the kinds produced, and inspires them with her own enthusiasm;

only the Tesco staff, she says, are fairly well primed because of the efforts of Juliet Harbutt, whose help in this and other ways she very freely acknowledges.

In fact, it was customers' needs which originally pointed her towards cheese. Ever since working at a chemist's before she married, she has believed in holistic medicine rather than drugs; then, when her youngest child went to nursery school, she took a job as receptionist at an osteopath's and was struck by the number of people who are allergic to cows' milk. Initially, she saw sheep's products as mainly for this market, and sold not only cheese but yoghurt and milk. As her husband is a farmer and was used to managing sheep, raising a milking flock presented no difficulties: she bought forty British Friesland lambs plus eight lactating ewes and spent the summer practising milking the ewes. As she did not know how to make cheese, she used some of the milk to help out her Rhodesian Ridgeback bitch, who had eleven puppies, and froze the rest.

The next summer, like Suzanne Stirke (page 245), she discovered that it is almost impossible for one person alone to milk and make cheese: she therefore froze her entire output until the winter, when the sheep were dry. After taking a cheesemaking course in Devon, she experimented intensively all through the winter, during which, like everyone else, she became hooked; however, still feeling 'in a bit of a fog', she joined a food and drink producers' group called the Yorkshire Pantry, where she met the late Les Lambert, then the cheesemaking director at Fountains Dairy. He gave her three pieces of advice: to revive the original sheep's Wensleydale, to produce a range of cheeses rather than just one, and to go to shows so that she became known and could gauge customers' reactions at first hand.

The range she has developed includes not only white sheep's Wensleydale but two blue Wensleydales, a sheep's and a cows', which were effectually revivals too, since at that time blue as opposed to white Wensleydale had similarly lapsed: she can thus fairly be said to have reinvented the original Wensleydale (until the end of the last century, Wensleydale was always blue). In addition, she has recently introduced two new blue cheeses, a creamy, relatively mild cows' cheese, Shire Blue, and a buffalo cheese, Buffalo Blue. The other Shepherd's Purse cheeses are a Cheddar-style cheese called Yorkshire Lowlands, feta, and plain and flavoured versions of a fresh sheep's cheese, Olde York. She says that Olde York was often made in the 1920s and '30s, but only for domestic use or local sale because of its perishability: she overcomes this by waxing, which increases its shelf-life from ten days to six weeks. For four or five years she produced her own milk, but partly because of bereavement she dispersed her flock in 1994 and now buys milk from wherever it is available, which in turn has led her to pasteurize. She works with her son and husband, who keeps the accounts, and a cheesemaker called Mark whose grandfather used to be the chief cheesemaker at Fountains, and an assistant: in 1996 they processed 4,500 litres/nearly 1,000 gallons of milk a week and have recently won two Gold Medals at the British Cheese Awards.

THE ORIGINAL FARMHOUSE WENSLEYDALE

A semi-hard sheep's cheese; wax rind; pasteurized milk; vegetarian rennet. 250g/9oz and 1.5kg/3lb 5oz rounds

The Original Wensleydale has a moist, flaky, open texture and is very mild; the sweetness of the milk is offset by a gentle, lemon-like tang.

After the addition of starter and rennet, the curd is cut fairly coarsely (sheep's milk tends to dry out if cut finely); it is then stirred and left to settle, the acidity checked, and all but enough of the whey to bring the acidity to the correct level run off. When the right acidity is reached, the curd is milled and salted, moulded, and lightly pressed overnight. The maturing time for most of the cheeses is two months, but a longer-matured version is also made which is constantly turned rather than pressed.

YORKSHIRE BLUE

Bronze Medal, British Cheese Awards 1996 and 1997
A blue cows' cheese; full-fat, pasteurized milk; vegetarian rennet.
3kg/6lb 10oz rounds

Yorkshire Blue has a soft, creamy texture; its medium strong, slightly salty blue taste contrasts with the sweetness of the cheese itself, which is typical of the area. The effect is rich but fresh, delicate, and altogether softer and lighter than either Stilton or the stronger sheep's version.

As the sweetness of the cheese suggests, the milk, although not produced by the Bells themselves, comes from nearby. None of the Shepherd's Purse blue cheeses is called Wensleydale because the farm is not in the Dale but the Vale of York (besides the fact that the sheep's milk is no longer from the area); also, Judy had a problem over the method. As no blue Wensleydale had been made for some time, she could not find a local recipe: after experimenting on her own, she ended up with a few 'brilliant' failures, and therefore adopted the Roquefort method (from which Wensleydale is in fact descended). For all the cheeses, *Penicillium roqueforti* is added to the milk with the starter; after renneting, the curd is left to set for an hour, cut, and allowed to stand until the acidity starts to rise. It is then ladled directly into tall, chimney-pot moulds (which are actually pieces of drainpipe) and turned three times on the first day and twice on the second. The cheeses are then unmoulded, rubbed with salt, and left in a drying room until piercing four or five days later: Judy now has a machine, but until two years ago they were stuck with skewers in the old-fashioned way. Four weeks later they are wrapped in foil to inhibit further blueing; the total maturing time is about three months.

SHIRE BLUE

A blue cows' cheese; full-fat, organic pasteurized milk; vegetarian rennet. 125g/4½oz wedges

This is a consummate cheese: in particular, the texture is remarkably smooth and creamy, making it a real semi-soft cheese (blue cheeses are usually classified as such but are often not in fact as soft as that suggests). The blue, because of the properties of the milk, is fairly mild, which makes it a good choice for the cheeseboard, since you can eat it and still appreciate the other cheeses which may be served.

MRS BELL'S BLUE

Bronze Medal, British Cheese Awards 1996; Gold Medal, 1997 and 2001
A blue sheep's cheese; pasteurized milk; vegetarian rennet. 3kg/6lb 10oz rounds

In the past, the cheese was sometimes seriously strong, but recently Judy has achieved the perfect balance between the blue and the actual cheese, which is gloriously rich, creamy, and sweet. It is now as good a blue as you will find anywhere, both for the cheeseboard and for cooking.

Yorkshire Blue and Chicken Mousse with Watercress

The mousse has a frothy, melting texture which is achieved entirely by means of whipping cream, without raw egg white. You can use pre-cooked chicken (e.g. from that used for the stock), but freshly poached breasts will give a smoother texture.

Cooking time: 30 minutes; allow 3–4 hours for the mousse to set
For 6–8 as a first course

150g/5¼oz skinned chicken breasts, washed
600ml/1 pint strong chicken stock (page xxvii)
salt
200ml/7fl oz (⅓pint) dry white wine
½ tsp Cayenne pepper
15g/½oz (1 sachet) gelatine
225ml/8fl oz whipping cream
50g/1¾oz watercress, washed, left to dry, and shredded, plus a little
    extra for garnishing
2 or 3 spears dill, washed and finely chopped
6 spring onions, peeled and finely sliced
100g/3½oz Yorkshire Blue sheep's cheese, finely grated

Poach the chicken in the stock with a pinch of salt for 25–35 minutes or until it is tender and no pink liquid emerges when it is pierced in the thickest part. Keep it covered as it cooks and allow the stock to simmer only very gently (if the chicken is boiled instead of simmered, it will be tough). Leave the chicken to cool; keep the stock to hand.

In another pan, reduce the wine to about a third of its original volume. Add the stock with 1 teaspoonful of salt and the Cayenne. Bring it to the boil, allow it to cool for a moment or two, and sprinkle in the gelatine: stir until it has dissolved. Leave the mixture to become cold and chill it for 2–2½ hours, until it has half-set.

Stiffly whip the cream and keep it chilled until needed. Dice the chicken as finely as possible. Mix together the watercress, dill, onions, and cheese and stir in the half-set stock; gently fold in the cream. Chill the mousse for at least another hour and serve it decorated with extra watercress.

BUFFALO BLUE

A blue buffalo cheese; full-fat, pasteurized milk; vegetarian rennet.
125g/4½oz wedges

Like Shire Blue, this is a relatively mild, genuinely semi-soft blue, although because of the richness of the buffalo milk, it is more compact and hence slightly less creamy than Shire.

YORKSHIRE LOWLANDS

A hard sheep's cheese, either wrapped in muslin or with a red wax rind;
pasteurized milk; vegetarian rennet. 280–350g/10–12oz and
1.4–1.8kg/3–4lb rounds

Yorkshire Lowlands is a moist cheese with a satisfyingly nutty, slightly gritty texture. The taste is sweet and similarly nutty, freshened with a faint citrus tang.

The milk is left for an hour after the addition of starter and fifty to ninety minutes (depending on the weather) after renneting. The curd is cut moderately finely, stirred and scalded by about 7°C/45°F (9°C/48°F for muslin-wrapping), and most of the whey drained off; the rest is removed when the acidity has risen sufficiently. It is then blocked and piled at the sides of the vat, milled, salted, moulded, and pressed hard overnight; finally, the cheeses are wrapped or coated with wax, and matured for six months.

YORKSHIRE FETA

Gold Medal, British Cheese Awards 1996; Silver Medal, 2002
A soft sheep's cheese with a green/natural wax rind; pasteurized milk;
vegetarian rennet. 300g/10½oz and 1.8kg/4lb rounds

The cheese is soft, rough, and nutty, with a pleasantly sharp, citrus taste; unlike traditional feta, it is not particularly salty and can be served or used for cooking directly, without soaking. It is excellent for salads and dishes such as stuffed aubergine, spinach pie, or on top of roast vegetables.

Feta is customarily preserved in brine, which was (and still is) convenient in a hot climate: instead Judy's is rubbed twice with dry salt and, like the other non-blue Shepherd's Purse cheeses, preserved by waxing. Starter and rennet are added and the curd left to set for fifty or more minutes: it is then cut, stirred, and allowed to settle. Thereafter, it is moulded and left to drain for thirty-six hours before being salted and waxed.

OLDE YORK

Silver Medal, British Cheese Awards 1996 and (Garlic) 1997
A fresh, soft sheep's cheese; wax rind; pasteurized milk; vegetarian rennet.
450g/1lb rounds

Olde York is very light but, like Judy's Feta, with a slightly textured, nutty feel. It comes plain or flavoured with green peppercorns, chives, parsley and garlic, or mint. The plain is mild but with a herbal tang just strong enough to give it interest; peppercorns add zest, and chives strengthen the flavour considerably. It develops quite a strong lemon-like tang when heated and is delicious fried in egg and breadcrumbs (page xxix): serve the plain version with red-currant jelly or the herb flavours with salad.

This cheese is made very simply by the free-draining Coulommiers method. After the addition of starter and rennet, the curd is left to set for fifty minutes or longer, according to the weather, and ladled directly into the moulds. The cheeses are then turned three times on both that and the following day, rubbed with salt, and left to absorb it for two hours at room temperature before being chilled, shaped, and waxed.

Swaledale Cheese Co.

DAVID REED, SWALEDALE CHEESE CO., MERCURY ROAD, RICHMOND DL10 4TQ. TEL: 01748 824932

Like Judy Bell (page 247), David's success with Swaledale has been remarkable. He puts it down to luck, although others attribute it to hard work; either way, it was only by coincidence that he came to make cheese at all. He started out as a chef: after training, he went to the Black Bull Inn at Moulton (about equally known for seafood and a dining room in a stranded Pullman railway carriage). After five years, feeling that it was time to move on, he left and took a job as development chef with a large company; by then, he had also married. Four days before his first child was due, he was made redundant: thus when he stopped at the Black Bull on the way home from the hospital to tell the staff that he had a daughter, he was 'rather desperately' wondering what to do.

Aside from fish, one of the specialities of the Black Bull was

Swaledale cheese, which was so popular that customers who ordered it often ended up buying whole cheeses to take away. Until that time, it had been made by a Mrs Wagstaff and her husband; however, it so happened that Mr Wagstaff had just died and his widow, feeling unable to continue with it alone, had given up. David went to see her and persuaded her to give him the recipe.

His training as a chef perhaps helped him to master the cheese quickly; however, he puts special emphasis on the fact that he took it over at exactly the right time. 'We started making Swaledale just when there was a cheese boom, 1986–7, when gourmets and cheese-sellers were touring Britain looking for native cheeses.' Randolph Hodgson of Neal's Yard Dairy seized on it at once: 'We were made.' Within eighteen months, David was able to buy the unit in Richmond where his dairy still is. He now makes Swaledale not only with cows' and sheep's milk but also with goats', plus smoked and flavoured versions, and Beamish, a crumbly cheese made at the Beamish Open Air Museum near Chester-le-Street, a little further north, where the dairy is open to the public. When I went to see him, he was hoping to make a new soft cheese but felt that for a soft cheese, where the quality of the milk is especially important, it was essential that he produced the milk himself. He was then living in rented accommodation because he had made an offer for a suitable farm and sold his house. The purchase fell through and he later bought another house, but without a farm, so that the cheese was put on hold. However, he started to experiment with a blue cheese instead, and has now produced Blue Swaledale, which won a Gold Medal and the trophy for the Best Blue Cheese at last year's (2002) British Cheese Awards. He has also introduced an organic version of the plain (cows') Swaledale.

SWALEDALE COWS'

Silver Medal, British Cheese Awards 2001; Bronze Medal
(Swaledale Organic) 2002
A semi-hard cows' cheese; full-fat, pasteurized milk; vegetarian rennet.
225g/8oz, 450g/1lb, and 2–2.5kg/4lb 6oz–5lb 8oz truckles; Richmond
Peculiar: 450g/1lb and 6kg/13lb 3oz truckles; Richmond Smoked:
450g/1lb and 1.6kg/3lb 8oz truckles

Swaledale Cows' has a moist, soft, deliciously melting texture: it
dissolves to cream on the tongue. The taste is mild but with a
gentle herbal sharpness and definite overtone of the moors. The
flavoured versions are garlic and herbs, apple-mint, and Richmond
Peculiar (with a black rind), for which the curd is soaked in
Theakston's Old Peculiar Ale: the mint is subtle and delicate, the
garlic and herbs stronger, and the Old Peculiar Ale definitely evident. The smoked version, Richmond Smoked (red wax rind) is
smoked over oak and applewood: the taste is mild and the texture
pleasantly moist and nutty.

Like that from Cotherstone (see page 259) the Swaledale recipe is
very similar to Wensleydale. The gentle, melting texture of the
cheese, which is part of its particular attraction, can only be
achieved by making it entirely by hand. About eighty per cent of
the plain and herb-flavoured cheeses have natural rinds, but David
waxes a few to protect them from storage at the wrong temperature (some customers also favour wax because it avoids wastage
when cutting off the rind).

SWALEDALE EWES'

Silver Medal, British Cheese Awards 1997
A semi-hard sheep's cheese; pasteurized milk; vegetarian rennet. 225g/8oz,
450g/1lb, and 2–2.5kg/4lb 6oz–5lb 8oz truckles

Like the cows', the sheep's version of the cheese has a soft, moist texture; the mild but beautifully balanced taste is just salty enough to offset a gentle herbal tang. The milk is not necessarily local but apparently comes from moorland areas: three samples bought at different times and places tasted unmistakeably of heather.

SWALEDALE GOATS'

A hard goats' cheese; full-fat, pasteurized milk; vegetarian rennet.
225g/8oz, 450g/1lb, and 2–2.5kg/4lb 6oz–5lb 8oz truckles

In contrast to the other two, the goats' cheese has a compact, almost grainy, satisfyingly nutty texture. It tastes subtly of flowers and the moors, with a suggestion of peat. I think it is delicious.

BEAMISH

A semi-hard cows' cheese; natural rind; full-fat, pasteurized milk;
vegetarian rennet. 450g/1lb truckles

Beamish is moist and crumbly rather than creamy, with a mild, sweet, flowery taste: in fact, it is very like a handmade white Wensleydale. It goes well with fruit, e.g. bananas.

THE NORTH OF ENGLAND

Cotherstone

JOAN CROSS, QUARRY HOUSE, MARWOOD, BARNARD
CASTLE, CO. DURHAM DL12 9QL. TEL: 01833 650351

As you drive north from Richmond, the country becomes larger-scale, with long ranges of hills spaced by wide valleys. Quarry Farm is in a stunning situation, nearly 300m/1,000 feet up on the edge of a dramatic drop overlooking a view south towards the Dales. The farm is quite small but orderly and as clean as if it had just been vacuumed, which Joan said is because they have given up their dairy herd and now raise stock only for meat, so that the cows no longer come in twice a day for milking. The other particularly striking feature about it was the garden, which glowed with pinks, oranges, and reds worthy of David Hockney.

Like Mrs Appleby and Ruth Kirkham (pages 206 and 229), Joan was brought up to cheesemaking and, although she did not practise it for a time after she married, has produced a steady supply of Cotherstone for over twenty-five years. Everyone in the area (as in the Dales) used to keep a cow and make cheese, including Joan's mother, who took it for granted that as long as Joan was living at home, she would help. When she married, Joan thought, 'Thank goodness I won't have to make cheese any more' – but, as her husband is a farmer, she naturally went back to it rather than see surplus milk go to waste. She used their own milk for many years but now buys it from a particular farm via Northern Milk. She does not make cheese continuously but in bursts, whenever the storeroom looks empty: at the time of our visit, she had just finished a ten-day run.

Except for the use of starter and vegetarian rather than natural rennet, she makes the cheese in exactly the same way as her mother. As with Swaledale, the recipe is similar to that for Wensleydale and depends for its texture on being completely handmade. Next to her dairy is a long room, or barn, containing twenty-two cheese-presses, all local and all at least 100 years old, many of which, after her recent run, were in use. In the store-room, since she has no humidity control, the cheeses are kept moist by wrapping them in damp cloths. The cooler the weather, she says, the better the cheese: 'Mind you, we don't get many heat waves up here, so it isn't a problem.'

COTHERSTONE

A semi-hard cows' cheese; wax or natural rind; full-fat, unpasteurized milk; vegetarian rennet. 450g/1lb, 900g/2lb, and 2.7kg/6lb rounds

Like Swaledale, the texture is irresistibly moist, soft, and creamy, melting in the mouth like mousse or the very finest shortbread. The taste is mild and sunny, with a fresh, gentle tang and hints of grass, flowers, and herbs. With recipes in mind, I bought the largest size while I was there; however, we were going on to stay with friends in Scotland, and before I had had time to think about cooking, every delicious crumb was gone.

Northumberland Cheese Co.

MARK ROBERTSON, THE CHEESE FARM, GREEN LANE, BLAGDON, SEATON BURN, NORTHUMBERLAND, NE13 6BZ. TEL: 01670 789798

When Mark moved to his present farm, it was called Make Me Rich, apparently because the soil is sandy loam, which was easily worked with a horse-drawn plough and yielded early harvests. Before moving there, he had made cheese for twelve years at

Soppitt Farm, only 24km/15 miles from the Scottish border: Make Me Rich is less than 16km/10 miles from Newcastle upon Tyne. The new dairy is four times as big as the old; there is a shop with windows overlooking the cheesemaking area, and a tea- and coffee-shop, where dishes made with the Northumberland cheeses are served. The dairy was converted at a cost of £15,000, with the aid of grants from the Department of Trade and Industry and the Ministry of Agriculture, Fisheries and Food (as it was then): the second of these was to enable him to recruit a board of non-executive directors, which he especially values because it means that instead of being alone, he has the support of a group of people with an interest in the business. The scheme has parallels with the cooperative formed by Plaw Hatch and Tablehurst Farms (page 17).

Originally, Mark was a sheep-farmer; he was tempted into cheese by Olivia Mills's book (page 9) and eventually gave up the sheep in favour of the cheese. When I visited him five years ago, all his milk was bought, as is still the case; however, he now uses sheep's milk from the Blagdon estate, where his farm is situated. Altogether, he makes nine different cheeses, including Elsdon and Brinkburn, which are goats', Redesdale, a sheep's cheese, and five cows' cheeses, one of which, a soft, mould-ripened cheese called Chevington, is made to a recipe over 100 years old. In addition, his signature cheese, Northumberland, comes in a number of different flavours (chives, garlic, chilli, nettle, and smoked as well as plain).

REDESDALE

A hard sheep's cheese; pasteurized milk; vegetarian rennet.

Redesdale has a velvety texture with a few small holes. The taste is beautifully balanced and strong enough to be bracing, like the invigorating Northumbrian air, with quite a strong, salty tang and slightly peppery aftertaste. It is excellent for cooking, since it keeps its flavour when hot and can be used as an alternative to pecorino for sprinkling.

 Cod and Redesdale Fish Cakes with Chives

The cakes can be made a day in advance. Serve with a tomato sauce.

Cooking time: 1 hour (potato only)
Makes 8–9 cakes

250g/9oz (1 small) baking potato, e.g. Estima, Cara, Marfona, washed
250g/9oz cod, washed, skinned, and boned
salt and pepper
1 large, or 2 small (85g/3oz) shallot/s, peeled and very finely chopped
1 small handful chives, washed and very finely snipped
175g/6oz Redesdale, finely grated
25–30g/1–1¼oz white flour
1 large free-range egg, beaten
55g/2oz finely grated fresh breadcrumbs
oil for frying

Pre-heat the oven to 200°C/400°F/Gas 6. Prick and bake the potato for an hour, until it is soft all the way through. As soon as it is cool enough to handle, peel it or scoop out the inside, discarding the hardened flesh next to the skin.

Season the fish lightly with salt and pepper and wrap it in a parcel of cooking foil. Bake the fish at the same temperature as the potato for 12 minutes or until it flakes easily with a fork and is opaque all the way through. Thoroughly drain and mash it with the potato, a little salt, and rather more pepper. Stir in first the shallot and chives, then the cheese.

Spread the flour over a plate and season it moderately with salt and pepper. Crack an egg into a bowl or saucer and season it. Spread the breadcrumbs over another plate. Form the fish mixture into cakes and coat them very thoroughly with the flour, egg, and crumbs, making sure that the entire surface is covered but shaking off any surplus. Warm the oil over fairly high heat and fry the cakes until golden on both sides. Serve at once.

ELSDON

Bronze Medal, British Cheese Awards 1997
A hard goats' cheese; full-fat, pasteurized milk; vegetarian rennet.
850g/1lb 14oz and 3kg/6lb 10oz truckles

Elsdon has a deliciously smooth, soft, sometimes almost semi-soft texture; the taste is mild and creamy, with virtually no trace of goat.

BRINKBURN

Gold Medal, British Cheese Awards 2001; Bronze Medal, 2002
A hard goats' cheese; full-fat, pasteurized milk; vegetarian rennet.
365g/12½oz truckles and 2.4 kg/5lb 4½oz rounds

Brinkburn too is notable for its light, caressing texture and in this case the complete absence of the flavour of goat; instead, it tastes predominantly creamy, with gentle herbal undertones.

NORTHUMBERLAND

Bronze Medal, British Cheese Awards 1997 (Smoked) and 2002 (Plain)
A hard cows' cheese; full-fat, pasteurized milk; vegetarian rennet.
450g/1lb, 1kg/2lb 4oz, 3kg/6lb 10oz and 10kg/22lb truckles

Like Elsdon, part of the attraction of Northumberland is its smooth, creamy, melting texture, which contrasts interestingly with a pronounced herbal flavour and crisp, bracing northern tang. It comes plain, smoked, or flavoured with nettles or chives: necessarily, the herb-flavoured versions have a slightly less smooth, creamy feel than the original and although apparently more popular, I think are less successful.

 ## Northumberland Potato Omelette

This omelette is quick rather than elegant, but it is totally delicious, mainly because of the cheese.

Cooking time: about 15 minutes
For 2

1 medium onion (about 150g/5¼oz), peeled and thinly sliced
150g/5¼oz waxy new potatoes (e.g. Charlotte), scrubbed or peeled
     and very thinly sliced; if peeled, use slightly more
2 tbsp virgin olive oil
salt and pepper
3 cloves garlic, peeled and thinly sliced
1 green pepper, washed, cored and with seeds removed, cut into thin
     half-rings
3 large free-range eggs, beaten and seasoned moderately with salt
     and pepper
100g/3½oz plain Northumberland cheese, very thinly sliced
hot brown bread for serving

Put the onion and potatoes into a large wok or frying pan with the oil, season moderately with salt and pepper, and fry over medium heat, turning constantly, for about 2 minutes. Add the garlic and green pepper and fry for about another minute; then reduce the heat to very low. Cover and cook for 8–10 minutes or until all the vegetables are soft, turning them from time to time. Raise the heat a little and continue to cook the vegetables until the potato and onion begin to show traces of gold. Beat and pour in the eggs; raise the heat a little more, tilt the pan, and push back the egg as it sets so that the part which is still liquid runs to the bottom. When most of it has set, spread the cheese on top. Continue to cook until the bottom is firm and golden and the top has just set; cut the omelette in half, fold it gently (it is very thick but folds easily) and serve it with hot brown bread.

COQUETDALE

Bronze Medal, British Cheese Awards 1997 and 1998
A hard cows' cheese; full-fat, pasteurized milk; vegetarian rennet.
650g/1lb 7oz and 2kg/4lb 6oz truckles

Coquetdale has a similar creamy, melting texture to North-umberland, but instead of the fairly robust tang of both Northumberland and Redesdale, a mild, fresh taste of grass and herbs.

CHEVINGTON

Bronze Medal, British Cheese Awards 2001
A semi-soft Jersey cheese; full-fat, pasteurized milk; vegetarian rennet.
300g/10oz truckles; 1.25kg/2lb 9oz rounds

This has a lovely, gentle feel on the tongue and tastes chiefly of butter, overlaid with a mild, grassy tang.

CHEVIOT

A hard cows' cheese; full-fat, pasteurized milk; vegetarian rennet.
125g/4½oz wedges, 400g/14oz truckles, or 2.4kg/5lb 4½oz rounds

This is rather different from the other cheeses in having a pleasantly short, fudgy, slightly nutty texture and a soft northern tang.

North Doddington Farm

NEILL MAXWELL, NORTH DODDINGTON FARM, WOOLER, NORTHUMBERLAND NE71 6AN. TEL: 01668 282081

North Doddington is a very large mixed farm: the need for specialization is not felt here. Neill and his family raise cereals as well as livestock and, besides sheep, have a small beef herd and a dairy herd of 250 Friesians and Normandies. The Normandies are especially suitable for cheese because their milk is higher in protein than Friesian, but not proportionately fattier, and coagulates very easily. The cows are managed by one of Neill's two brothers, Robert, whose feelings for them extend not only to knowing each one individually but also to giving them names. When I remarked that thinking of so many names must be difficult, Neill replied, 'Oh, he's called them after all his girlfriends.' (Later Robert said, 'Yes, it's an odd thing: I mean it as a compliment, but they don't always see it that way.') The herd has been with the family since before the war: it was brought to Doddington in 1944, but before that was kept by Neill's parents in Dumfries. The farm is now run jointly by Neill, his two brothers and sister, and their mother, whose parents were dairy-farmers in Ayrshire, traditionally Scotland's main dairying area. She remarked that whereas early in the century everyone there made cheese, as in Yorkshire, cheese-making had been eroded by the easier transport of milk in the period between the wars, and finally killed by the establishment of the Milk Marketing Board.

Neill's enthusiasm for cheese is electric. He started making it six years ago, initially experimenting, like everyone else, with a bucket and spoon in the kitchen; he then took a cheesemaking course and when we visited him had just returned from studying how to make farmhouse Gouda in the Netherlands. He has evolved three cheeses: the first, Doddington, is of the open-textured, Leicester type; the second, Berwick Edge, of the Gouda type; and the third, St Cuthbert's Cave, based on a Caerphilly recipe. St Cuthbert's Cave is named after a local cave said to have been used by the saint as a resting-place but is always referred to by Neill as 'Cuddy's Cave'. To achieve the creamy, semi-hard texture for which it is notable, he makes it with milk taken only at the beginning and end of lactation, when the yield is low but the fat content relatively high. For all the cheeses, he uses half as much starter as usual and leaves the milk to ripen for twice as long, which may help to account for their distinctive flavour.

DODDINGTON

A semi-hard cows' cheese; full-fat, unpasteurized milk; traditional rennet.
2kg/4lb 6oz, 5kg/11lb and 20kg/44lb truckles

Though of different types, Neill's three cheeses share an exceptionally light, melting texture and bold, interesting, totally unique flavour, combined in the case of the first two with a herbal, almost spicy tang. Doddington is fairly dry and almost but not quite crumbly, with flavours suggestive of the earth, grass, and sea air (the sea is about 19km/12 miles away). The tang is fairly strong when the cheese is younger, and powerful by the time it reaches nine months. Altogether, it is different and memorable. Toasted, it is delicious in another way, since the tang is subdued and the cheese becomes much sweeter.

BERWICK EDGE

A hard cows' cheese; full-fat, unpasteurized milk; traditional rennet.
2.5kg/5lb 8oz and 5kg/11lb

At seven to eight months, this has an airy, insubstantial, lace-like texture, with small holes; at a year, it becomes more compact and creamier. Like Doddington, the younger cheese tastes of earth and grass, with a moderately strong tang; when older, the tang becomes deep, mellow, and vigorous, almost hot, as if seasoned with chilli. I served the older version to guests on Christmas Day and everyone agreed that it was quite exceptional.

ST CUTHBERT'S CAVE (CUDDY'S CAVE)

A semi-hard cows' cheese; full-fat, unpasteurized milk; traditional rennet.
1.5kg/3lb 5oz and 4kg/8lb 13oz

Cuddy's Cave is semi-hard verging on semi-soft, light, melting, mousse-like, and above all creamy. The creaminess carries through to the taste, making it milder than the other cheeses but with an interesting range of grassy and herbal flavours and background hints of both spiciness and flowers. It is possibly my favourite of the three. If it is not already very soft, store it at room temperature covered by a dish to keep it moist.

CHAPTER 7

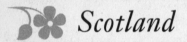 *Scotland*

LOCH ARTHUR CREAMERY

GALLOWAY FARMHOUSE CHEESE

H. J. ERRINGTON

DUNLOP DAIRY PRODUCTS

ISLE OF MULL TRADITIONAL FARMHOUSE CHEESE

WESTER LAURENCETON CHEESES

HIGHLAND FINE CHEESES LTD

SEATOR'S ORKNEY

LAIROBELL GOATS

WHEEMS

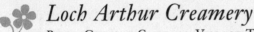

Loch Arthur Creamery

BARRY GRAHAM, CAMPHILL VILLAGE TRUST, BEESWING,
DUMFRIES DG2 8JQ. TEL: 01387 760296

The Camphill Village Trust is part of the Camphill Movement, which was founded by an Austrian paediatrician, Dr Karl König, to provide education and a family environment for children with learning difficulties. The Village Trust extends his ideas to adults: there are six village communities in England, one in Ireland, and two in Scotland, where the other is at Newton Dee, near Aberdeen. Residents with difficulties live in family houses with co-workers and their children, sharing domestic life and types of work which vary according to location and circumstance. At Loch Arthur there is a weaving workshop, bakery, and two farms: on one beef-cattle, sheep, and pigs are reared, and the other has a market garden and a herd of Ayrshires which supplies the milk for the Creamery. We visited the bakery just as trays of little oat biscuits scented with honey were being taken from the oven; in the market garden we could see every kind of vegetable, soft fruit including raspberries and strawberries, and huge clumps of herbs, all interspersed with the bright colours of marigolds and nasturtiums. The movement holds Rudolf Steiner's ideas 'in special respect': thus a school for the younger children is run on his principles and the farms are biodynamic.

When Barry and his wife joined the Community, two years after it was founded in 1984, a dairy for making butter and soft cheese had already been set up by a Trust worker called Vivian, chiefly to provide employment for a Community member who was paralysed from the waist down but could churn butter; however, Vivian left soon after Barry arrived, leaving him as her obvious successor. In response to the general feeling of the community, he set about reorganizing the dairy to make hard cheese, and gradually built up a team which at the time of my visit included four co-workers and six members with difficulties. Watching them working together, I was deeply impressed by their commitment and efficiency; I was also astonished at the confidence and maturity of a group of Community children who joined them for tea. They seemed to prove the value of early contact with adult occupations and, perhaps even more, of having both parents near to hand for most of the day, although their Steiner schooling perhaps deserves some of the credit.

For some years, Barry concentrated on the hard cheese, for which most of the milk is still used; however, he also continued Vivian's soft cheese, and recently, feeling that it could be improved, asked Iain Mellis in Edinburgh for advice (although he now sells rather than makes cheese, Iain used to be a cheesemaker). Between them, they devised a semi-soft version. Between them they devised a rind-washed version, Criffel; recently, Barry has also developed a second rind-washed cheese, Kebbuck. In addition, he makes a fresh cheese called Crannog, a cream cheese, ricotta, and butter.

LOCH ARTHUR ORGANIC FARMHOUSE CHEESE

Silver Medal, British Cheese Awards 1995; Bronze Medal, 1996; Gold Medal, 2001
A Cheddar-style cheese; full-fat, unpasteurized organic milk; vegetarian rennet. 9kg/20lb truckles; smaller sizes also available

At six months, which I consider to be its optimum age, this cheese is moist, mild, rich, and wonderfully multi-flavoured, with a creamy background against which herbal and flowery tastes are evenly balanced. Its varying tones and subtleties mean that you could eat it every day for years without being bored. At a year, it is drier and has developed a tang, but to some extent at the expense of the sub-flavours, which become subordinate and less lively.

It is made according to a Cheddar recipe and bound with cloth which is stuck on by 'burning' or scalding rather than with lard or flour-paste. The maturing time is six to twelve months. For the soft cheese, Crannog, some of the curd is scooped off before being cut for the hard cheese and left to free-drain: it then is ripened for two to three weeks. The new cheese, Criffel, is made similarly, but rind-washed in brine and matured for at least a month.

Loch Arthur Potatoes

This can be made with almost any Cheddar-type (and other) cheese, but Loch Arthur gives a gentle flavour which does not overwhelm the taste of the potatoes. Waxy potatoes that will not disintegrate are essential; it is also important to slice them thinly, partly to reduce the time they take to cook. If you are in a hurry, the slices can be boiled in water, which takes 4–5 minutes, rather than simmered in the sauce; however, the result will not have quite the same richness and unity. The dish can be prepared in advance up to baking.

Cooking times: 18–25 minutes for the potatoes in sauce; 20–25 minutes for baking
For 2–3 as a main course or 4–6 as a vegetable

450ml/16fl oz milk
salt and pepper
400g/14oz preferably organic waxy new potatoes, e.g. Charlotte or
    Jersey Royal, scrubbed and very thinly sliced
125g/4$\frac{1}{2}$oz shallots, preferably organic, peeled and finely chopped
20g/$\frac{3}{4}$oz butter
20g/$\frac{3}{4}$oz white flour, preferably organic
1 tsp Dijon mustard
150g/5$\frac{1}{4}$oz Loch Arthur Organic Farmhouse Cheddar, finely grated
nutmeg

Heat but do not boil the milk; season the potatoes moderately with salt and pepper. Fry the shallots in the butter over medium to low heat – if possible in a non-stick pan – for 2–3 minutes or until they are soft but not brown; add the potatoes, stir-fry for about half a minute to coat them with oil, and stir in the flour gently but thoroughly off the heat. The pan will be very dry, but because of the cheese the finished dish might become greasy if more butter is used. Pour in the milk gradually, stirring continuously; return the pan to the heat and stir until the sauce has thickened. Lower the heat to a simmer, season lightly with salt and a little more generously with pepper, and cook until the potatoes are just tender, turning them often to ensure that they do not stick to the pan. Gently stir in the mustard; allow the potatoes to cool briefly before adding and stirring in the cheese.

Turn the potatoes into a lightly greased soufflé or other baking dish and grate a little nutmeg over the top. Bake the potatoes at 190°C/375°F/Gas 5 for 20–25 minutes, until they are lightly browned. Serve at once.

CRIFFEL

Silver Medal, British Cheese Awards 2001
A semi-soft cows' cheese; full-fat, unpasteurized organic milk; vegetarian rennet. 25–30cm/10–12-inch discs

Criffel has a smooth, consistent texture not quite soft enough to flow. The taste is fairly strong, tangy yet sweet, with a wide range of flavours among which butter and wild flowers predominate. It is a lovely cheese but regrettably scarce.

CRANNOG

Bronze Medal, British Cheese Awards 1996; with chives, 2001
A fresh, wax-coated cows' cheese; full-fat, unpasteurized organic milk;
vegetarian rennet. 280g/10oz rounds

Crannog has a firm, compact, nutty texture. Thanks to the organic
Ayrshire milk, the taste is surprisingly distinctive, with flavours of
grass and wild herbs combined with an earthy, almost mushroom-
like sweetness. It comes plain or flavoured with organic herbs or
green peppercorns.

Galloway Farmhouse Cheese
ALLAN BROWN, MILLAIRIES FARM, NEWTON STEWART,
WIGTOWNSHIRE DG8 8AL. TEL: 0198 885 0224

When I visited him, some five years ago now, Allan had a flock of
400 Frieslands or Friesland crosses, of whom he milked 100 for
eight months of the year: during that time, he made 112kg/250lb
of cheese a week, which, given that he had no one to help with the
milking, kept him 100 per cent busy all and every day. The fact that
we arrived at Millairies (the name means watermill) on Bank
Holiday Monday was irrelevant to him.

He was originally inspired to keep Frieslands by Olivia Mills's
book (page 9) and, like Ann Dorward (page 281), started out simply
intending to sell the liquid milk. Surprising as it may seem now,
neither of them could find a market: to begin with, Allan, entering
the field later than Ann, froze his milk and took it to her dairy,
where she made cheese for him. Soon, however, he started making
his own, using a recipe from *The Smallholder*. In addition, he set up
a smokery and opened a shop called From Ewe to You, selling a

range of products connected with sheep. At that time, his aims were to employ an assistant (or install a carousel: see next entry) so that he could milk twice as many sheep; he also planned to make ricotta and a cows' cheese while the sheep are dry in the winter.

Then came foot-and-mouth, which meant that he has had to put all his plans on hold: his entire flock, which by then consisted of 430, plus 100 beef cattle and calves, were culled. He admits that at the time he almost had a breakdown; however, he is now rearing a new flock of young ewes and for the time being makes his cheese with bought milk.

I did not discuss all the details of his cheese recipe with him; however, an aspect of it which I found particularly interesting is that he matures all his cheeses in vacuum-packs, which considerably retards the ripening process. After six months, some are left plain and coated with wax, some are flavoured or smoked before waxing, and some matured on for another four months. By then, they have formed a natural rind with brownish mould, which, combined with a drier texture and the extra maturing time, effectually transforms them into a completely different cheese.

CAIRNSMORE (NATURAL RIND)

Bronze Medal, British Cheese Awards 1996; Silver Medal, 1997 (Smoked)
A hard sheep's cheese; unpasteurized milk; vegetarian rennet.
900g/2lb and 1.8–2.3kg/4–5lb truckles

The ten-month-old cheese is pure delight, with a soft but pronounced sweet, creamy taste and undertones of nuts and earth. It is not in the least like the more usual pecorino-style sheep's cheeses: the sweetness, which also distinguishes Ann Dorward and Humphrey Errington's cheeses, seems to be characteristic of the area. The wax-rinded version is less distinctive.

H. J. Errington

BRAEHEAD FARM, WALSTON, OGSCASTLE, CARNWATH,
STRATHCLYDE ML11 8NF. TEL: 01899 870266

By now, BSE and the American attempt to persuade the European Union to adopt compulsory pasteurization have pushed the Errington case into history, but three years ago cheeselovers all over Britain joined in a campaign to help Humphrey Errington to save his sheep's cheese, Lanark Blue, from extinction. Humphrey has already given his own account of what happened in *Lanark Blue: a Brief History of the Battle*, available from the Specialist Cheesemakers' Association. Very briefly, however, he was asked by the local council to recall all the cheese on the market from sale and cease trading because a sample test showed that it was so heavily contaminated with *Listeria monocytogenes* that it could have caused 'a UK-wide outbreak ... with a possible fatality rate of 40%'. (*Lanark Blue*, p. 4) Astonished and appalled, Humphrey of course complied and waited with dread for the predicted reports of illness. None came, and independent tests on the cheese showed that it was perfectly normal (it was later alleged that a patient had died of listeria which could have been transmitted by it, but the claim was shown to be false). After several months, Humphrey informed the council that he proposed to start trading again. The ensuing series of hearings lasted a year, with a final judgement in his favour. He says that he could never have sustained the strain of the legal proceedings without the tremendous public support he received, which in cash terms totalled £35,000.

Two points proved by the case were that it is possible for a small producer to challenge the authorities and win, and that consumers really value good cheese: 'If anyone needs convincing that in Britain there is an enormous desire for artisan cheese, despite the best attempts of the regulatory authorities to frustrate that desire,

he has only to study the case of Lanark Blue...'. (*Lanark Blue*, p. 14)
A further point which emerged was that unpasteurized cheese contains natural controls which can make it safer than pasteurized.
Humphrey says: 'Fresh raw milk contains "bacteriostats", i.e. sub-
stances which prevent the growth of pathogens during the critical
stage when the milk is warm in the vat but before starter activity
has begun. There are no bacteriostats in pasteurized milk. Also,
many raw milk cheese processes include the production of various
organic acids in addition to lactic acid: for example, acetic acid,
well known as an effective agent against pathogens, is often present. Thirdly, the microflora present in raw milk cheese after it has
been made (and absent in pasteurized cheese) will include significant populations of organisms such as enterococci, which are
highly inhibitory to invading pathogens.'

The farm which gave rise to the drama is in a sternly beautiful situation in the Pentland Hills; battle-scars remain in the form of large
notices at either end of the cheesemaking area forbidding the entry
of unauthorized persons for reasons of hygiene (Lanark Blue is now
also sold with a sticker warning pregnant women and those who are
immuno-compromised not to eat blue cheese – which, with equal
justification, should be on every cheese matured for less than four
months). At present, Humphrey has 300 Friesland sheep, but aims at
500: the problem of the time it takes to milk them, which haunts
Allan Brown and Ann Dorward (pages 275 and 281) simply does not
exist here. The shepherd, Walter Robertson, showed me the item of
equipment which every sheep-cheesemaker needs: a carousel, or
revolving milking-parlour. It does not float on water, like the
Applebys', and is fairly noisy, but the sheep apparently do not mind.
Twenty-five can be accommodated at once and the total milking
time is reduced to thirty or forty minutes in the morning and thirty
minutes in the afternoon. The milk for the cows' cheese, Dunsyre
Blue, comes from a herd of Ayrshires on the farm next door.

LANARK BLUE

A blue sheep's cheese; unpasteurized milk; vegetarian rennet.
1.4–1.8kg/3–4lb rounds; seasonal: available April–Christmas

I am told that the cheese can be fairly strong, but the examples I have tried have been moderate, with blue which does not overpower the gentler tastes of sheep, grass, herbs, and somewhere in the background a slightly smoky suggestion of peat. It is particularly good with plums or pears; it is also excellent for adding a subtle piquancy to cooked dishes.

Marrow Rings Stuffed with Plums and Lanark Blue

This is a brilliant way of finishing up remains of the cheese, since you only need 40g/1½oz: the result is quite surprisingly full and rich-tasting.

Cooking time: 35–40 minutes
For 2 as a light main dish or 4 as a vegetable

400–450g/14oz–1lb piece of a small or long, thin marrow, washed
salt
1½ tbsp oil
150g/5¼oz (1 medium) onion, peeled, quartered, and finely sliced
100g/3½oz (2) red plums, washed and diced
1 fairly sharp eating apple, peeled and diced
2–3 sage leaves, washed and finely chopped
40g/1½ oz walnuts, crushed or chopped
½ tsp Dijon mustard
4 tbsp whipping cream
40g/1½ oz Lanark Blue, finely grated

Chop the marrow into slices 2.5cm/1 inch thick, barely cover them with slightly salted water, and boil for 9–10 minutes, until the marrow is tender but still firm. Drain the slices and leave them on a plate to drain further.

Warm the oil over low heat and fry the onion for 8–10 minutes or until it is soft and starting to change colour. Add the plums and apple and fry them for 4–5 minutes; add the sage and cook for about another minute; add the nuts, turn up the heat slightly, and stir for a few seconds. Add the mustard and cream and stir gently until the liquid is slightly reduced. Remove the pan from the heat.

Cut the fibrous centres, with the seeds, from the slices of marrow. Lay the slices in a baking dish and fill the holes with the plum stuffing. Cover the stuffing with the cheese and bake in a pre-heated oven at 200°C/400°F/Gas 6 for 9–12 minutes or until the cheese is melted and golden. Serve at once.

DUNSYRE BLUE

A blue cows' cheese; full-fat, unpasteurized milk; vegetarian rennet.
1.4–1.8kg/3–4lb rounds

Dunsyre Blue is milder, sweeter, and creamier-tasting than the Lanark; probably partly because of the Ayrshire milk, it has an unusually wide range of rich, grassy flavours. On a cheeseboard, it is particularly well partnered by Bonnet (hard goat: page 283) or Cairnsmore (sheep: page 276): the background tastes of both harmonize with it beautifully.

Dunlop Dairy Products

ANN DORWARD, WEST CLERKLAND FARM, STEWARTON, STRATHCLYDE KA3 5LP. TEL: 01560 482494

The drive up to West Clerkland Farm leads past very, very green fields, with kids in one and lambs in the next, all adolescent and quite large but still looking as perfectly white and clean as when they were born. At present, Ann keeps 100 milking Saanen goats and sixty Friesland sheep, and besides a goats' and sheep's cheese makes a farmhouse Dunlop which at the time of writing was the only one I had tasted in Scotland; she also has a shop where she sells the cheese, and two children, aged three and eight. Her husband manages his own farm next door; her parents live with them at West Clerklands, which means that she has help with the children, and she has a part-time student assistant, but she acknowledges that she has far too much to do. Like Allan Brown (page 275), she started out with the intention simply of selling liquid sheep's milk but found that there was no demand; having embarked, first on sheep's, then on goat's cheese made with milk from a neighbour, she decided to keep goats only when two successive suppliers let her down. 'Often, oh often, I wish I hadn't – they're so lively, and I haven't time to entertain them!'

If only from necessity, her approach to cheesemaking is relaxed. When someone needs serving in the shop, the cheese has to wait; she is not concerned about 'touch' (she does not need to be) and is pragmatic about pasteurization. When she started, eleven years ago, she pasteurized all her cheese because she was told not only that the authorities preferred it but also that unpasteurized products would soon be made illegal – whereas in fact, as she said, feeling seems to have gone the other way. She now makes all her cheeses in a pasteurized and unpasteurized version; the former are matured in vacuum-packs and rindless and the unpasteurized ones (with rinds) are matured normally. As is traditional, she uses Ayrshire milk for the Dunlop; initially, she bought it from Scottish Milk, but now produces her own, as for the goats' and sheep's cheeses. As well as the three described below, she has now developed two new white mould-ripened cheeses, Aiket (cows') and Glazert (goats').

SWINZIE (WITH RIND)

> *Gold Medal and trophy for the Best Modern British Cheese,*
> *British Cheese Awards 2001*
> *A hard sheep's cheese; full-fat, unpasteurized milk; vegetarian rennet.*
> *2.5kg/5lb 8oz truckles*

Swinzie is sweet and rich-tasting, with a predominantly nutty flavour: like Cairnsmore (page 276), it is completely different from pecorino, although if matured for a long time it acquires a smoky tang. Ann's cheesemaking may sometimes have to take its turn, but instinct and judgement compensate: this is a wonderful cheese. She won first prize with it at Nantwich in 1992, and first prize with Bonnet (below) for three consecutive years, but has never entered for the British Cheese Awards: she should. The pasteurized version (rindless) is milder and less distinctive.

All the cheeses are made by the Dunlop method, which is similar to Cheddar but the curd is cut larger and scalded to a slightly lower temperature, which gives a moister result. After starter and rennet have been added, the curd is cut into 1.5cm/$^1/_2$-inch squares; it is then scalded to 38°C/100°F and stirred 'for a wee while' before being left to settle. Draining and piling in blocks follow, as for Cheddar, until the acidity has risen; finally, it is milled and salted, moulded, and pressed. The unpasteurized cheeses are wrapped and matured in muslin: except for the larger Dunlops, which need longer, the maturing time is a minimum of six months.

BONNET (WITH RIND)

Silver Medal, British Cheese Awards 2001; Bronze Medal, 2002
A hard goats' cheese; full-fat, unpasteurized Ayrshire milk;
vegetarian rennet. 2.5kg/5lb 8oz truckles

This has virtually no flavour of goat, but tastes of blossom and herbs, with a soft lemon-like tang: it is very unusual and utterly delicious. When matured beyond six months, it becomes dryish and, like Swinzie, acquires a soft, smoky tang. The name originates from the local craft of making bonnets for Scottish regiments. As with Swinzie, the rindless pasteurized version is much milder.

DUNLOP (WITH RIND)

Gold Medal, British Cheese Awards 2001
A hard cow's cheese; full-fat, unpasteurized Ayrshire milk; vegetarian
rennet. 2.5kg/5lb 8oz and 50kg/110lb truckles; pasteurized 2.5kg/5lb 8oz
truckles only

The cheese has a slightly fudgy, cohesive texture and mild but deep taste, predominantly of nuts but with earthy tones and a hint of smokiness; unlike Cheddar, it has virtually no salty tang.

The pasteurized version is almost unrecognizably different, with a silky texture and fresh, grassy flavour; if matured for over six months, it develops a caramel-like overtone faintly reminiscent of Emmental.

Isle of Mull Traditional Farmhouse Cheese

CHRIS AND JEFF READE, SGRIOB-RUADH FARM, TOBERMORY,
ISLE OF MULL PA75 6QD. TEL: 01688 302235

We crossed to Mull on the small Lochaline ferry, which operates
without fuss or formality: you simply drive to the water's edge and
pay on the way over. The road to Tobermory is a 'major road with
passing-places': on one side were woods carpeted with fern and on
the other the Sound, with the silhouette of the mountains stretching northwards like the teeth of a saw, their peaks echoed by a
magnificent cloudscape above. The Reades' farm is on a hill with
a view not only of the mountains but south over the island to Ben
More, from the top of which you can see as far as Ireland. In front
of the house is a curiously shaped tall, gabled conservatory filled
with hanging baskets and urns of flowers, which is used as a shop
and tearoom; besides the flowers, it is furnished with a cheese-dale,
or cheese storage-dresser, now used as the counter, and an old
turning-dale for turning cheeses. The reason for its pointed shape
is that it was the framework of the local village hall, transported up
the hill and filled in with glass instead of boards.

Jeff and Chris were dairy-farmers in Somerset, producing milk
only until, like Mike Davies (page 77), they became discouraged by
the size of the milk lake: cheese was an obvious possibility, but
competition in Somerset is harsh. As they were then approaching
forty, 'the age when you start saying, "If I don't do it now, I never
will"', they decided to fulfil a long-standing wish and set up a
cheese-farm in Scotland. They bought Sgriob-ruadh (the name
means 'red furrow') on sight, even though it had been unoccupied
for sixteen years and was almost a ruin: as the house had no roof,
they began by living, with all four sons, in a caravan. By degrees,

with the sons' help, they renovated it entirely themselves. Their final achievement has been to dig an underground cheese-store, the nearest possible equivalent to a cave; when we were there it was visible as a patch of concrete in the grass, but they were planning to turf it over, not only for aesthetic reasons but also to increase the humidity. Another imaginative touch, inspired by the need to keep the cows indoors for seven months of the year, is their four-star luxury cow-shed. The floor is covered with a six-inch-thick rubber carpet which is as springy and comfortable as a mattress; on top of this, instead of straw, is a colourful layer of shredded recycled paper, collected from all over the island.

They now have a closed herd of 100, mainly Friesians, but with a sprinkling of coffee-coloured Swiss cows, plus the odd Jersey and Ayrshire. As Jeff is the only dairy-farmer on Mull, they sell liquid milk as well as cheese, half the herd being used for each. Chris took lessons in Cheddar-making before leaving Somerset and makes the cheese, working entirely by herself, to a conventional Cheddar recipe. She is one of the only two cheesemakers I have met who prefers using winter to summer milk: she says that in winter, when she has complete control over the cows' diet, the quality is predictable, but when the cows are out at grass the taste can vary considerably. One year, she said, when they had just been let out to eat the new grass in May, the curd was completely unusable: she has never been able to work out exactly why. As well as large truckles, she makes a few small ones coated with wax called Tobermory Truckles, some of which are flavoured; the large cheeses are cloth-bound and matured for ten to twelve months.

ISLE OF MULL

A hard cows' cheese; full-fat, unpasteurized milk; traditional rennet.
22kg/48lb truckles

The Reades do not call their cheese Cheddar because it is not
made in the traditional area and therefore tastes different from
the Somerset version; however, it is sufficiently Cheddar-like to
have been included in a tasting of six Cheddars organized by the
Specialist Cheesemakers Association. It is paler than the West
Country cheeses and distinguishable for a clean, light feel and
flavours of the sea: the tang, which is strong, is correspondingly
salty. It often has blue veins, especially under the rind: rather than
being undesirable, these are a sign of maturity. Mail order is welcomed.

Wester Lawrenceton Cheeses

PAM AND NICK RODWAY, WESTER LAWRENCETON, BY
FORRES, MORAY IV36 ORL. TEL: 01309 676566

I first heard about the Rodways' venture through a friend, Jane
Heape, who used to make goats' cheeses but recently gave up and
sold some of her goats to Pam. At the time of my visit, the dairy
was still being converted, although sufficiently advanced to show
that it would be spacious and well planned, with a milking-parlour
for cows at one end and the goats' down the side. As she could not
yet use it, Pam was making soft cows' and goats' cheeses in the
kitchen which, because of the other food prepared there, she had
(very rightly) pasteurized. Much to my surprise, I found that they
were nevertheless quite exceptional, with a very unusual taste and
varied sub-flavours. Subsequently, she developed two hard cheeses,

a cows', Sweetmilk, and a goats'. Now, some five years on, she is still making Sweetmilk, plus two versions of a semi-soft cheese and a white mould-ripened cheese, Brierley, which is still under development. Sadly, after several years she and Nick decided that they would have to give up the goats, mainly because the land at Wester Lawrenceton did not suit them, so that she no longer makes goats' cheeses.

The Rodways are deeply committed to organic principles: Nick has been a member of the Soil Association for thirty years and Pam has already made cheese on two organic farms. On one of the farms, near Edinburgh, she worked with ex-prisoners, drug abusers, and others in need of rehabilitation: 'Working on an organic farm turned around the lives of some of them quite dramatically,' she remarked. On the other, in Devon, she taught for the Yarner Trust and made a cheese called Welcome Barton. At Wester Lawrenceton, she and Nick have a flock of nearly 300 very free-ranging hens, and a herd of eighteen Ayrshires plus a Jersey. To help finance the cows, they have launched a cow-share scheme by which ten families have bought a £500 share and in return receive £50-worth of products a year: for the moment, this means cheese, but eventually Pam will also make butter and yoghurt. (It should be added that the farm is ideally placed, since the organic community at Findhorn is only a few miles away.)

WESTER LAWRENCETON FRESH CHEESE

Fresh cows' cheese; full-fat, organic pasteurized milk; vegetarian rennet. Sold by weight in tubs

The cheese is sweet and rich-tasting, with hints of herbs and nuts and a texture slightly firmer than thick cream.

Seville Orange Caramel Cream

This is as unusual as it is delicious: however, you have to remember that Seville oranges are only in season in February.

> *Cooking-time: 3½–5 minutes to make the caramel. You also need to allow at least an hour for chilling.*
>
> *For 4*

> *5 tbsp Seville orange juice (the juice of 3 small oranges)*
> *1 tbsp lemon juice*
> *125g/4½oz caster or granulated sugar*
> *100 ml/⅙ pint double cream, lightly whipped*
> *100g/3½oz Wester Lawrenceton fresh cheese*

Put two tablespoonsful of the orange juice, the lemon juice, and the sugar into a small saucepan and set over very low heat until the sugar has melted. Make sure that the rest of the orange juice is conveniently to hand. Raise the heat to moderate, bring the syrup to the boil, and boil for 3½–4½ minutes or until the bubbles on top have changed from white or pale primrose yellow to deep amber, which will happen fairly suddenly. After about 2½ minutes, a smell rather like coconut may rise from the pan. As soon as the bubbles change colour, add the remaining 3 tablespoonsful of orange juice: stand back, as the addition of cold liquid to the syrup causes it to spit. It will also, however, prevent it from setting, which would make it impossible to mix with the cheese. Leave it to become cold.

Lightly whip the cream and fold it into the cheese. Stir in the syrup. Chill for an hour or so before serving.

WESTER LAWRENCETON SWEET-MILK

Gold Medal, British Cheese Awards 2000
A Dunlop-style semi-soft cows' cheese; full-fat, organic unpasteurized milk;
vegetarian rennet. 3kg/6lb 10oz and 5kg/11lb

At seven weeks old, the cheese has the most delicious moist, semi-soft texture and a mild, pure, sweet taste with flavours of cream, butter, and wild flowers; by five months, it was hard, although moist, with a predominantly buttery taste and the promise of flowers to come. Older samples were not available at the time of writing: of the two I tried, I preferred the first.

CAROLA

Silver Medal, British Cheese Awards 2000
A semi-soft cows' cheese; unpasteurized, organic, mainly Ayrshire milk;
vegetarian rennet.
800g–1kg/1lb 12oz–2lb 3oz rounds

This is a delightful cheese with a taste which brings to mind cream and heather, moorland, moss, and wild herbs. The texture is similar to Duckett's matured Caerphilly: just, but only just soft enough to be described as semi-soft.

GLEN MORAY CAROLA (which also won a Silver Medal at the British Cheese Awards 2000) is rind-washed in Glen Moray whisky, which gives it a creamier texture and a much deeper, sweeter taste.

BRIERLEY

A white mould-ripened cows' cheese; unpasteurized, mainly Ayrshire
organic milk; vegetarian rennet.
340g/12oz and 220g/8oz rounds

Opinions seem to be divided on this cheese, probably because it is
still being developed and different samples vary very widely. The
one I tried, however, had a gloriously creamy, flowing texture,
with a contrastingly crisp rind and an interesting medley of flowery and herbal flavours, again with a hint of moss somewhere in the
background. I thought it was delicious. Its numerous flavours are
also a good illustration of the advantages of unpasteurized organic
milk.

Highland Fine Cheeses Ltd
SUSANNAH STONE, KNOCKBRECK, TAIN, ROSS &
CROMARTY. TEL: 01862 892034

We drove to Tain from Ballater in late August, when the heather
was just coming out and the moors, instead of blazing with colour,
were a soft greenish purple. The hills were dotted with the white
bodies and black faces of sheep; here and there were dark fir plan-
tations which on the one hand interrupt the natural flow of the
landscape, but on the other add contrast and scale. We crossed the
Moray Firth at Inverness, and the Cromarty Firth via a long, low
bridge like a causeway which makes you feel almost as if you are
skimming the water. Knockbreck is a house to die for, large enough
to seem spacious but small enough to be comfortable, with a view
over a wide lawn and low-set double bow windows to make the

most of the sun. Susannah told us that it is a sixteenth-century foundation, but had been devastated by raids and rebuilt around 1790 by her husband's ancestors. Later, they sold it, and it was eventually bought back by her father: she inherited it just at the point when she and her husband needed more space for the cheese (and, to begin with, privacy from the prying eye of the authorities).

Her account of how she started to make cheese was so racy that I wished I had brought a tape-recorder and could transcribe it verbatim. Before the war, everyone in the Highlands, including her mother-in-law, had made crowdie or, to give it its local name, 'gruth'; afterwards, mainly because of the Milk Marketing Board, it disappeared. However, her husband had a nostalgic longing for it and asked her to make some. She knew how because she had watched her mother-in-law, but had never actually tried, and started by buying a churn of 45 litres/10 gallons of milk, which she almost immediately realized was far too much. It was supposed to be left to sour naturally in the sun or by the fire: instead, she stood it in warm water in the bath. After two days it showed no sign of curdling; on the third, her husband, fed up with not being able to use the bath, went to the chemist and bought a packet of lactophyllic acid pills (normally used for babies), which curdled it very effectively. The next stage is to cook the curds to the consistency of scrambled eggs: Susannah achieved this by simply running in the hottest possible bath water. Finally, she hung up the curds to drain in a pillowcase. The result was delicious, but even her husband could not eat it all: they therefore took the surplus to the local grocer, who was very scathing, remarking that nobody liked crowdie any more. It sold out immediately, so the Stones, who were chronically short of money, made more, first with two churns and 90 litres/20 gallons of milk, then with three.

However, as its popularity grew, so did the Stones' worry about the local sanitary inspector. Soon after graduating to three churns, they moved to Knockbreck, where, unable to afford a proper dairy, they made the cheese in the secrecy of the cellar and, as a further precaution, took to working at night. Even after they built a dairy, their troubles were not over, chiefly because, while it was under construction, the sanitary inspector asked the builder where the drains would be, and the builder jokingly replied that there were not going to be any. This seemed to confirm the inspector's worst suspicions, and thereafter he harassed them on every possible occasion. They were also threatened with competition from the Milk Marketing Board, which began to manufacture a rival brand of crowdie, but this turned out to be to their advantage, since the Board's version went mouldy and they were able to pick up all its customers.

Susannah now has an impeccable modern dairy, a staff of ten (part-time so that mothers can look after their children), and makes five varieties of cheese: crowdie, two cheeses flavoured with garlic, Hramsa and Galic, and two cream cheeses, Gruth Dhu and Caboc. She pasteurizes because the milk is bought, but compensates by using a custom-made starter designed to give the traditional flavour of the cheese by reintroducing specific local bacteria. The crowdies are still made to her mother-in-law's recipe, with a jacketed vat to replace a fire or the bath, and Caboc to a recipe said to have been used in the sixteenth century by her ancestor Mariota de Ile, daughter of The Macdonald, Lord of the Isles.

HIGHLAND CROWDIE (LOW-FAT)

A soft, fresh cows' cheese; low-fat, pasteurized milk; rennet-free.
140g/5oz pots and 2kg/4lb 6oz tubs

Crowdie is made with skimmed milk to which enough cream has been returned to bring the fat content to the equivalent of hand-skimmed milk. The texture is as light, mousse-like, and melting as fresh sheep's cheese; presumably thanks to the starter, the taste includes not only the lemon-like tang which is characteristic of the northern Highlands and Orkney, but also undertones of earth and flowers. It is a delight, and invaluable to anyone watching fat intake or calories. The traditional partner to crowdie is oatcakes; but weight watchers may prefer Wheat Wafers (p. xxii: only 16 k cal per biscuit). The cooked, low-fat curds are unsuitable for heating but can be mixed into excellent creams or pâtés.

 ## Highland Whisky Cream

For 4

125g/4¹/₂oz low-fat Highland Crowdie
100g/3¹/₂oz icing sugar
142ml/¹/₄ pint whipping cream, stiffly whipped
1 tbsp freshly squeezed lemon juice
1 tbsp whisky

Beat the cheese and sugar together: the mixture will seem very stiff at first but will become moist as mixing proceeds. Fold in the cream; then stir in the lemon juice and whisky. Chill for 2 hours or more before serving.

HRAMSA AND GALIC

A soft, fresh cows' cheese flavoured with wild garlic; full-fat, pasteurized milk; rennet-free. 140g/5oz pots or 1kg/2lb 4oz logs; Galic: 110g/3³/₄oz or 1kg/2lb 4oz logs

The garlic comes from Black Rock Gorge, near Evanton (the name 'Hramsa' is the Saxon word for wild garlic). The texture of the cheese is again deliciously light and frothy; the flavour of the garlic, although quite strong, is soft and aromatic.

Galic is similar to Hramsa but is rolled in toasted hazlenuts: the name is derived from 'garlic' and 'Gaelic'.

GRUTH DHU

A soft, fresh cows' cheese; 50%-fat, pasteurized milk; rennet-free. 110g/3¾oz or 1kg/2lb 4oz logs

Gruth Dhu is made of two-thirds Crowdie and one-third double cream, and rolled in pin-head oatmeal and peppercorns. It has an exceptionally light texture and rich taste, with a faint lemon tang and strong earthy undertones.

CABOC

A soft, fresh double-cream cows' cheese rolled in toasted oatmeal; full-fat, pasteurized milk; rennet-free. 110g/3¾oz or 1kg/2lb 4oz logs

Caboc has a light, melting texture like the other cheeses, but with a sharp lemon tang. It is particularly good with digestive biscuits.

The story associated with this cheese is that the heiress Mariota de Ile was hidden under a cheese-barrel at the age of twelve in the attempt to save her from a rival family, the Campbells, who planned to abduct and marry her for the sake of her castle and lands. The Campbells found her and carried her off to Cawdor Castle but it seems that she had the last word, since she outlived her first husband and married again, this time perhaps according to her own choice.

The Company also makes a blue cheese, Strathdon Blue, which won a Gold Medal and was judged the Best Scottish Cheese at the British Cheese Awards 2000 and 2002.

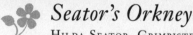

Seator's Orkney

HILDA SEATOR, GRIMBISTER FARM, GRIMBISTER,
FINNSTOWN, KIRKWALL, ORKNEY KW15 1TT.
TEL: 01856 761318

The east coast of Scotland above Tain is relatively flat, although higher-lying than it seems, as one realizes from the periodic descent of the road into steep, wooded estuary valleys; except in the shelter of the valleys, trees become sparser the further north you go. Leaving the coast, the country is featureless bog and grassland, relieved only by the blackened area of a peat farm and the silhouette of a group of hills to the west. The ferry to Stromness, in contrast, takes you close to the nearest Orkney island, Hoy, which has a volcanic-looking mountain and extraordinary red sandstone cliffs horizontally seamed and worn into pillars and milk-bottle shapes reminiscent of the rock formations in the Painted Desert: most eye-catching of all is a gigantic pillar standing alone in the sea, the Old Man of Hoy, which looks like some grand, prehistoric monument.

Grimbister Farm is on the main island about halfway between Stromness and Kirkwall, standing on the side of a hill overlooking the sea and a vista of islands which includes Garsay, Shapinsay, and two tiny ones in the bay below, one of which is uninhabited. Only Hoy is mountainous; the rest of Orkney is rolling or flat, and almost completely treeless. Once you have become used to it, you realize that treelessness is the essential ingredient in the openness and sense of space which is the islands' peculiar charm. At one time, there were more trees than today, but early settlers who migrated from mainland Scotland were attracted by the fact that they could graze their animals without having to clear the land of forest.

The Seators keep a herd of Charolais and Aberdeen Angus

cattle for beef and fourteen Friesians for the cheese; they also have two handsome chestnut horses, ridden by Hilda, and grow barley. The dairy herd is kept to fourteen, with calving in rotation, because she could not handle more milk without an assistant. She has made the cheese every day for twenty-seven years, using a traditional recipe absolutely unchanged except for the replacement of animal rennet, which she can no longer buy, with the genetically engineered equivalent, Chymosin. Neither she nor the other Orcadian cheesemakers given here use starter, which helps to account for the unusually distinctive local taste of their cheeses: in her case, the acidity is given plenty of time to develop by the fact that cheesemaking is spread over twenty-four hours.

SEATOR'S ORKNEY

A fresh cows' cheese; unpasteurized; vegetarian rennet.
675g–3.2kg/1½–7lb truckles

Seator's Orkney is crumbly and fairly moist, especially when just made. When new, it is gentle and delicate, tasting mainly of milk, but after a few days it develops the lemon-like tang characteristic both of crowdie and the other Orkney cheeses. The one I bought on the day of my visit was relatively mild, even at two weeks old, but others I have tasted have been surprisingly deep and powerful, with a taste like a mixture of lemon zest and the sea shot with the sweetness of honey and wild flowers. The plain version, particularly when mature, is delicious accompanied by bananas. As the cheeses are sent to Neal's Yard by post, they are not available from July to early September because of the weather.

Chymosin is added while the milk is still warm from the cow and the curd is left to set for three to four hours; it is then broken by hand and allowed to stand for another three to four hours before being drained and left overnight. Next morning, it is broken by hand again and salted; flavouring is also added when required (flavourings include chives, garlic, caraway, walnut, and pineapple). Moulding and pressing follow, after which the cheeses can be eaten straight away or kept for up to two weeks. Most are sold locally; the rest (plain only) go to Neal's Yard Dairy in London.

 ## Wheems

CHRISTINA SARGENT AND MIKE ROBERTS, WHEEMS,
EASTSIDE, SOUTH RONALDSAY, ORKNEY KW17 2TJ.
TEL: 01856 831537

Mike and Christina are among the very few who carry on the pre-industrial tradition of making cheese with the surplus milk of just one household cow, although in fact they have two so that they have milk all the year round. Less because of small output than Mike's principles, which dictate that food should be produced and eaten locally if possible, the cheese is only to be had in Orkney: we tasted it at the Creel Inn, St Margaret's Hope, where the cooking is equalled only by the excellence of the ingredients (I can testify to the perfectly fresh fish, full-flavoured Orkney steak served that night with slices of black pudding, and not only local cheeses but strawberries which actually had flavour).

Before coming to Wheems, Mike and Christina tried communal organic farming in Devon and considered settling in Shetland, but were attracted to Orkney by the survival of the custom of mixing different activities together and the lively atmosphere it creates. There is not much demand here for landscape architecture, which is Mike's original profession; however, Christina, as both artist and musician, generates a string of commissions and concert and teaching engagements: 'I'm afraid it's all very rushed here – overflowing with vegetables and now school has restarted and I have to think flutes and clarinets when I haven't finished felt commissions and the shops are running out of cards...'. Most of Mike's time is devoted to looking after a large market garden and organizing a vegetable box scheme: extra help is supplied by WWOOFers (Willing Workers On Organic Farms), who come to the islands from all over the world. This, in turn, means that, along with her other commitments, Christina necessarily runs a hostel.

They also keep ducks and hens, and, until lack of time forced them to give up, milked and made cheeses from sheep. Christina fell in love with the first cow, Gretel, a Jersey, twelve years ago and gave her to Mike as a birthday present; the second, Gelda, is Gretel's daughter. Christina makes the cheese daily in summer and two or three times a week in winter from one milking; the other milking is used for drinking, yoghurt, and butter.

WHEEMS

An organic, semi-hard Jersey cheese; unpasteurized milk; vegetarian rennet. 1.25kg/2lb 12oz truckles

The texture of Wheems is crumbly and aerated with tiny holes, almost like a soufflé. At only a few days old, the cheese has a sharp lemon tang; after two weeks, however, it has developed a wonderfully rich, creamy taste with a strong suggestion of honey and only a faint hint of lemon. When toasted, it leaches fat, like other Jersey cheeses, but gains rather than loses flavour and has a pleasantly gritty, nutty feel. (See page 178 for a lemon tart recipe.)

The cheese is made without starter for the sake of organic purity; at the moment, the rennet is ordinary vegetarian, but Mike would be happier if they could find an alternative made from ingredients which he could trace to source. After rennet is added and the curd has set, it is cut into 1.5cm/$^1/_2$-inch squares and left to stand for about two hours while the acidity rises; this is followed by gentle scalding, during which, instead of the usual stirring, it is broken by hand. It is then left to settle, drained, and hung up in a cloth overnight. In the morning, it is broken up by hand again, salted, and finally moulded and pressed. The usual maturing time is about two weeks.

INDEX

Cheeses

Organic cheeses are marked with an asterisk (*)

cows'

soft and fresh

Caboc (Highland Fine Cheeses), 294

Cornish Pepper, Herb and Garlic (Lynher), 123

*Crannog (Loch Arthur Creamery), 275

Elmhirst (Sharpham Creamery), 114

Galic (Highland Fine Cheeses), 293

Gruth Dhu (Highland Fine Cheeses), 294

Highland Crowdie, 292

Hramsa (Highland Fine Cheeses), 293

Seator's Orkney, 296

Wealden Round (Neal's Yard Creamery), 195

Wester Lawrenceton Fresh Cheeses, 287–90

mould-ripened

Bath Soft (Park Farm), 72

Brierley, 290

Cooleeney, 135

Finn (Neal's Yard Creamery), 196

Kelston Park (Park Farm), 73

St Killian (Carrigbyrne Farmhouse), 133

Sharpham, 113

Somerset Brie (Lubborn Cheese), 97–100

Somerset Camembert (Lubborn Cheese), 101

Windwhistle Organic Brie, 100

semi-soft

Carola, 289

Chevington, 266

Make Me Rich (Northumberland), 260

May Hill Green, 60

Starvall Royal, 60

Taurus, 101

Waterloo (Village Maid), 5–6
Wester Lawrenceton Sweet-milk, 289
semi-hard
Avalon (Chris Duckett), 94
Beamish (Swaledale), 258
Caerphilly (Teifi), 173
Carron Lodge Lancashire, 235
Caws Cenarth, 182
Caws Mamgu (Caws Cenarth), 183
Cornish Garland, 120
Cotherstone, 260
Doddington (North Doddington Farm), 268
Duckett's Caerphilly, 92
Duckett's Smoked Caerphilly, 95
Gorwydd Caerphilly, 178
Hereford Hop (Malvern), 187
King Richard III Wensleydale (Fortmayne), 246
Kirkham's Lancashire, 230
Llangloffan Coloured Cheshire, 171
St Cuthbert's Cave (North Doddington), 269
Sandham's Lancashire, 232
Swaledale Cows, 257
Tiskey Meadow, 121
Tiskey Meadow (Lubborn), 121
Wedmore (Chris Duckett), 95
*Wheems, 297
White Wensleydale, 242
hard
Appleby's Cheshire, 208
Appleby's Double Gloucester, 210
*Ashdown Foresters (Sussex High Weald), 27
Berwick Edge (North Doddington Farm), 268
Cheviot, 266
Coolea, 161
Coquetdale (Northumberland), 265
Cornish Yarg (Lynher Dairies), 119
Desmond (West Cork), 155
Double Berkeley (Charles Martell), 62
Double Worcester (Ansteys of Worcester), 189

Dunlop, 283
Gabriel (West Cork), 154
Harefield (Smart's), 52
Hereford Hop (Charles Martell), 58
Isle of Mull, 286
Keen's Cheddar, 86–7
Lincolnshire Poacher, 227
Llanboidy, 166
Llangloffan, 169
*Loch Arthur Organic Farmhouse Cheese, 272
Menallack, 124–5
Montgomery's Cheddar, 82
Mrs Rhodes' Farmhouse Toaster, 236
Northumberland, 264
*Old Plaw Hatch Organic 18
Old Worcester White (Ansteys), 188
Olde Sussex (Mike Turner's Dairy), 38
*Penbryn, 164–5
Quicke's Traditional Cheddar, 104
Quicke's Traditional Oak-smoked Cheddar, 106
Quicke's Traditional Red Leicester, 106
Remarkable Valley (Teifi), 176
Sharpham Rustic, 114
Single Gloucester (Charles Martell), 57–8
Single Gloucester (Smart's), 51
Smart's Double Gloucester, 49
*Staffordshire Organic, 224
Teifi, 173
Worcester Gold (Malvern), 187
blue
Blue Wensleydale (Wensleydale Dairy), 244
Cashel Blue, 138–9
Colston Bassett Stilton, 220
Devon Blue (Ticklemore), 108–9
Dorset Blue Vinny, 79
Dunsyre Blue (H. J. Errington), 280
Exmoor Jersey Blue, 75
Partridges (Exmoor Blue), 76
Somerset Blue (Exmoor Blue), 76

Yorkshire Blue (Shepherd's Purse), 250
washed-rind
Ardrahan, 143
*Criffel (Loch Arthur Creamery), 274
Durrus, 151
Gubbeen, 159
Milleens, 148
Stinking Bishop (Charles Martell), 59–60
Sussex Dew-Pond, 20
Tornegus (Eastside Cheese Co), 15

sheep's
soft and fresh
Fromage Frais (Sussex High Weald), 26
Marlow (Berkswell), 214
Nanterrow (Menallack Farm), 125
Olde York (Shepherd's Purse), 254–5
Ricotta (Sussex High Weald), 24
Sussex Slipcote (Sussex High Weald), 23
Yorkshire Feta (Shepherd's Purse), 254
mould-ripened
Flower Marie (Greenacres Farm), 31
Kelsey Lane, 214
Marlow, 214
semi-soft
Wigmore (Village Maid), 6
semi-hard
Acorn, 180–1
*Halloumi (Sussex High Weald), 24
Lady Llanover (Little Acorn), 181
Skirrid (Little Acorn), 181
Swaledale Ewes', 258
The Original Farmhouse Wensleydale, 249–50
hard
Berkswell, 213
Cairnsmore (Galloway Farmhouse), 276
Crockendale, 16
Duddleswell (Sussex High Weald), 22
Feta (Sussex High Weald), 25

Lord of the Hundreds (Mike Turner's Dairy), 38
Malvern, 186
Redesdale (Northumberland), 261–2
Spenwood (Village Maid), 7
*Staffordshire Organic Sheep's Cheese, 224
Swinzie (Dunlop Dairy Products), 282
Tala, 116–17
Walda (Brebilait), 10–11
Yorkshire Lowlands (Shepherd's Purse), 253
blue
Beenleigh Blue (Ticklemore), 109
Lanark Blue (H. J. Errington), 279
Yorkshire Blue (Shepherd's Purse), 250

goats'
soft and fresh
Baby Brendon (Exmoor Blue), 77
Cerney, 63–4
Cerney Starter, 65–6
Dorstone, 195
Fingals, 127
Innes Button and Curd Cheese, 216–17
Innes Log, 218
Neal's Yard Creamery Goats' Curd, 191
Perroche (Neal's Yard Creamery), 193
St Tola (Inagh Farmhouse), 141
Sleight, 68
Ticklemore Soft Goat, 111
Vithen, 127
Wester Lawrenceton Fresh Cheeses, 287–9
mould-ripened
Bosworth (Innes), 218
Capricorn (Lubborn Cheese), 102
Chabis (Greenacres Farm), 29
Clifton Leaf (Innes), 218
Golden Cross (Greenacres Farm), 30
Laughton Log (Greenacres Farm), 30
Mine-Gabhar (Croghan Goat Farm), 131
Ragstone (Neal's Yard Creamery), 194

St Francis (Womerton Farm), 198
St George (Nut Knowle Farm), 34
Somerset Goat (Lubborn Cheese), 102
Tymsboro' (Sleight Farm), 68
semi-soft
　　Croghan, 130
semi-hard
　　Ribblesdale Original Dairy Cheese, 238
　　Wealden (Nut Knowle Farm), 35
hard
　　Bonnet (Dunlop Dairy Products), 283
　　Brinkburn, 263
　　Carraig, 160
　　Elsdon (Northumberland), 263
　　Ribblesdale Goat Cheese, 238
　　Swaledale Goats', 258
　　Ticklemore, 110
　　Tilleys (Sleight Farm), 69
　　Womerton, 198
washed-rind
　　Sussex Yeoman (Nut Knowle Farm), 34–5
blue
　　Harbourne Blue (Ticklemore), 110

buffalo
　　Blissful Buffalo (Exmoor Blue), 77
　　Soft Cheese with Herbs (Menallack), 127
　　Ribblesdale Buffalo Cheese, 240

cows' and sheep's
　　Mrs Finn's Farmhouse (Menallack), 126
　　Wensleydale Ewes' and Cows', 244

Recipes and Makers

Ansteys of Worcester, 187

Appleby's Cheshire, 206

Appleby's Jerusalem Artichoke Soup, 210

Ardrahan, 142

Ardrahan Potato Casserole, 144–5

Avalon and Sultana Tea Bread, 94

Beenleigh Blue Pâté with Sage, 109–10

Berkswell, 211

Butternut Squash and Tomato Soup with Jersey Blue, 75

Carrigbyrne Farmhouse Cheese Co., 131

Carron Lodge, 234

Cashel Blue and Fish Salad, 139

Cashel Blue Farmhouse Cheese, 137

Caws Cenarth, 182

Cerney Cheeses, 62

Cerney Chicken or Pork in Pastry, 64

Cheese Fondue, 155

Cheshire Rarebit with Whisky, 209

Cod and Redesdale Fish Cakes with Chives, 262

Colston Bassett and District Dairy, 218

Cooleeney and Fish Salad, 136

Cooleeney Farmhouse Cheese, 134

Cotherstone, 259

Croghan Goat Farm, 129

Dorset Blue Cheese Company, 77

Duckett, Chris, 91

Dunlop Dairy Products, 281

Durrus, 150

Eastside Cheese Co., 12

Errington, H. J., 277

Exmoor Blue Cheeses, 73

Finn and Watercress Soup, 196

Fortmayne Farm Dairy, 245

Fruit Cheeses, xxx–xxxi

Frying Cheese in Breadcrumbs, xxix–xxx

Galloway Farmhouse Cheese, 275

Goats' Curd and Strawberry Fool with Maraschino, 191–2

Gorwydd Caerphilly, 176–7
Gorwydd Lemon Tart, 178
Gougère, 174
Greenacres Farm, 28
Grilled Innes Button with Cherries in Brandy, 217
Grilling Cheese, xxviii
Gubbeen, 157
Hereford Hop Chive and Bacon Creams, 59
Highfields Farm Dairy, 215
Highland Fine Cheeses Ltd, 290–2
Hot Chocolate Creams, 193
Hurst Farm Cheeses, 15
Inagh Farmhouse Cheeses, 139–40
Isle of Mull Traditional Farmhouse Cheese, 284
Keen, S. A. & G. H., 84–6
Kirkhams Lancashire, 229
Lincolnshire Poacher, 225
Little Acorn Products, 179
Llanboidy Cheesemakers, 165
Llangloffan and Spinach Pies, 170
Llangloffan Farmhouse Cheese, 167–9
Loch Arthur Creamery, 271
Loch Arthur Potatoes, 273
Lord's Fish Soufflé, 38–40
The Lubborn Creamery, 96
Lynher Dairies, 118
Malvern Cheesewrights, 185
Marrow Rings Stuffed with Plums and Lanark Blue, 279–80
Martell, Charles, 56
Mary Quicke's Celeriac Chowder, 104–5
Menallack Farm, 123–4
Milleens, 145
Montgomery Ltd, J. A. & E., 81–2
Neal's Yard Creamery, 190
North Doddington Farm, 266–7
Northumberland Potato Omelette, 264
Northumberland Cheese Co., 260
Nut Knowle Farm Cheeses, 32–4
Old Plaw Hatch Organic, 17

Park Farm Cheeses, 70–2
Penbryn, 64
Plaw Hatch Scones, 19–20
Polenta with Blue Vinny and Tomatoes, 80
Puff Pastry, xxvi–xxvii
Putlands Farm Sticky Lemon Pudding, 26
Quicke and Partners, J. G., 102–3
Ribblesdale Cheesemakers, 236–7
Ribblesdale Lemon Cheesecake, 239
Sandham Ltd, J. J., 231–2
Seator's Orkney, 295–6
Seville Orange Caramel Cream, 288
Sharpham Creamery, 112
Shepherd's Purse, 247–9
Short Pastry, xxv–xxvi
Sleight Farm, 66–8
Smart's Gloucester Cheese, 47–8
Somerset Brie and Garlic Mushrooms, 99
Spaghetti with Berkswell, Basil, and Courgettes, 213–14
St Tola and Avocado Salad, 142
Staffordshire Organic, 222–3
Stilton Mashed Potatoes, 221–2
Stinking Bishop Fritters with Cider, 61
Stock, xxvii–xxviii
Strawberry Curd Ice, 192
Sussex High Weald Dairy Products, 21–2
Swaledale Cheese Co., 255–6
Tagliatelle with Spenwood and Spring Vegetables, 7–8
Teifi, 172
Ticklemore and Apple Mousse, 111
Ticklemore Cheese, 107
Tiskey Meadow Courgettes, 121
Traditional Cheese Dairy, The, 36
Trout and Double Gloucester Fish Cakes, 50
Veronica Steele's Puff-Balls, 149
Village Maid, 4–5
Walda and Anchovy Salad, 11
Warm Salad of Tilleys with Hazlenuts, 69
Welsh Rarebit, 93–4

Wensleydale and Whisky Walnut Cake, 243
Wensleydale Dairy Products Ltd, 240–1
West Cork Natural Cheese, 152–4
Wester Lawrenceton Cheeses, 286
Wheems, 298
Wield Wood Farm, 9
Wine, with cheese, xxxii–xxxiv
Womerton Farm, 14, 197
Yorkshire Blue and Chicken Mousse, 252

COOKING FOR BLOKES

D. Anderson & M. Walls

HUNGRY?

Can't find the menu from the takeaway up the road? Can't face beans on toast again? Trying to convince someone that men aren't completely hopeless in the kitchen?

DON'T PANIC!

Cooking for Blokes tells you all you need to know – from what knife to buy, which pots you need in your cupboard, what spoons you need in your drawers, to what to put in the spice rack . . .

From the simplest of 'half-eleven on a Friday night, drunk, absolutely starving' snacks (cheese on toast) to dishes that might even impress Mum (Trout & Almonds) the simple, short recipes in *Cooking for Blokes* take you through the process step-by-step.

From beginner to cordon bleu chef (well, nearly), it's all there: Indian, Chinese & Far Eastern, Italian, Tex-Mex, Vegetarian, Salads, Party Food, Drink (from lager to punch, and even something called water) . . .

FLASH COOKING FOR BLOKES

D. Anderson & M. Walls

For those about to wok . . .

You know your basil from your rosemary. Your tender curried chicken has impressed the ladies. You don't need to be told how to do toast. What next for the laughing gastronome?

From 'sorry I forgot the Millennium' dishes (scallop tagliatelle) to the greatest pudding in the world™ (Black Forest Gateau), Duncan Anderson and Marian Walls take the budding chef a stage further into their epicurean odyssey, where devilish desserts, vibrant vegetables and posh pasta remain within the bounds of the enthusiastic amateur.

Containing all you need to know to create perfect profiteroles, superlative shrimp gumbo, and even some fancy booze, *Flash Cooking for Blokes* is the definitive book for the man in the modern kitchen. Why, there's even a chapter on power tools . . .

FAST CAKES

Mary Berry

Cakes Are Simple

The recipes in *Fast Cakes* are *really* fast! Most of them can be prepared in less than ten minutes and baked in under an hour. These are *not* instant cakes but proper cakes of all kinds – from old nursery favourites such as Fruit Cake, Gingerbread and the reassuringly named Can't-Go-Wrong Chocolate Cake to the more adventurous but equally speedy delights of Praline Meringue, Iced Queen Cakes and Mocha Gâteau.

This tempting selection includes delicious chapters on tray bakes, no-bake cakes, tea breads, scones and biscuits as well as an invaluable introduction, a sensible emergency section, useful hints and straightforward children's recipes. Altogether this is the complete book for busy bakers.

'Interesting and unusual suggestions for cakes that can be created in minutes . . . Many are simple enough for children to make.' *Good Housekeeping*

'Will appeal to anyone who loves baking but does not have time to wade through laborious techniques.' *Ideal Home*

Sphere now offers an exciting range of quality titles by both established and new authors. All of the books in this series are available from:

Sphere
P.O. Box 121, Kettering,
Northants NN14 4ZQ

Fax No: 01832 733076
Telephone No: 01832 737525
Email: aspenhouse@FSBDial.co.uk

Payments can be made as follows: cheque, postal order (payable to Sphere) or by credit cards, Visa/Access. Do not send cash or currency. All U.K. orders free of charge. E.E.C. and Overseas: 25% of order value.

NAME (Block Letters) ....

....

ADDRESS ....

....

....

☐ I enclose my remittance for ....

☐ I wish to pay by Access/Visa Card ....

Number ☐☐☐☐☐☐☐☐☐☐☐☐☐☐☐☐

Card Expiry Date ☐☐☐☐